REVISING SHAKESPEARE

# Revising
# Shakespeare

GRACE IOPPOLO

Harvard University Press
Cambridge, Massachusetts
London, England
1991

Library of Congress Cataloging-in-Publication Data
Ioppolo, Grace, 1956–
Revising Shakespeare / Grace Ioppolo.
p.   cm.
Includes bibliographical references and index.
ISBN 0-674-76696-2
1. Shakespeare, William, 1564–1616—Criticism, Textual.
2. Shakespeare, William, 1564–1616—Adaptations. 3. Shakespeare, William,
1564–1616—Editors. 4. Editing—History. I. Title.
PR3071.I62 1991
822.3'3—dc20
91-12627
CIP

For Carmela and Gaetano Ioppolo
and
For R. A. Foakes

# Contents

# Acknowledgments

I must pay the many debts I have promised and prove myself much better than my word.

For permission to reprint published material, I thank the *Huntington Library Quarterly* and *Analytical and Enumerative Bibliography*. For permission to cite from unpublished dramatic manuscripts, I thank the Victoria and Albert Museum, National Art Library; Trinity College Library, Cambridge; the Bodleian Library, Oxford; the British Museum; and the Huntington Library, San Marino, California. For permission to reproduce unpublished dramatic manuscript material in the form of photographs, I thank the Huntington Library.

For generous professional support, advice, and guidance, I must gratefully thank: the British Academy, for awarding me a travel grant, and the Trustees of the Huntington Library, for awarding me two dissertation fellowships, which allowed me to complete this study; the dedicated staff and readers of the Huntington Library, especially Martin Ridge and Robert Middlekauff; Fredson Bowers; Susan P. Cerasano; Jerome McGann; Randall McLeod; G. R. Proudfoot; James Riddell; John Sutherland; James Thorpe; and Steven Urkowitz. I would also like to thank Elizabeth Story Donno, E. A. J. Honigmann, T. H. Howard-Hill, John Jowett, Paul Stevens, and Guilland Sutherland for graciously reading and commenting on portions of Chapters 1 and 2. *Con amore,* I thank my parents, Gaetano and Carmela Ioppolo, and my family for their loving support and understanding.

I am most indebted to the readers of this manuscript who painstakingly reformed it: George R. Guffey and Michael Hackett, who contributed to the manuscript in its apprentice form; Thomas D'Evelyn, my editor at Harvard University Press, who assigned the manuscript a glittering value; Lauren M. Osborne, my copy editor, who brightened the manuscript; Margreta de Grazia, Gary Taylor, and Michael Warren, who generously redeemed the manuscript's meanings and forms; and, most especially, R. A. Foakes, who offered me throughout the writing and rewriting of this manuscript his brilliance as a literary and textual critic, teacher, and mentor.

# REVISING SHAKESPEARE

# Introduction: Canonizing and Constituting Shakespeare

With the publication of Steven Urkowitz's book, *Shakespeare's Revision of "King Lear,"* in 1980 and that of *The Division of the Kingdoms,* edited by Gary Taylor and Michael Warren, in 1983, the critical debate about Shakespeare as a reviser of his own plays has been reopened and theories of authorial revision are being seriously reconsidered by both textual and literary scholars. Both of these critical works propose that Shakespeare was motivated by theatrical demands and his own aestheticism in revising the original *King Lear,* printed in the 1608 Quarto 1 text, to produce the new version which appeared in the 1623 First Folio. Urkowitz and the contributors to *The Division of the Kingdoms,* including Stanley Wells, John Kerrigan, Taylor, and Warren, argue that Shakespeare revised *King Lear* in order to re-present both the play's major themes, kingship, familial relationships, and war, and its major characters, Lear, Kent, Albany, Edgar, and the Fool.

Although Paul Werstine asserted, in a recent article arguing for authorial revision in *Hamlet* and against it in *King Lear,* that "the notion of revision had its heyday in the nineteenth century just as it is having another one now; what's more, discussion of the question has hardly languished in the last three decades,"[1] the critical discussion of the type, degree, and consequence of authorial revision in Shakespeare's plays has been a crucial issue for editors and critics since the appearance of the First Folio. Theories of authorial revision were loudly and exhaustively articulated, debated, defended, and dismissed from the seventeenth century to the early twentieth century by such figures as Alexander Pope, Dr. Samuel Johnson, Edmond Malone, Samuel Taylor Coleridge, Charles

Knight, F. G. Fleay, J. M. Robertson, and John Dover Wilson. However, E. K. Chambers's reverberatingly harsh condemnation in 1924 of any exploration of authorial revision (on the grounds that it would "disintegrate" the Shakespearian canon by revealing non-Shakespearian material underlying some of the plays[2]) effectively silenced modern discussion of revision.

Michael Warren first reopened this long-closed debate in 1976 when he argued convincingly that changes in the roles of Albany and Edgar between the Quarto 1 and Folio texts of *King Lear* signaled "authorial reworking" and revision.[3] In 1980, three sets of scholars continued the debate and provoked further study of Shakespearian revision. A Shakespeare Association of America seminar took up the textual "problem" created by the variant Quarto and Folio editions of the play. In addition, Gary Taylor published "The War in *King Lear,*" which strongly concluded that Shakespeare had systematically replaced references to the foreign war with France found in the Quarto text with references to the domestic war in the Folio text.[4] Finally, Steven Urkowitz cogently traced a theory of more extensive revisions than those discussed by Warren and Taylor, as he claimed that the Folio text represented "a careful and dramatically sensitive revision of the Quarto" made by Shakespeare himself.[5]

This renewed critical discussion of authorial revision resulted in the publication of *The Division of the Kingdoms,* which presents arguments supporting a thesis very similar to Urkowitz's—that Shakespeare deliberately revised his Quarto version of *King Lear* to produce the separate and alternative version in the Folio. Although their theories have not received universal acceptance, by advocating that the recognition of authorial revision demands changes in the ways scholars study, edit, and teach Shakespeare's plays, these "revisionists" have succeeded in forcing an urgent and far-reaching crisis in and reexamination of the critical and editorial approaches to all literature which exists in multiple states and texts.

The central aim of the contributors to *The Division of the Kingdoms* is to reject these five standard views of *King Lear:*

> that Shakespeare wrote one play about *King Lear;* that this play is imperfectly represented in both the Quarto and the Folio texts; that each of these texts contains genuinely Shakespearian passages which are missing from and should have been present in the other; that comparison of the variant readings of the

two texts must form the most important basis for the correction of errors of transmission; and that conflation of the two texts, along with such correction, will bring us as close as we can hope to get to the lost archetype which each is supposed imperfectly to represent.[6]

Although these revisionists still debate among themselves various textual issues, including whether Shakespeare's act of "deliberately rewriting" a play resulted in a "new," an "improved," or simply a "distinct" version of that play, they all defend the independent dramatic integrity of the two texts of *King Lear*.[7]

Yet the bold assertions in these scholarly works have not merely added to or quietly taken an assigned place in the breadth of Shakespearian criticism, to be debated only by elite textual scholars and cited by a few specialized critics; instead, these arguments represent a manifesto which has rebelliously overthrown all modes and all discourses of textual and literary criticism of *King Lear* as well as other Shakespearian plays extant in variant versions.

The new revisionists have achieved a *coup d'état* which offers a new constitution for how scholars read, study, and teach Shakespeare's canon and also redefines the canon itself. The very concept of what is and is not "Shakespearian" has been shattered, not because these scholars disintegrate Shakespeare by arguing that he did not write the plays in the canon but because they prove that in the case of one play, and by implication several others, Shakespeare's *editors* since 1623 have not rewritten what Shakespeare wrote. The previously canonized Shakespeare is an author who was created by textual and literary scholars eager to make sense of his sanctity; the revisionists have begun to return the canon to its real constitution. This "new" Shakespeare is not the editorially and eclectically reduced one whose early and later compositions and revisions have been diluted and dissolved, but the "old" one, the creative and re-creative artist who displayed his genius in original texts that resist dissolution, reduction, finiteness, finality, and, ultimately, being edited away. Shakespeare's plays, as the Quarto and Folio texts attest, are ever self-revising products, objects, and subjects.

Rather than "reconstructing" Shakespeare by piecing together the "best" passages from "faulty," "fraudulent," and "inferior" variant versions of plays which have served as major cultural, social, and historical icons for centuries, the new revising editors now construct Shakespeare by resurrecting and respecting the value of variant Quarto and Folio texts as representations of Shakespeare's own constantly creating and multiplying artistic process and of his canon. In reporting on the new revolution and defending its constitution by placing it in a much broader historical, theatrical, textual, and literary context, I will both revise Shakespeare and allow him to revise himself on a scale much larger than that offered by the individual and isolating case of *King Lear*. I will present studies of his texts and those of his contemporaries which show Elizabethan and Jacobean dramatists at work revising themselves, their plays, and their audiences, producing a new conception of the author as a creator and re-creator, viewer and re-viewer, writer and re-writer of his dramatic world.

Such a perception of the authorial process proceeds from the recognition that the author identifiably constructs himself within the texts; the texts do not produce or even identify the author, he produces and identifies the texts. Yet, new historicists and deconstructionists have used the new textual criticism to assert that the theoretical mode of discourse, rather than the dramatist, is the genuine author of the form and the meaning of the text. Stephen Orgel, for example, presents what he terms a "self-evident" argument: that the authority of a Renaissance text does not derive from the author because "the very notion of 'the author's original manuscript' is in such cases a figment"; the author's manuscript is transformed and altered without the author's cooperation into a "performing text." From this general argument Orgel concludes that "we know nothing about Shakespeare's original text."[8] Jonathan Goldberg similarly argues that the new textual criticism forces scholars to recognize that "there never has been, and never can be, an unedited Shakespearean text. Textual criticism and poststructuralism agree therefore: we have no originals, only copies. The historicity of the text means that there is no text itself; it means that a text cannot be fixed in terms of original or final intentions."[9]

Yet the author has not "died," nor has he "disappeared" from his "work."[10] These arguments, which decentralize the author and centralize the critical discourse used to strip him of his power, ignore the main tenets of the new revisionists: the Quarto and Folio texts, with each granted an authorial integrity, origin, and historicity, are not unfixed or unfixable copies but specific and particular products fixedly descending from the author. The texts of Shakespeare's plays, many of which encompass the compositional and revisional processes, exist as original and seminal physical products of the authorial process, a process that does not require poststructural criticism or any other externally imposed theoretical mode to seek its actual meaning or existence. Contrary to the argument that "it is the *manuscript* that is the immaterial abstraction, an enabling figment of the bibliographic and critical imagination,"[11] it is the mode of literary criticism that immaterially abstracts the authorial production of the text. Many Quarto and Folio texts, including Quarto 1 *Love's Labor's Lost, Troilus and Cressida, Othello,* and *King Lear,* Quarto 2 *Hamlet* and *Romeo and Juliet,* and Folio *All's Well That Ends Well,* were printed from Shakespeare's foul papers; these texts thus serve as more immediate manifestations of the manuscript than the critical discourse designed to discount it as a figment.

This book is the first to establish in a materially concrete way that William Shakespeare was a deliberate, consistent, and persistent reviser who worked in an infinite variety of ways, and to recognize his career-long practice of revision as he himself recognized and practiced it. I use the five standard views of *King Lear* and their rejection by the contributors to *The Division of the Kingdoms* as the starting point to examine the old and the new constitutions not just of the single, unparalleled case of *King Lear,* but of the entire canon of Shakespeare. In order to understand how these views became standardly entrenched in Shakespearian study, why arguments for authorial revision subject them to treacherous attack, and what role revision plays in the transmission of a Renaissance play-text, I will cite evidence of the composition, theatrical, and printing practices of Shakespeare and his contemporary dramatists and outline both the causes of the current debate about authorial revision and its consequences for *all* who are engaged in the study of Shakespeare.

## "As He Conceiued Them"

The very nature of the evidence left by Shakespeare of what he wrote, when he wrote it, and how he wrote it has contributed to the uncertainty of how to treat the extant printed texts of his plays, many of which share complicated printing histories. As none of his manuscripts survives, with the exception of the few pages which have been ascribed to him in the collaborative manuscript of *The Book of Sir Thomas More,* scholars have no evidence in his own hand that he revised passages or scenes in the plays in the canon. Also, very few contemporary records document the theatrical and printing practices which may have introduced revisions into his plays. Thus, the editorial and critical methodologies developed to deal with Shakespeare's printed texts have often been based on scholarly speculation and conjectural reconstruction which succeeding scholars can only with uncertainty accept or challenge.

Eighteen of the Folio plays had appeared in some previous printed form, in either spurious or genuine Quartos or Octavos[12] (some of which served as copy for the Folio printers) before being collected in the 1623 First Folio.[13] However, these Quarto texts do not provide any consistent information about Shakespeare's composition practices; his name did not always appear on Quarto title pages, and evidently first appeared in 1598 on the first Quarto of *Love's Labor's Lost* and the second Quartos of *Richard II* and *Richard III*. In the cases of plays with more than one Quarto text, the later Quarto was often nothing more than a reprint of the earlier Quarto with increased compositorial errors, as in the case of *King Lear*.

Yet some of the later Quartos show substantial variants and differences when compared to the earlier Quartos. Three "good" Quartos which contain variants not found in the preceding "bad" (possibly memorially reported) Quartos advertise on their title pages that they have been altered. The 1598 Quarto 1 of *Love's Labor's Lost* states that it was "newly corrected and augmented *By W. Shakespere,*" leading some critics to argue that a non-extant earlier Quarto was printed; the 1599 Quarto 2 of *Romeo and Juliet* states that it was *"newly corrected, augmented, and amended,"* perhaps suggesting that Quarto 1 was a "bad" Quarto; and the 1604 Quarto 2 of *Hamlet* states that it was "newly imprinted and enlarged to almost as much againe as it was, according to the true and perfect Coppie," also implying that Quarto 1 was a "bad" Quarto.[14] These advertisements had varying and variant objectives: some may have been designed only to help sell the new edition, to proclaim the previous editions obsolete or pirated, or to establish that in some way the plays had been changed. Some later reprints of Quartos which contain no major variants also misleadingly announce that they have been "augmented."

Most Quartos (both early and later) show substantial variants and differences when compared to their counterpart Folio texts. Eighteen plays were apparently printed for the first time in the Folio, although it is conceivable that some (including *Love's Labor's Won,* a Shakespearian play noted by Francis Meres in his 1598 tract, *Palladis Tamia*) appeared in Quarto form and are no longer extant. Two plays now considered to have been at least partially written by Shakespeare, *Pericles* and *The Two Noble Kinsmen,* were not included in the Folio, although *Pericles* appeared in Quarto editions beginning in 1609. The existence of several apocryphal plays attributed to Shakespeare and extant in manuscript or Quarto form, such as *The Troublesome raigne of John King of England, The True Tragedy of King Richard the Third,* and *The Taming of a Shrew,* further confuses textual reconstruction of Shakespeare as author and reviser. He may have had some hand in the composition of these plays or later revised, adapted, or borrowed from them when he wrote his own plays.

The 1623 Folio, the first collected edition of Shakespeare's plays, printed seven years after his death, contains thirty-six plays, although only thirty-five are listed in the "Catalogve." The title of *Troilus and Cressida* is omitted, probably because the printers only secured the rights to the play late in the printing of the volume.[15] The advertisements and editorial remarks in this edition, collected and edited by Shakespeare's friends and fellow actors in the King's Men, John Heminge and Henry Condell, present no more certain a picture of Shakespeare's writing practices than the evidence offered in the Quartos. The title-page advertisement in the Folio that the Comedies, Histories, and Tragedies have been "Published according to the True Originall Copies," suggests that these particular texts were printed from Shakespeare's own authoritative "foul" or "fair" copies. However, it is not clear which type of text, printed or manuscript, served as the "true Originall" printers' copy, or whether these texts were authorized by Shakespeare, who died in 1616, or by Heminge and Condell. As some "good" Quarto texts of some of the plays which had followed "bad" Quarto texts into print also announce that they were printed from the "true copies," this advertisement in the Folio cannot verify the authority of these particular texts.

Heminge and Condell's Folio preface, "To the great Variety of Readers," contains two other seemingly authoritative editorial assertions about the quality of these texts. The reader is carefully advised:

> As where (before) you were abus'd with diuerse stolne, and surreptitious copies, maimed, and deformed by the frauds and stealthes of iniurious impostors, that expos'd them: euen those, are now offer'd to your view cur'd, and perfect of their limbes, and all the rest, absolute in their numbers, as he conceiued them.

Heminge and Condell also add admiringly of Shakespeare, "What he thought, he vttered with that easinesse, that wee haue scarse receiued

from him a blot in his papers." Heminge and Condell may be an-
nouncing here that their texts supersede all other printed versions of the
plays, including "good" and "bad" Quartos and Octavos, or that they
supersede only the "surreptitious copies," that is, "bad" texts that were
printed by piratical "impostors," or they may simply be engaging in
shrewd advertising without saying anything specific. Who, for example
has "cur'd" the texts? Heminge and Condell may be claiming that they
have used Shakespeare's papers to print the plays in the volume, rather
than their acting company's promptbooks, and that the plays are thus
completely free of all types of scribal, theatrical, and literary revision, or
the editors may simply be praising their former friend and playwright
and increasing the commercial appeal of their product. The fact that
some Folio texts appear to have been printed from from foul papers
while others are set from theatrical manuscripts or Quarto copy belies
the Folio editorial claim of setting *all* of the plays from the same type
of "true Originall" copy, including Shakespeare's papers.

Although the authority in and the meanings of these three editorial
comments are not completely clear or certain, Shakespeare's subsequent
editors and critics clearly and certainly seized upon them to build two
arguments: first, that the Folio texts represent the single "best" extant
copies of the plays as Shakespeare intended them to appear and were
only to be corrected by Quarto texts in passages with obvious corruptions;
and second, that Shakespeare was a natural and spontaneous writer who
wrote out a play once and only once in foul papers without making any
kind of alteration whatsoever and thus left uncorrected and unblotted
manuscripts because he neither needed nor wanted to revise. Ben Jonson,
the first to interpret the claims of the Folio editors of having received
unblotted papers, mused, "*I remember,* the Players have often mentioned
it as an honour to *Shakespeare,* that in his writing, (whatsoever he penn'd)
hee never blotted out line. My answer hath beene, would he had blotted
a thousand. Which they thought a malevolent speech."[16] Later scholars,
including most recently J. M. Nosworthy and David Bevington,[17] have
paid more attention to Jonson's acknowledgement of the "unblotted
lines" than to his own response to them and the malevolent reaction it
created.

Since 1623 and until the current "revisionism" debate, editors and
critics investigating these two arguments concerning the authority of the
Folio texts and the unblotted manuscripts of Shakespeare have often been
willingly or unwillingly sidetracked by some of the plays' bibliographic

puzzles. An editor's or a textual critic's desire to trace the "transmission of the text" may become more important than his or her inquiry into the author's possible reworkings of the text. Eighteenth-century scholars began to challenge successfully the theory that the Quarto texts were less authoritative than those in the Folio. However, these and later scholars felt it necessary to choose between Quarto and Folio texts in order to reconstruct the single, lost version upon which their edition would be based and refused to acknowledge the individual integrity of the extant multiple editions of a play. Thus revision theories have been seen as only tangential and often worthless pursuits of Shakespearian study. G. E. Bentley explains that there is "fairly clear evidence" of revision in Shakespeare's plays by the author or other dramatists but the fact has been obscured because "most Shakespearean scholars have been less interested in the clear evidence that the play has been revised at some time or other than in the much more difficult problem of who wrote what lines and when."[18]

Some scholars have argued that multiple texts are the result of authorial revision; however, their theories have been especially obscured and discredited. Modern scholarship has preferred to concentrate on the complex publication histories rather than the complex writing processes of the plays, perhaps because slightly more is known about how certain printers worked than about how Shakespeare worked. An editor who argues, for example, that a certain Shakespearian Quarto edition was derived from the author's foul papers and the Folio edition from an emended promptbook can easily sidestep questions of authorial revison, correction, or interference, claiming instead that the bookkeeper's or actors' interpolations or the printing process rather than the author produced the extant text.

Other factors which complicate the distinction between authorial and nonauthorial revision include the classification of variant readings and the sources which produced them. Discrepancies between an earlier and later text of the same play are generally classified as "variants" (either "accidental" or "substantive"), "differences," "omissions," and "appearances," rather than intended "revisions," "cuts," and "additions," and the discussion of their origins can be swallowed up in determining what kind of material served as the printer's copy. The several types of manuscripts that could have served as printer's copy for a play include the author's foul papers, his and/or a scrivener's fair copy, the acting company's promptbook,[19] and any transcript of any of these manuscripts.

Printers may have also used a "memorial reconstruction" or "memorial report" made by members of an acting company or of the audience to print a play, or they may have used one or a combination of existing printed versions of the text, whether pirated, spurious, unauthorized, or authorized. When collating different editions of the same play, a modern editor notices variants between them but is usually unwilling to consider or explain them as revisions. Thus, in various calculated and uncalculated ways, scholars have shifted the emphasis on revision from that of an integral factor in the authorial process to a tangential by-product of the printing process.

E. A. J. Honigmann only begins to suggest the complexities of the transmission of the text when he concludes:

> McKerrow observed that even if a scrivener did the copying the author would probably correct the manuscript, especially if he occupied Shakespeare's position in the company. Both Shakespeare's foul papers and fair copy, or his foul papers and a scribal transcript corrected by him, could thus come into the possession of the players, and both, or descendants of both, might ultimately find their way to the printers—so that the Quarto and Folio of one play could easily record variants stemming from Shakespeare.

Honigmann accepts W. W. Greg's and E. K. Chambers's "skepticism"[20] about literary revision, but at the same time, in canvassing, as he was in 1965, for "another form of textual instability," he argues that "to submit that Shakespeare introduced verbal changes in copying out a play is not to assert large-scale revision."[21] However, critics have not usually seen the presence of variants in Shakespeare's printed texts as signs of authorial change. Unlike Honigmann, Sidney Thomas cites the problems of determining the transmission of the text to argue that variants are most certainly nonauthorial in origin. In rejecting theories of authorial revision in *King Lear,* Thomas assigns many of the differences between the texts to "corruption" in the Quarto or "theatrical cuts" in the Folio, none of them "necessarily attributable" to Shakespeare.[22] Yet, all Folio variants cannot stem from nonauthorial origins, such as printing errors; as Paul Werstine has shown, "no play in the Folio is a simple reprint of an earlier printed text; no play thought to have been set from quarto copy contains only compositorial variants from printed copy."[23] Although editors have argued that there is no extant evidence of Shakespeare's revisions, they have failed to produce extant evidence that any agent other than Shakespeare was resonsible for all of the variants, and probable revisions, found in the texts.

Even some of the editors who have built a case for authorial revision of a passage or a scene seem unwilling to argue that Shakespeare intended to make the changes for his own artistic reasons; for example, after establishing "major revision and amplification" by Shakespeare in one scene of the Folio text of *Julius Caesar* and "minor revision" in another scene, Fredson Bowers asserts that the changes were "forced on Shakespeare."[24] While the theory of minor revision during composition in the form of the marginal additions and duplications found in such texts as the first Quartos of *Titus Andronicus, Love's Labor's Lost,* and *A Midsummer Night's Dream* has won a grudging acceptance from textual critics, theories of later revisions which appear as substantive variants between printed editions of a play, such as Quarto 1 and Folio *King Lear,* have usually been rejected. As John Kerrigan points out, "almost all scholars accept the idea of rethinking within foul papers, and the majority believe that, in copying, Shakespeare made changes"; however, revision between foul papers and a transcript, resulting in variants between texts, provokes more scholarly "resistance."[25] Stanley Wells similarly does not see any consistency

> in an editorial tradition which allows us to accept and act upon the hypothesis that Shakespeare altered his original conception when his first and second thoughts sit side by side in a single text (as in the duplicated passages at the end of Act Two, Scene Two and the opening of Act Two, Scene Three of *Romeo and Juliet,* or in Act Four, Scene Three and Act Five, Scene Two of *Love's Labour's Lost,* or in the opening speeches of *Titus Andronicus*), but which does not allow us to admit the hypothesis of Shakespearian revision when the first and second thoughts occur in different texts (like the quarto and Folio *King Lear, Troilus and Cressida,* or *Titus Andronicus*).[26]

Resistant scholars have not even accepted the evidence about Shakespeare's composition and later revision practices derived from the pages of the manuscript of *The Book of Sir Thomas More,* which they believed to be in Shakespeare's hand. Of the *More* pages, E. K. Chambers concluded:

> What one does not find is that absence of 'blots' for which Heminges and Condell especially lauded Shakespeare. There are a score of places which show alterations made either *currente calamo* or as afterthoughts. And even then there were some oversights left for Hand C to correct. Perhaps the writer did

not take the play he was tinkering [with] very seriously. I do not take the
statement of Heminges and Condell very seriously.

However, in discussing the printed texts of Shakespeare's plays, Chambers supported only the possibility of afterthoughts during composition
and sharply rejected theories of "wholesale" or "self" revision made after
the completion of the foul papers.[27]

Curiously, skeptical editors and critics do not extend this argument
that Shakespeare did not revise to other later sixteenth and early seventeenth-century dramatists. Textual scholars have uncovered and accepted
significant evidence of the types of and causes for the authorial revision
practiced by Shakespeare's contemporaries. Manuscripts of plays such as
Anthony Munday's *John a Kent & John a Cumber,* Philip Massinger's
*Believe As You List,* and Thomas Middleton's *A Game at Chesse* show
evidence of authorial revision. Other manuscript and printed plays,
including *The Book of Sir Thomas More* and Thomas Kyd's *The Spanish
Tragedy,* show revision by at least one other hand.

Revision of existing plays by company dramatists, including in many
cases the original author, was commonplace, as plays belonging to an
acting company could undergo alteration, expansion, revision, or cutting
in order to serve the company's current needs or those of the censor, the
Master of the Revels, or even the author. G. E. Bentley cites evidence
provided by Philip Henslowe's *Diary* to argue that revision "seems to
have been the universal practice in the London theatres from 1590–
1642."[28] The *Diary,* which lists some of Henslowe's business dealings with
acting companies, records payments and loans made to authors for their
"adicians" to and "alterynge" and "mending" of existing plays for revival,
as in this famous example:

> Lent vnto m$^r$ alleyn the 25 of septemb[er]        $\Big\}$   +
> 1601 to lend vnto Bengemen Johnson vpon
> h[is] writtinge of his adicians in geronymo              xxxx
> the some of . . .[29]

Although the precise meaning of such terms as "mending" is unclear,
the *Diary* proves that an existing play could undergo several types of
later theatrical revision.

Besides employing resident dramatists of acting companies, Henslowe
appears to have paid hack and free-lance writers to make alterations or
additions, as reworking a play became a lucrative trade for both the

dramatist and the acting company. Some critics argue that Robert Greene's satirical warning to his fellow playwrights about the *"Iohannes fac totum"* and "vpstart Crow, beautified with our feathers, that with his *Tygers hart wrapt in a Players hyde,* supposes he is as well able to bombast out a blanke verse as the best of you,"[30] castigates the young Shakespeare, dressed in borrowed feathers and revising the plays of other authors.[31]

Other comments about or within plays demonstrate that actors also made changes, frequently adding to, interfering with, or borrowing from an author's manuscript. Authors often bemoaned such changes, as Thomas Nashe did in his anecdotal essay, "The Praise of the Red Herring," in which he calls his controversial play, *The Ile of Dogs,* an "imperfit Embrion," as, "I hauing begun but the induction and the first act of it, the other foure acts without my consent, or the least guesse of my drift or scope, by the players were supplied, which bred both their trouble and mine to."[32] Although Nashe may have been exaggerating here to save himself from prosecution, these types of authorial remarks are common in the period. Hamlet, for example, warns the players that they should perform the court play as he has given it to them: "Let those that play your clownes speake no more than is set downe for them." Shakespeare's character terms any nonauthorial tampering with his play "villanous."[33] However, a large number of the plays recorded in Henslowe's *Diary* and in the Stationers' Register do not survive in print or in manuscript; therefore, many editors and critics remain skeptical about the value of the *Diary,* of anecdotes by authors, and of allusions to revision in dramas and other documents of the time in determining precisely how plays were treated by their authors and by the acting companies and printers who purchased them.

Given the lack of verifiable and precise information on the authorial practices of Shakespeare, the theatrical practices of his acting company, and the editorial practices of his Quarto and Folio printers, his editors have struggled for more than three centuries against dangerous uncertainty and imperiling vulnerability. Beginning with Nicholas Rowe in 1709, editors have collated variant editions of the plays in an attempt to reproduce the text that Shakespeare originally wrote but have often found their task impossible. Most have worked under the assumption that "where two substantive readings differ one or both must be corrupt."[34] Many of the very editors who refused to believe that Shakespeare himself revised certain passages actually revised for him by introducing their own emendations into passages they considered corrupt and un-

Shakespearian. Finally, the early practitioners of the twentieth century's "New Bibliography" applied modern research methods to Elizabethan and Jacobean texts in order to establish some type of standard editorial theory and to assert some form of textual authority. R. B. McKerrow, W. W. Greg, and other New Bibliographers examined the current state of the textual scholarship begun in the early eighteenth century and studied the composition, theatrical, and printing histories of Renaissance plays in an attempt to deal definitively with the varied theories relating to single, multiple, and revised texts.

In order to elude the uncertainty and vulnerability implicit in editing Shakespeare, the New Bibliographers attempted to impose a strict formula on textual study by reducing all of the often contradictory theories into one standard theory which would suit most if not all of Shakespeare's plays. In 1950, W. W. Greg established the specific standard and the rationale for the "copy-text" from which to set an edition of a play with or without extant manuscripts. Basing his work on that done by McKerrow, Greg advocated a modern editorial practice in which an editor chooses "whatever extant text may be supposed to represent most nearly what the author wrote and to follow it with the least possible alteration." Greg argued that for texts which do not involve revision, the first edition should stand as copy-text; for texts which show or suggest revision, "if the original be selected, then the author's corrections must be incorporated . . . If the reprint be selected, then the original reading must be restored when that of the reprint is due to unauthorized variation."[35] Yet in spite of this uniform and standardized advice to editors, Greg and his followers remained extremely hesitant about recognizing "suggested" revision in the plays of Shakespeare.

Greg's definition of the task of the dramatic editor was reinterpreted by later textual critics, beginning with Fredson Bowers,[36] to include the determination of authorial intentions in establishing a copy-text. Bowers argued that for modern texts with extant prepublication documents an editor should choose an author's manuscript as copy-text as it most clearly represents his "final intentions."[37] When dealing with a revised text, Bowers cautioned an editor

> to heed Greg's advice and to choose a revised derived edition as his copy-text only in cases of the sternest necessity when to select an earlier document would pile up lists of emendations of staggering proportions.

However, Bowers did find Greg's rationale of copy-text too narrow to apply to cases, exemplified by some of Shakespeare's plays, in which two extant texts are not related to each other but derive from different documents radiating from a lost archetypal manuscript.[38] James Thorpe agreed with Bowers that "the ideal of textual criticism is to present the text which the author intended."[39] Yet, this ideal of reproducing what an author actually "intended" is not synonymous with Greg's advice to reproduce what he actually wrote, or with McKerrow's advice to reproduce what is actually published as and accepted to be his writing, as an editor should "present Shakespeare's work as nearly in the form in which he left it as the evidence which we have permits."[40] Determining "authorial intention" has proved to be even more problematic and digressive than determining a single copy-text.

The current revisionists, led by Michael Warren, Gary Taylor, and Stanley Wells, have chosen to reject rather than to reinterpret the theories of McKerrow, Greg, Bowers, Thorpe, and other editors and critics who argue that only *one* form or *one* text can represent what an author intended to write or actually wrote. Although Steven Urkowitz acknowledges that the New Bibliographers made significant gains in the study of the texts of Shakespeare's plays, he believes that in essence "the textual specialists who were marvelously trained in the arcane mechanics of manuscript transmission and typesetting inadvertently neglected to learn much about the dramatic art embedded in the texts they were supposed to be preserving and explaining."[41] Rather than argue about which state of the text best represents a dramatist's one single vision of his play by finding its lost original, the revisionists grant equal textual integrity to each extant version, including, for some plays, what has been termed a "bad" Quarto, and they see each as representing a particular vision at a particular time. The revisionists further question whether the existence of multiple versions of a play indicates that the dramatist deliberately produced these versions when he rewrote his play for a variety of reasons.

This critical reconsideration of textual revision, which includes the argument that through revision Shakespeare deliberately produced two versions of at least one play, *King Lear,* each possessing its own textual integrity, not only questions the editorial methods used to deal with all of his works, but also the critical interpretation which has been dependent on them. The literary interpretation of a play's imagery, themes, plot, setting, structure, and characters, or any other crucial, interlocking dramatic element, must change when textual scholars demonstrate that any of these aspects was altered by the author in a later version of the text. Thus, the war in textual study does not merely represent a skirmish among textual critics alone but enlists and threatens the profession and the power of literary critics who find their traditional or their nontraditional theories challenged by the conclusions of the new revisionists.

Yet the readers of Shakespeare's texts are not the only audience that has been conscripted into the textual revolution; current theatrical audiences of Shakespeare's plays are now instructed that they are watching revised and revising Shakespeare. In an essay in the London *Times,* Nicholas Hytner, the director of the 1990 Royal Shakespeare Company production of *King Lear,* confirmed his belief that the play was authorially revised and exists in two versions, and he cautioned that now "the first decision any company approaching *King Lear* has to make is which play to do." The souvenir program for this production, which is based on the Folio text of the play, includes a lengthy discussion of authorial revision suggesting that Shakespeare "revised the play after seeing how it worked in performance."[42] Shakespeare can no longer be read or watched or studied or scrutinized outside of the context of revision when even commercial newspapers and souvenir theatre programs are spreading the new doctrines of revision to mass audiences. Thus, this debate about revision, once confined to textual scholars, has now radically and essentially revised the presentations and interpretations of Shakespeare for his literary and his theatrical audiences, for his scholarly and his popular audiences.

This irreversible and irrevocable movement toward Shakespearian revision also challenges the very foundations of textual and literary theories for *all* disciplines of literature. Jerome McGann observed in 1983 that the continuing *King Lear* controversy had caused a "crisis in editorial theory" and a reformulation of textual and literary criticism:

> If scholars were misguided in their assessments of the two original printed texts of *King Lear*—if for example, these are not two *relatively corrupted* texts of a pure (but now lost) original, but two *relatively reliable* texts of two different versions of the play (as we now think)—then our general methods for dealing with such texts is called into serious question. Furthermore, since Shakespearean and Elizabethan studies constitute the central field in which our theories of textual criticism seek their ground, a crisis in that field involves a general crisis of the discipline.[43]

This crisis in editorial policy extends beyond Renaissance drama to all literature which exists in multiple versions. Editors now choose to construct a composite text which shows within it rather than in footnotes all variants of the different versions and to present an edition which can no longer be regarded in terms of Greg's concept of "copy-text." For example, Bernard Brun decided not to construct a copy-text for his edition of Marcel Proust's *A la recherche du temps perdu* but to produce all forms of the text in *"une édition génétique"* that reflects its "alchemical" composition process: *"Miroir de ce qui était en train de s'écrire, du travail que seule la publication du roman ou la mort de l'auteur ont arrêté, elle s'intéresse à la rature autant qu'au mot conservé, à l'histoire du texte plus qu'à celle du romancier."*[44]

Bernard Brun's conception of literature as a mirror of the author's creative process and this new method of editing an unstable text by giving it a pre- and postpublication integrity have been employed by other editors, including Hans Walter Gabler, whose 1984 "critical and synoptic" and genetic edition of James Joyce's *Ulysses* continues to provoke intense controversy.[45] Gabler explains that his synoptic presentation, in recording inter- and intradocument changes, "places every revisional variant in relation to others as well as in a compositionally invariant context. Details of the autograph inscription—deletions, erasures, insertions and illegible words or letters—are recorded."[46] Central to Gabler's editorial procedures is his distinction between authorial "correction" and "revision"; he claims that Joyce "corrected" but did not "revise" his text after 1922.[47] Gabler's methods have been both violently attacked and strongly supported, and the scholarly community has been forced to take sides in the debate of "copy-text" versus "genetic-text" and the role that authorial revision in any field or discipline of literature plays in establishing both. For example, in 1989, two editors cited revisions made by John Donne to urge that "editors provide, rather than a single 'authoritative' text, the entire texts of all authoritative versions of works when the entire texts are essentially variant."[48] Although these new rejections of traditionally conflated editions undoubtedly have critical consequences for scholars, they, more importantly, may have major economic consequences for those who publish and those who purchase scholarly works: if the currently available eclectic editions are rejected, they are no longer marketable, creating an economic crisis for publishers and consumers as well a theoretical crisis among literary and textual critics.

This current editorial, critical, and commercial debate about authorial revision engendered by the new Shakespearian revisionists in *The Division of the Kingdoms* and by Steven Urkowitz in *Shakespeare's Revision of King Lear* has now broadened to include the more complicated issues presented in Stanley Wells and Gary Taylor's *William Shakespeare: A*

*Textual Companion* to the new Oxford *Complete Works*. Although David
Bevington has concluded that their arguments contribute to today's
editorial "phenomenon of indeterminate Shakespeare,"[49] Wells and
Taylor present a determinate authorial rationale for and editorial acceptance of revision in Shakespeare's plays.[50] Michael Warren's recently
published parallel edition of the Quarto and Folio *King Lear* texts, *The
Complete "King Lear," 1608–1623,* also containing facsimiles of the Quarto
1, 2, and Folio texts, aims through photography to return to the source
of information for previous editions of the play and thus "permits
comprehension of how those editions were composed by historically and
socially conditioned yet idiosyncratic intelligences and may moreover
enhance our understanding of our own behavior in relation to texts."[51]
This edition will serve not merely as a way to "recharge the batteries of
the debate," as E. A. J. Honigmann has argued,[52] but as a revolutionary
document canonizing Shakespeare's deliberately variant versions of *King
Lear* and constituting the center of textual and literary criticism for the
canon of Shakespeare's plays. Taking this argument one step farther, my
own textual study in the pages that follow of the Quarto and Folio texts
of Shakespeare's plays can serve not as a battleground but as a proving
ground for the dramatist's creation and re-creation of his canon.[53]

## ❧ 1 ❧

# Theories of Revision,
# 1623–1990

In his essay "Shakespeare's Supposed Revision of *King Lear*," Sidney Thomas labels the editors and contributors to *The Division of the Kingdoms* and the author of *Shakespeare's Revision of King Lear* "new revisionists"[1] because they have reopened the critical discussion of Shakespeare as a reviser of his own plays, particularly *King Lear*. This "new" Shakespearian revisionism has become within the past few years a persuasive, if not a completely accepted, "orthodoxy,"[2] and Jerome McGann argues that this current *King Lear* controversy has caused an editorial crisis.[3] Yet is there really anything new about this new revisionism or its conjectures that Shakespeare produced two separate and "relatively reliable" versions of some of his plays?

Alexander Pope in 1725 first raised the issue of Shakespearian authorial revision, but his conclusions that Shakespeare was a wholesale and continual "double" reviser and "remodeller" of his own and others' plays, responsible for "insertions," "deletions," and "alterations" in nearly all of his plays, produced a tradition best labeled "old" revisionist theory. Pope's school of "old" revisionists, who were eager to regard most textual variants, no matter how accidental or substantive, as authorial, and who saw preexisting plays underlying many of Shakespeare's plays, included such eighteenth century figures as Dr. Johnson, George Steevens, and Edward Capell, and developed into the late nineteenth and early twentieth-century doctrines of the "disintegrators" (to borrow E. K. Chambers's contemptuous term), F. G. Fleay and J. M. Robertson.

The arguments of those now regarded as "new" revisionists follow in a scholarly tradition begun in the late eighteenth century by Edmond

Malone. Rather than "disintegrating" the Shakespearian canon, as critics such as Sidney Thomas have charged, by reinterpreting or re-presenting the faulty, limited, and limiting textual hypotheses of Pope and his followers, the current revisionists hold positions which were anticipated in many respects by Malone. Malone is already accepted by at least one "new" revisionist as "the father of modern Shakespearian criticism,"[4] and should also be accepted as the father of modern Shakespearian revision criticism, since his arguments, as do those of today's revisionists, distinguish between theatrical "adaptation" and "authorial revision" in order to recognize how and when Shakespeare "revised" versions of a single play. Malone did not subscribe to a theory of double or wholesale revision and, with the exception of the *Henry VI* plays, now considered by many to be partly collaborative, and a few other plays, he refused to "disintegrate" the canon by claiming that Shakespeare took over his plays from predecessors, reworked them, and at some later period touched them up once again.

As an editor, Malone struggled to determine the editorial value of a conflated edition and of a version of a play resulting from authorial revision, issues so central to the discussion of today's revisionists. More important, Malone was the first editor of Shakespeare to recognize that the age of Shakespeare was one of rich learning, and so rescued Shakespeare from his reputation as a *lusus naturae,* who wrote instinctively in an age of barbarism. Rather than depending "largely on ingenuity in emendation and the exercise of contemporary 'taste' in grammar and language" to solve what seemed to be the problems of the text, as earlier editors had done,[5] Malone set editorial standards which respected the early editions of Shakespeare's plays and investigated the role of authorial revision in producing their textual variants. Thus Malone can be recognized as the first to establish that revision played a vital role in Shakespeare's creative and artistic process, and the "new" revisionists can be recognized not as peripheral or atraditional protesters, but as the most recent contributors to a crucially important and richly substantive Shakespearian editorial tradition.

## "The True Originall Copies"

Eighteenth-century as well as nineteenth- and twentieth-century editors and critics who have argued for authorial revision in Shakespeare's plays have had to battle the textual fortress constructed in 1623 by the Folio printers' defensive claim that their edition was set from the authoritative, true original copies, which were cured and perfect in limb; by Heminge and Condell's protective injunction that Shakespeare scarcely blotted a line in his papers; and by Ben Jonson's immediately misunderstood buttressing remark of how wonderful it would have been if Shakespeare had blotted a thousand. The mandate that Shakespeare did not revise, compounded from these problematic praises from his friends and business partners, effectively deterred any critic wanting to object that it overconfidently or underestimatedly misinterpreted the evidence of the texts themselves.

Yet both Shakespeare's theatrical and literary audiences were being badly misled about what he was capable of writing, rewriting, and not writing; although he supposedly did not need to revise his plays because he was a natural genius who spontaneously generated perfect texts, his admirers and successors generously decided to revise his perfect texts for him. At least nineteen of Shakespeare's plays were rewritten by late seventeenth- and early eighteenth-century playwrights and producers, including William Davenant, Nahum Tate, Charles Gildon, John Dryden, and Colley Cibber. The plays were "refined," "improved," and "reformed" into operas, spectacles, masques, and dramatic presentations, often bearing little resemblance to the plays on which they were based. Tragedies such as *King Lear* were reworked to provide happy endings, while romances such as *The Tempest* were revised to reflect current mores, tastes, and political climates.[6] Thus, by the beginning of the eighteenth century, many critics and most of the general public were unaware of what was "genuinely Shakespearian" in the productions they saw, as the dramatist who did not need to revise himself now needed to be revised by others.

However, his literary editors undertook to document and reproduce the genuine Shakespeare, even though through the editorial process they also subjected him to the very revision that they refused to see him performing himself. In 1709, his first "editor," Nicholas Rowe, claimed to "have taken some Care to redeem him from the Injuries of former Impressions," but he used the textually corrupt Fourth Folio to produce his first complete and corrected edition of the plays. Rowe's task was to "restore" the texts, which had become mangled through subsequent printings and theatrical adaptations, and he advised that, as Shakespeare's "Original Manuscripts" had been lost, he had compared several printed editions to give the "true Reading": "In some of the Editions, especially the last there were many Lines (and in *Hamlet* one whole Scene) left out together; these are now all supply'd." Rowe was satisfied to attribute textual "corruptions" (often and erroneously synonymous with "variants" in the eighteenth century) to printers' errors.

Although misguided in his choice of copy-text, Rowe was the first to collate different editions of the same texts in order to arrive at some type of "true Reading." He did however work on the assumption that the latest text presented the best readings, and did not comment on the plays' textual histories or on Quarto/Folio variants, probably because he did not have access to many of the original Quarto texts. Rowe found Shakespeare incapable of revision or even correction, as "what he thought, was commonly so Great, so justly and rightly Conceiv'd in it self, that it wanted little or no Correction," and he accused Ben Jonson of jealously belittling Shakespeare: "The Praise of seldom altering or blotting out what he writ, which was given him by the Players who were the first Publishers of his Works after his Death, was what *Johnson* could not bear."[7]

It was left to Alexander Pope, Shakespeare's second editor, to attempt to produce in 1725 the first edition based on collation of all of the available extant Quarto and Folio texts, and thereby raise the issue of how to treat variants between Quartos and between Quartos and Folios. In his preface, Pope noted Heminge and Condell's reference to the "unblotted lines" and testified:

> There never was a more groundless report, or to the contrary of which there are more undeniable evidences. As, the Comedy of the *Merry Wives* of *Windsor,* which he entirely new writ; the *History of* Henry *the 6th,* which was first published under the Title of the *Contention of* York *and* Lancaster; and that of *Henry the 5th,* extreamly improved; that of *Hamlet* enlarged to almost as much again as at first, and many others.

Pope proposed that an editor work from the earliest texts printed during the author's lifetime, rather than the latest texts, to produce a correct edition (although he himself did not accomplish this task). He questioned the authority of the First Folio texts, which he decided had been printed from theatrically corrupted prompt-copies and *"Piece-meal Parts,"* and instead considered the Quarto texts the "Originall Copies."

Pope's examination of Quarto texts, a major step in Shakespearian textual study, led him to some conclusions which have remained controversial. For example, confronted with the incomplete Quarto 2 of *The Merry Wives of Windsor,* he agreed with Charles Gildon that it had been hastily composed, and assumed that it was "the first imperfect sketch of this Comedy," later "alter'd and improved by the Author almost in every speech" in the Folio. Pope extended this theory to other plays which now are considered by many editors to have "bad" first Quartos, including *2 Henry VI, 3 Henry VI, Henry V,* and *Hamlet* (although Quarto 1 of this play was not seen by Pope or any other eighteenth-century editor), and to *King John* and *The Taming of the Shrew.*[8]

Without exploring theories of piracy or memorial reconstruction, and having had access to only nine first Quartos,[9] Pope made the most astute judgment he could: plays with substantive Quarto and Folio variants which he considered valuable were probably "altered" by the author, and these variants were incorporated into Pope's edition, while variants resulting in "whole heaps of trash" could be ascribed to bookkeepers, actors, printers, and editors, and rejected. For example, Pope advised readers in the footnotes to his editions of *Richard III, Henry V, Romeo and Juliet, 2 Henry IV,* and *King Lear* of the probable "Alterations or Additions which *Shakespear* himself made."[10]

Claiming that some plays, particularly *Love's Labor's Lost, The Winter's Tale,* and *Titus Andronicus,* were only partially written by Shakespeare, Pope treated him as a working dramatist who, in addition to collaborating with others, adapted numerous preexisting plays and later doubly revised them again. Pope's edition nobly attempted to "restore" what was lost to Shakespeare's Quarto and First Folio texts in the subsequent Second, Third, and Fourth Folios, but, in effect, he undermined his arguments for the authority of the earliest texts and for authorial revision by setting his texts largely from the second edition of Rowe,[11] and by bringing his own revisions, emendations, alterations, and additions to the "restored" texts, and by relegating to the foot of the page passages he believed were "excessively bad."[12] Nevertheless, Pope's revision theories became immediately and immovably entrenched in a new textual tradition for succeeding decades of editors and critics to adopt or abandon, and his popular edition was frequently reprinted during the eighteenth century, often with a new editor's preface tacked on and the original notes, including those on revision, left intact.

In his 1726 answer to Pope's edition, pointedly titled *Shakespeare Restored,* Lewis Theobald attacked many of Pope's emendations in specific plays (for which he was promptly satirized by Pope in *The*

*Dunciad*). In his 1733–34 edition of the plays, Theobald was openly
contemptuous of Pope's claims of authorial revision and, like Rowe, did
not consider Shakespeare capable of blotting lines: "his Fire, Spirit, and
Exuberance of Imagination gave an Impetuousity to his Pen: His Ideas
flow'd from him in a Stream rapid, but not turbulent; copious, but not
overbearing its Shores." Theobald attempted to elucidate the troubled
printing history of the plays in order to explain their variants, and in the
process proposed the theory that an audience's desire to see a play in
print and the players' desire to "secrete" it produced pirated Quartos
with nonauthorial corruptions, deformities, and "blemishes."[13] He also
suggested that the Folio texts had been assembled and followed Pope
(who followed Gildon) in accepting the early Quartos of *The Merry Wives
of Windsor* and possibly *Love's Labor's Lost* only as first sketches[14] and in
using later Folios and later Quartos to emend the plays.

Pope's edition was reissued in 1744–47 by Thomas Hanmer[15] and in
1747 by William Warburton, who in one astute sentence summed up the
current state of Shakespearian editing: "So that, as then, he was thought
not to deserve a Cure, he was now supposed not to need any." Motivated
to protect the integrity of Pope's textual work, Warburton criticized both
Theobald and Hanmer for their failure to collate and correct texts in
case they harmed Shakespeare's reputation as a natural genius, and he
credited Pope with having "separated the genuine from the spurious
Plays."[16] In 1748, Zachary Grey[17] and Thomas Edwards[18] rebutted many
of Warburton's charges.

Samuel Johnson's preface to his 1765 edition of the collected plays
likened Shakespeare's composition to a "forest, in which oaks extend
their branches and pines tower in the air, interspersed sometimes with
weeds and brambles, and sometimes giving shelter to myrtles and to
roses; filling the eye with awful pomp, and gratifying the mind with
endless diversity."[19] In spite of his consciousness of "weeds and brambles"
in the texts, Dr. Johnson's limited access to early Quartos[20] rather than
his reverence for Shakespeare prevented him from giving much attention
to the question of revision and caused him to use later (and derivative)
Folios and Quartos to edit the plays, a practice rejected by modern
editors. Johnson lacked the first Quartos of *Richard II, Henry V, Love's
Labor's Lost,* and *Othello,* and the first and second Quartos or Octavos
of *2 Henry VI, 3 Henry VI, Hamlet, Romeo and Juliet,* and *Titus Andronicus.* He thus depended on the speculations of his predecessors,
including Pope and Theobald, for his own conclusions on authorial

revision.[21] Johnson described *Richard II* as "one of those which *Shakespeare* has apparently revised," and also cited scenes in *2 Henry IV, Henry VIII, Troilus and Cressida, Othello,* and *King Lear* which Shakespeare may have "inserted" or "expunged."

Johnson's high regard for the Folio texts as the true texts is exemplified in his repeating Pope's standard critical theory of the transmission of their "errors": the chain was begun by Shakespeare's "ungrammatical" style, continued by transcribers, copiers, and actors, and permanently anchored by printers. Johnson did offer a stunningly modern critical explanation for the dramatic inconsistencies in texts which he suspected had been revised:

> An authour, in revising his work when his original ideas have faded from his mind, and new observations have produced new sentiments, easily introduces images which have been more newly impressed upon him, without observing their want of congruity to the general texture of his original design.[22]

However, Johnson's edition, and particularly its theories of what was and was not "Shakespearian," prompted critical and satirical attacks. For example, William Kenrick assailed Johnson for noting the line, "I'th name of me," in *The Winter's Tale* and remarking "I believe *me* should be blotted out,"[23] by retorting, "This scheme of blotting out was originally suggested by . . . BEN *Johnson,* who only expressed his wish that Shakespeare had done, what SAM *Johnson* boldly determined to do for him."[24] Yet in berating Dr. Johnson, Kenrick attacked an editor who had unexceptionally taken a theory of authorial revision over from previous editors; for example, Johnson's most convincing argument for revision in a play (*King Lear*) was developed from observations first made by Pope.

In 1766, George Steevens printed twenty of the plays; the title page advertised his edition as "being the whole Number printed in Quarto During his LIFE-TIME, or before the RESTORATION." Steevens agreed with Pope that the Folio texts were corrupted by the players and transcribers without supervision by Shakespeare, "for he would hardly have unnerved a line in his written copy," and followed previous editors in assigning blame for difficult words and passages to nonauthorial interference. In denigrating the Folio texts, Steevens seemed motivated to protect the commercial success of his edition; he conceded that although Shakespeare may have revised his Quarto texts before or after their publication he did not produce revised Folio texts. In the Folio, in comparison with Quartos, Steevens did not "see on the whole any greater marks of a skilful revisal, or the advantage of being printed from unblotted originals in the one, than in the other." He agreed with Pope that *The Merry Wives of Windsor* and *Henry V* were altered by Shakespeare, and conjectured that Shakespeare had revised the most "ancient" version of *King John* (*The Troublesome raigne of John*) to produce a later, superior version in the Folio: "The author seems to have been so thoroughly dissatisfied with this Play as to have written it almost entirely anew, reserving only a few of the Lines and the Conduct of several Scenes."[25]

However, not all critics and editors were as eager as Pope and his followers to debate authorial revision, an issue as "extremely sensitive"[26] in the eighteenth century as in the twentieth. Dr. Richard Farmer's 1767 "Essay on the Learning of Shakespeare," which was reprinted in a few subsequent editions of the plays, discussed Elizabethan stage history and dramatic practice at length but summarily dismissed Pope's questioning of the "unblotted lines" in a mere footnote.[27] Walter Whiter defended Shakespeare against charges of "a foolish quibble, or an impertinent allusion" (including those caused by variants?) by applying Locke's Association of Ideas to the author's composition process. Thus Shakespeare worked "with words and with ideas, which have been suggested to the mind by a principle of union unperceived by himself, and independent of the subject, to which they are applied."[28] Farmer and Whiter serve as extreme examples of eighteenth-century editors and critics determined to protect Shakespeare from any charges of corruption, bad writing, or even rewriting.

Advertised solely as *"a companion to the theatre,"* John Bell's 1774 edition intended to capture the "essence" of Shakespeare as his plays were currently being performed at the Theatres Royal in London. The editors anticipated antagonism and criticism from literary purists but did not apologize for offering modern theatrical corrections and emendations. Although they acknowledged that Shakespeare was a "most spontaneous author," the editors followed Pope *verbatim* in admitting revision in some plays: "We have undoubted proof, the *Merry Wives of Windsor,* the three parts of *Henry the Sixth, Henry the Fifth,* and *Hamlet* were not only improved, but almost re-written." However, the editors indignantly dismissed Pope's attribution of other "errors" to actors and instead blamed Shakespeare, as all previous editors had, for his "unparalleled neglect of the correction and publication of his works."[29]

In his 1767–68 edition, Edward Capell had also attributed Folio corruptions to the players and variants to "player editors," who "studiously heighten'd" them and who "had the means in their power, being masters of all the alterations,—to give at once greater currency to their own lame edition, and support the charge which they bring against the quarto's." Capell appeared to accept Pope's general theories of revision and collaboration and added several non-Shakespearian plays to the canon. Capell explained: "To the thirty six plays in this collection, we must add seven, (one of which is in two parts) perhaps written over again," plus fourteen other plays, "making in all, fifty-eight plays; besides the part that he may reasonably be thought to have had in other men's labours, being himself a player and manager of theatres." Although willing to argue for revision in collaborative plays, of the plays written (according to Capell) entirely by Shakespeare, only the early Quarto copies of *Henry V, King John, The Merry Wives of Windsor,* and *The Taming of a Shrew* were conceivably allowed to have been "first draughts" later enlarged by the author after the first performances,[30] and Capell saw only very limited revision in other plays.

While the 1778 reissue of Johnson and Steevens's joint edition offered no new editorial comment on revision, it did contain Edmond Malone's essay, "An Attempt to Ascertain the Order in Which the Plays Attributed to Shakspeare Were Written," which provided the first significant reexamination and restatement of authorial revision since Pope's remarks on the subject in the first edition of his *Works of Shakespear* in 1725. Malone later revised "An Attempt" at least three times: first for the 1788 *Prolegomena* (produced to follow the 1785–86 reissue of Johnson and Steevens's edition), then for his own 1790 edition, and again sometime prior to an 1821 posthumous edition.[31] He continually revised his chronology of the plays, and by 1790 dropped six apocryphal plays, *Titus Andronicus,* and *Pericles* from the list, renaming the essay "An Attempt to Ascertain the Order in Which the Plays of Shakspeare Were Written." In spite of these other changes, his comments on revision varied only slightly.

Because Malone made the first editorial distinction between authorial/theatrical "cuts," "additions," "emendations," and "alterations" and printer/compositor "omissions" and "appearances," he should be recognized as the father both of the modern school of Shakespearian textual criticism and of revision criticism. In his 1778 "Attempt to Ascertain the Order," he stated in a discussion of *Henry V,*

> I have not indeed met with any evidence (except in three plays) that the several
> scenes which are found in the folio of 1623, and are not in the preceding
> quartos, were added by the second labour of the author.—The last chorus of
> *K. Henry V.* already mentioned, affords a striking proof that this was not
> always the case. The two copies of *the Second Part of K. Henry IV.* printed in
> the same year (1600) furnish another. In one of these, the whole first scene of
> Act III. is wanting; not because it was then unwritten, (for it is found in the
> other copy published in that year) but because the editor was not possessed of
> it. That what have been called *additions by the author,* were not really such,
> may be also collected from another circumstance; that in some of the quartos
> where these supposed additions are wanting, references and replies are found
> to the passages omitted.[32]

The great strength of Malone was that he carefully discriminated between additions in printed texts for which other explanations could be
found and authorial revising; thus he did not accept what so many editors
had taken for granted, that Shakespeare "revised" *Henry V* and *2 Henry
IV.* Malone was the first to contradict previous editors, who had all
accepted the absence or appearance of whole speeches or scenes as
primary and irrefutable evidence of authorial revision in the *Henry VI*
plays, *Henry V,* and other plays, and to urge caution in using variants
resulting from editorial addition or deletion to determine a text's provenance.

   Although Steven Urkowitz has argued that Malone rejected
"Johnson's exposition of Shakespeare as a revising artist,"[33] Malone did
in fact see Shakespeare as a revising artist and began carefully to "clas-
sify" variants in support of an argument for limited authorial revision:

> I do not however mean to say, that Shakspeare never made any alterations in
> his plays. We have reason to believe that *Romeo and Juliet, Hamlet,* and *the
> Merry Wives of Windsor,* were entirely new written; and a second revisal or
> temporary topicks might have suggested, in a course of years, some additions
> and alterations in all his pieces. But with respect to the entire scenes that are
> wanting in some of the early editions, (particularly those of *King Henry V. the
> Second and Third Part of Henry VI.* and *the Second Part of King Henry IV.*) I
> suppose the omissions to have arisen from the imperfections of the copies; and
> instead of saying that "the first scene of *King Henry V.* was *added by the author*
> after the publication of the quarto in 1600," all that we can pronounce with
> certainty is, that this scene is not *found* in the quarto of 1600.[34]

By 1788 Malone had substituted *Richard II* for *2 Henry VI* and *3 Henry
VI* in the list of plays "wanting" entire scenes which earlier editors had

cited as revised.[35] By 1790 he had become more conservative in his assessment of Shakespeare's revisions: his 1778 argument that the three plays "were entirely new written," Pope's exact term, was amended to "were revised and augmented by the authour," and his conclusion that Shakespeare's second revisal produced "some additions and alterations in all his pieces" was amended to "in some other of his pieces." He also questioned whether *Love's Labor's Lost,* as its Quarto 1 title page suggests, had been revised after performance and prior to its publication.[36] Malone's conservatism regarding revision may have been due to his increasing desire to establish fixed dates and a smooth chronology for the composition of the plays in the canon.[37]

In his 1790 Preface, Malone complained of the "arbitrary and capricious innovations made by our predecessors from ignorance of the phraseology and customs of the age in which Shakespeare lived." Malone did not see Shakespeare, as previous editors had, as a natural and spontaneous genius who wrote during an uncultivated age, but as a learned author writing and rewriting in a learned age. Malone agreed with Johnson that during Shakespeare's age the plays had been "mutilated" by transcribers, players, and compositors, but he stressed that only the first Quartos, except in the case of *Romeo and Juliet,* which was an "imperfect sketch," and *The Merry Wives of Windsor* and *Henry V,* which may have been first sketches or imperfect copies, should be considered the author's "*first* editions." Malone correctly rejected the authority of the later Folios, and questioned only the First Folio texts which had extant Quartos.[38] Unlike his predecessors, Malone respected the authority of these First Folio texts, demanding that they be collated with first Quarto texts, and usually refused to use post-First Folio and later Quarto texts in editing the plays. Thus, Malone insisted on the relative value of the variant texts for particular plays and on their correlative value for other plays in the canon. Though seemingly a minor point in his larger arguments for textual editing, Malone's distinction on the value of variant texts in determining authorial revision firmly established an editorial foundation which succeeding scholars have never been able to overturn.

Malone, who was the first editor to use Henslowe's *Diary,*[39] which detailed "mending" and "alterynge" of Elizabethan and Jacobean plays, recognized that Shakespeare and other dramatists worked as adapters, revisers, and collaborators. For example, he contended that Shakespeare had probably not entirely written but rather made additions to existing texts of *Titus Andronicus, 1 Henry VI,* and *Pericles.*[40] Also, in his "Disser-

tation on the Three Parts of *King Henry VI.*," Malone argued that
Shakespeare had adapted at least *2 Henry VI* and *3 Henry VI*, and
probably *The Taming of the Shrew* and *King John,* from preexisting plays.
Malone carefully distinguished between Shakespeare's patterns of
"adding to" and "new-modelling" another author's plays, explaining:

> He did not content himself with writing new beginnings to the acts; he
> new-versified, he new-modelled, he transposed many of the parts, and greatly
> amplified and improved the whole. Several lines, however, and even whole
> speeches which he thought sufficiently polished, he accepted, and introduced
> into his own work, without any, or with very slight, alterations.[41]

These comments, when contrasted with his statements in "An Essay"
and his "Preface," demonstrate that Malone considered revision by
Shakespeare of his own plays a different matter from his "rewriting" or
adapting plays by other dramatists. Malone had already decided by 1790
that Shakespeare had altered and not "entirely new writ" three of his
own plays, but *had* "entirely new writ" at least four plays that were not
his own. His argument here interestingly foreshadows that of a "new"
revisionist, John Kerrigan, who claims that generally a seventeenth-century adapter

> cut, inserted and substituted sizeable pieces of text without altering the details
> of his precursor's dialogue. Revising authors, by contrast, though they some-
> times worked just with large textual fractions, tended to tinker, introducing
> small additions, small cuts and indifferent single word substitutions.[42]

Malone established a number of other new Shakespearian textual
theories which reestablished the principles of scholarly editing.[43] In
arguing that alterations might be made to "topical" issues or allusions,
such as a reference to "the council" in the Elizabethan Quarto 1 of *The
Merry Wives of Windsor* changed to "the king" in the Jacobean Folio, he
anticipated the modern research which documents that political and
religious concerns prompted censorship of printed texts. Also, Malone
did not depend solely on the title pages of Quarto 1 of *Love's Labor's
Lost* and Quarto 2 of *Romeo and Juliet* and *Hamlet,* which advertised
augmentation, to decide which plays had been altered or adapted by
Shakespeare, but looked instead for what he considered "*internal
proof,*"[44] such as stylistic evidence. While Malone did not discuss revision
in *King Lear,*[45] and in "An Essay," devoted little attention to the play, he
was suspicious of the variants between what he assumed were all first

Quartos: "Of the tragedy of *King Lear* there are no less than three copies, varying from each other, printed for the same bookseller, and in the same year";[46] he perhaps also considered the Folio variants as editorial or compositorial in origin and thus was unwilling to commit himself to arguing for revision in this play.

Malone later gained greater fame and editorial prominence by proving in 1796 that the "Shakespearian" documents earlier "found" by Samuel Ireland were actually forgeries. Malone's landmark edition of Shakespeare's plays was edited and reissued by Boswell's son James in 1821, and the eighteenth-century edition had even greater impact as a nineteenth-century edition. The younger Boswell agreed with Malone that Quarto 1 of *Romeo and Juliet* was an "imperfect sketch by the author himself,"[47] but otherwise did not comment on revision. Boswell reprinted nearly every preface or advertisement from the major eighteenth-century editions, thus ironically placing side by side conflicting and contradictory theories of textual emendation, correction, and revision, including the prefaces of Theobald, Hanmer, and Warburton, all of which Malone had earlier dismissed as worthless.[48]

Malone's pioneering work in editorial theory soon became orthodoxy for nineteenth-century editors and critics, but rather than focusing on his primary argument that Shakespeare revised his own plays, his followers canonized his peripheral argument that Shakespeare had "new-modelled" existing plays. In an 1811 lecture on Shakespeare's "excellencies," Samuel Taylor Coleridge suggested that an examination of the style of a passage in the plays could be used to determine whether Shakespeare had originally composed the passage or adapted it from an "old" play:

> If we discovered a Play in which there were neither Shakespeare's defects or his excellencies, or defects or excellencies incompatible with his, or individual scenes so circumstanced, we should have strong reason to believe that it was not Shakespeare's & that they were taken either from the old plays which in some instances he reformed & altered; [or] that they were inserted by some underhand to please the mob.[49]

Coleridge, like Malone, was willing to recognize both defects and excellencies in Shakespeare's work, although Coleridge joined Pope in ascribing these inconsistencies to "double" revision. Coleridge was perhaps more eager than Malone to defend Shakespeare against charges of uncultivated or careless writing as his public lectures stressed that Shakespeare was an extraordinarily gifted writer. Coleridge apparently did not

discuss Shakespeare's revision of his own plays in these lectures, yet his
inclusion of style with the other types of internal evidence which could
locate revision prefigured much of the critical research done by twentieth-century scholars investigating authorial revision.

However, the issue of authorial revision in the plays originally written
by Shakespeare, and of the degree of caution exercised by the editor who
argued for it, soon resurfaced. In 1842–1844, John Payne Collier produced an edition of the plays based on what he advertised as newly
acquired and hitherto unseen manuscripts of Shakespeare's poems and
the private papers and theatrical documents that had belonged to Shakespeare and his acting companies.[50] In his edition, Collier used these new
documents, including Henslowe's *Diary,* to argue that Shakespeare "had
chiefly employed his pen in the revival, alteration, and improvement of
existing dramas." Collier listed *The Comedy of Errors, 1 Henry VI, 2 Henry
VI,* and *3 Henry VI* as having been adapted by Shakespeare from existing
non-Shakespearian plays, and *The Merry Wives of Windsor, All's Well That
Ends Well, Henry V, Romeo and Juliet,* and perhaps *Macbeth, Hamlet,* and
*King Lear* as having been "improved," "altered," or "added to" by
Shakespeare after performance or after publication of Quarto editions.[51]

Collier's later purchase of a 1632 Second Folio with what he termed
"authoritative" emendations in a "17th-century hand" encouraged him
to retract much of the editorial comment and criticism in his 1844 edition
when he printed *Notes and Emendations to the Text of Shakespeare's Plays*
in 1853. He conjectured that this Folio, inscribed "Tho. Perkins His
Booke" on the cover, had belonged to Richard Perkins, a member of the
King's Men, who had penned into it changes made in performance by
or with the consent of Shakespeare or his acting company. The emendations included corrections on nearly every page, changes in character
names, deletions of large blocks of text, and additions of explicit stage
directions.[52] Perhaps because the task of editing Shakespeare's plays and
reconstructing his original texts had by now become so difficult (due to
the lack of original manuscripts), many editors and critics immediately
accepted without question the authority of the Perkins Folio and to
incorporate its revisions into their own editions and critical work. However, others publicly attacked the quality and genuineness of its "corrections" and questioned the true identity of the "old corrector."[53]

In 1859, the Perkins Folio was subjected to a scientific study by
members of the British Museum (with whom Collier had strained relations), who concluded that the emendations had been made in two

different hands, one of which was later than seventeenth century, and that some of the inked words appeared to have been written over penciled tracings. In 1861, C. Mansfield Ingleby offered a "complete view" of the Shakespeare controversy and strongly reiterated earlier claims that, in addition to the Perkins Folio, other documents and manuscripts that had fallen into Collier's hands had been "falsified."[54] Collier steadfastly maintained that he was innocent of forgery or any other type of tampering,[55] and the debate continued for several decades. Yet the Perkins Folio truly represents the reconstructed Shakespeare. Although a few scattered annotations in the Folio, now in the Huntington Library, are probably in an early seventeenth-century hand, nearly all of the remaining annotations and emendations are written in two or three hands significantly later than the date of the Folio.[56]

The most important result of the Perkins Folio debate was that editors, critics, and the general public re-examined the nature of conjectural emendation; in the future, correction of *any* of the extant printed Quarto and Folio texts made without sufficient evidence would provoke strenuous objection. In other words, revising Shakespeare or allowing him to revise himself constituted fraud. Variants between Shakespeare's own texts therefore became suspect, were no longer regarded as certain signs of authorial revision, and were not automatically incorporated as authoritative corrections into an editor's text of the plays.

Prior to the Perkins Folio debate, editors saw their main occupation as restoring to Shakespeare's own plays what previous editors had removed, and their lesser occupation as restoring to other playwrights' plays what Shakespeare had added. Pope's and Malone's theories on the various types of revisions that Shakespeare made in plays that were not his own were carefully scrutinized and often rejected. Mid-nineteenth-century editors, reacting to Malone, reclassified the type of "remodelling" that Shakespeare would have performed. Charles Knight, in his 1839–1843 and subsequent editions, accepted the theory that Shakespeare "remodelled" rather than "revised" his own and his company's plays, but in commenting on Malone's conclusions that Shakespeare had "altered" *1 Henry VI, 2 Henry VI, 3 Henry VI, Richard III,* and *Henry VIII,* Knight insisted that Shakespeare was involved only in major revision:

> We can understand how Shakspere new-modelled the old Taming of a Shrew and the old King John, by completely rewriting all the parts, adding some characters, rejecting others, rendering the action at his pleasure more simple

or more complex, expanding a short exclamation into a long and brilliant
dialogue, or condensing a whole scene into some expressive speech or two.
This, to our minds, is a sort of remodelling which Shakspere did not disdain
to try his hand upon.[57]

Knight accepted authorial revision only to the extent that Shakespeare
could be seen as "improving" rather than "reworking" another's play and
making it his own by infusing it with his own style and genius.[58]

During the Perkins Folio debate, editors, content to leave the problems
of conjectural emendations to Collier, concentrated on recognizing the
previously unrecognized passages and scenes that they believed Shakespeare had worked into his plays from preexisting plays. Both Samuel
Weller Singer in his 1856 edition and Alexander Dyce in his 1857 edition
saw Shakespeare as a master "remodeller" of other dramatists' plays as
well as a shrewd actor-manager who made extensive revisions in his own
plays. After finding "traces of revision" in *As You Like It* and *All's Well
That Ends Well*, Singer concluded that Heminge and Condell's mention
of unblotted lines referred to revised copies "prepared by the author
himself" for publication, so that through such revision some plays "received a portion of the very latest poetry that fell from Shakespeare's
pen." Singer also found three types of "remodelling" of other playwrights' work performed by Shakespeare: abridgment, insertion of words
and lines, and recasting of speeches and scenes.[59] Rev. Dyce agreed that
there was every reason to believe that Shakespeare "commenced author
by remoulding the works of others, and not by original composition."[60]

Subsequent to the Perkins Folio debate, editors, in an attempt to
produce a straightforward edition of the plays, paid little attention to the
problems engendered by eighteenth- and nineteenth-century speculation
on emendations, including revision. W. G. Clark, John Glover, and W.
A. Wright, the editors of the 1863–1866 Cambridge Shakespeare, noted
that there had been 262 previous editions of the plays, and they attempted
to set Shakespearian scholarship in some kind of perspective by producing a corrected edition. These editors, the first to list variants on pages
of the text rather than in an appendix, discounted the veracity of Heminge and Condell's 1623 "Address to the Reader" and followed the Folio
texts only when Quartos were not extant, noticing possible and slight
revision in *Love's Labor's Lost, Richard III, Troilus and Cressida, Romeo
and Juliet,* and *Hamlet.*[61] In discussing revision, the editors were conservative and noncontroversial, as they attributed many variants to memo-

rial reconstruction and printers' and compositors' errors.[62] Their carefully collated and researched collection became a standard edition of the plays for several decades.[63]

However, a few later nineteenth- and early twentieth-century critics took the offensive in the revision battle by militantly carrying Malone's and Collier's theories of "adaptation" to an extreme and by subscribing to Pope's theories of double revision. Frederick Gard Fleay, first in his 1876 *Shakespeare Manual* and later in his 1886 *A Chronicle History of the Life and Work of William Shakespeare* and other books, argued that Shakespeare was a professional and indiscriminate reviser of preexisting plays. Fleay believed that prior to 1593, as a "journeyman" with acting companies, Shakespeare revived plays already held by the company by carefully replacing "in almost every instance the work of his quondam companions by other and certainly not weaker lines of his own." Once trained to revise preexisting plays, Shakespeare, Fleay argued, as resident dramatist for the Chamberlain's, later the King's, Men, would logically have extended this double revision training to all of his own subsequent plays.

Fleay was not bothered by other critics' beliefs that some of Shakespeare's plays were of a higher quality than others and thus would need less reworking. Instead, he saw the plays as commercial theatrical products subjected to revision before, during, and after their performances and publications. In order to explain variants and differences among Quarto and Folio texts of the plays, Fleay cited the example of *King Lear*. Its entrance in the Stationers' Register in 1608 with mention of its being played at court in 1606, he suggested,

> settles two important questions: first, the relation of the Quarto text to the Folio—the Quarto being the version played at Court, the Folio that retained by the players for the public stage; secondly, the existence of a custom in the Globe company of allowing, in cases of altered or revised plays, the version not required for future stage purposes to be issued to the public in print.[64]

Fleay's argument here about the states of the texts was not new, but he succeeded in using it to support his newly founded large-scale revision theories.

Fleay's contentious theories were wholly supported and expanded by John Mackinnon Robertson, who in the early twentieth century proposed that *all* of Shakespeare's plays, except *A Midsummer Night's Dream,* were adaptations of existing plays probably first written by Christopher Mar-

lowe. In arguing for a "pre-Shakespearean" and "Marlovian" structure
to Shakespeare's plays, Robertson commented:

> While he (with another) entirely recomposed LEAR, of which the old form
> is in print, and very fully rewrote MACBETH, OTHELLO, and ANTONY
> AND CLEOPATRA, even as he did HAMLET, and as he did the best
> comedies in the degree of his satisfaction with them, he rewrote ALL'S WELL
> much less than he did MEASURE FOR MEASURE, which would appeal
> more to him, as it should to us.

Robertson accepted the idea that Shakespeare provided "unblotted" papers, but attacked Heminge and Condell's Address to the Reader because
it "coerced" readers into believing that Shakespeare "wrote the whole of
every play in the Folio."[65]

Fleay's argument that Shakespeare had "vamped" his own and others'
plays[66] and Robertson's argument that Shakespeare had "transfigured"
others' plays were certain to provoke angry reaction and controversy
from already beleaguered critics eager to protect the Shakespeare they
had so diligently reconstructed. Malone's careful distinctions between
"theatrical adaptation" and "authorial revision" had now been obscured,
and the entire canon of Shakespeare had been labeled "not genuine."
Fleay's and Robertson's reckless overextensions of the carefully constructed and researched theories of Malone would soon discredit any
scholarly examination of revision theories.

The British Academy lectures of the first two decades of the twentieth
century took up this perilous "revision crisis" in Shakespearian textual
study caused by Fleay and Robertson and their followers. In 1916, J. W.
Mackail agreed that Shakespeare had begun his career by revising existing dramas:

> The amount of non-Shakespearian work in what is called Shakespeare is
> considerable; this is so alike in the earlier period when he was adapting and
> piecing out older men's work, in the later period when younger men were
> doing the same with his, and even between the two, where the stage-text that
> has survived has been altered for performance by members of the company or
> by irresponsible actors.[67]

However, not all of the British Academy defenders of revision theories
were defenders of "double" revision theory. In 1909, Alfred W. Pollard
had proposed a distinction between "good" and "bad" Quartos by iden-
tifying the first Quartos of *Romeo and Juliet, Henry V, The Merry Wives*

*of Windsor,* and *Hamlet* as "pirated" texts.[68] He later used this "bad Quarto" theory to propose a revision theory that was less radical than those of Fleay, Robertson, and Mackail, but still too radical for some traditional tastes. Pollard took the comments on "unblotted lines" to imply that the Folio texts were "original drafts" which were later revised.[69] Yet Pollard did not share Fleay's and Robertson's radically unscholarly treatment of the texts; instead, he scrupulously analyzed the texts using the methods of the New Bibliography.[70]

John Dover Wilson later applauded Pollard's refusal to accept the "three gloomy doctrines" of the old criticism, namely that all of the Quartos printed before 1623 were stolen and surreptitious; that the textual "idiosyncrasies" of the Quarto and Folio texts were due to the "drunken aberrations" of compositors; and that Heminge and Condell were either fools or "knaves in league with Jaggard to hoodwink a gullible public."[71] Thus, in his 1923 British Academy lecture, Pollard confidently argued that revision was most certainly a "Shakespearian" concept, and in most of his plays,

> we shall find enough discrepancies, enough evidence of what seems imperfect revision, enough diversity of style, to tempt us to believe that Shakespeare wrote all his plays in the years of his dramatic apprenticeship and spent the rest of his working life in constantly rewriting them.

He concluded that his theory was not much more untenable than "its opposite which envisages each play as the result of a continuous effort throughout so many weeks and then finished and done with."[72] Because Pollard's theories on "bad" Quartos had revolutionized Shakespearian textual study, his theories on revision were immediately awarded scholarly acceptance and privilege.

Yet in his 1924 Shakespeare Lecture to the British Academy, pointedly titled "The Disintegration of Shakespeare," E. K. Chambers responded to this new orthodoxy by contemptuously attacking and dismissing theories, most notably those of Fleay, Robertson, and Wilson, which suggested that Shakespeare revised his plays and/or those of his predecessors. Chambers acknowledged that the coexistence in a play of features belonging to different stages and lines of development presented problems which needed to be resolved. However, he attributed the source of these "eccentricities and dislocations" to inconsistencies in Shakespeare's style rather than to revision.

In order to bolster his own arguments and to provide the ending point for the arguments begun by his predecessors, Chambers attempted to historicize and contextualize the revision debate in this speech to the Academy. He very briefly traced the discussion of double revision by Pope, Theobald, Hanmer, Farmer, and Capell; applauded Malone's silencing of it; and listed the few heretical dissenters such as Coleridge, Knight, and the *Cambridge Shakespeare* editors, who had continued to argue for it in a few plays.[73] Chambers refused to accept scholars' claims of single revision by Shakespeare of his own plays because he believed that they led to the acceptance of Fleay's and Robertson's "devastating" claims of double revision. He ominously warned that "it is an easy step from Shakespeare as a reviser of Shakespeare to Shakespeare as a reviser of predecessors," and therefore succinctly concluded that "the amount of revision in the canon is not likely to be very great."[74] Chambers continued his attack on the revisionists as "disintegrators" in his subsequent books.

Chambers did not recognize and therefore did not separate the "old" revisionist school of Pope, which saw revision as the cause of the coexistence of good and bad passages in the plays, from the "new" revisionist school of Malone, which saw revision as part of Shakespeare's creative process. In congratulating Malone for attacking double revision theories, Chambers evidently had not noticed Malone's own conclusions that Shakespeare had revised three of his own plays, *Romeo and Juliet*, *Hamlet*, and *The Merry Wives of Windsor*. Yet Chambers's influence was so strong that even though he had failed to distinguish between those scholars who were willing to argue that Shakespeare had revised only his own plays from those who believed that he had revised others' plays, the fearful nondisintegrators were eager to distance themselves from the disintegrators.[75]

In his 1929 lecture to the Academy, Wilson responded to Chambers's attack on him by defending revision and revisionists against disintegration: "To show, for instance, that *Hamlet* had been rehandled once or even twice by Shakespeare is not surely to injure it in any way as a work of art." He repeated Pollard's argument that the players' comments on the "unblotted" lines could be used to support revision theory.[76] However, Chambers's rebuke of revisionists, including disintegrators, and his rejection of their arguments for Shakespearian revision had been too powerful for rebuttal or rescue. Because scholars supporting revision, such as Wilson, were now grouped together with such extremists as J. M. Robertson and Basil Lawrence, who claimed that the revision characteristics pointed to Francis Bacon as the author of Shakespeare's plays,[77]

revision theories again became subject to the overwhelming ridicule
heaped on them when Pope first argued for revision in 1725. The revision
theories which had degenerated from the careful, scholarly work of
Malone to the wild, unscholarly speculations of Fleay and Robertson
during the past one hundred years were now effectively silenced for the
next fifty years.

E. K. Chambers found wholehearted support in the work of two later
scholars, W. W. Greg and Fredson Bowers, who used New Bibliography
to develop the textual criticism that laid the foundation for modern
Shakespearian editing. In his final summation of Shakespearian textual
theory, *The Shakespeare First Folio*, W. W. Greg expressed the same
disregard for revisionists that Chambers had shown and agreed that

> we may freely admit the possibility of revision or collaboration in a few plays,
> but the fact remains that those who begin by accounting for everything that
> seems to them unexpected by the postulate of rewriting and recasting end by
> seeing each play as the outcome of a long process of rehandling of earlier
> material by the same or by some other hand.[78]

Greg, like many critics before and after him, explained textual differences
and anomalies in other, sometimes trivial, ways, admitting the possibility
of revision as a last resort and in very few instances. His concentration
on causes other than revision for Quarto and Folio variants helped to
terminate the critical discussion of Shakespeare as a reviser of his own
plays.

Similarly, Fredson Bowers, in *On Editing Shakespeare* (which with
Greg's book has served to canonize textual study), presented what has
become the standard explanation for the variant first Quarto texts of
*Hamlet, King Lear, Henry V, 2 Henry VI, Richard III, Romeo and Juliet,*
and *The Merry Wives of Windsor:*

> When these quartos were first distinguished they were assessed either as early
> Shakespearian drafts, or as old plays by another author in a partial state of
> Shakespearian revision. Subsequently, the estimate was completely reversed by
> the formulation of the 'bad-quarto' hypothesis, which took these versions not
> to be ancestors of the good texts but, instead, corrupt later derivations of the
> good-text manuscripts.

Bowers was willing to argue for some authorial revision for specific
theatrical reasons between the writing of the foul papers and their
transcription in a fair copy, but he attributed most of the variants in some

of the Folio manuscripts to nonauthorial "corruption, censorship, and sophistication."[79] In the same way, M. M. Mahood, in her Annual Shakespeare Lecture of 1972 (forty-eight years after Chambers's), pledged her lasting gratefulness to her predecessor for checking "the dismemberment of Shakespeare's texts into revisions and collaborations." Mahood applauded the "slovenliness" and "inspired carelessness" of Shakespeare's "unblotted lines," and recognized at least one "duplication" (in *Julius Caesar*) as Shakespeare's "doing deliberate violence to his own dramatic instincts."[80] Thus Shakespearian textual and literary criticism had come full circle since Lewis Theobald had first expressed his scholarly frustrations with the careless, incorrect, and distortive transmission of Shakespeare's plays.

Since 1924, a few critics, including John Dover Wilson, Madeleine Doran, Albert Feuillerat, Hardin Craig, E. A. J. Honigmann, J. M. Nosworthy, and Nevill Coghill, have courageously contested both the seventeenth-century mandate of Heminge and Condell and the twentieth-century mandate of Chambers and have continued to offer differing theories of the causes for and the extent of Shakespeare's revision of his own plays.[81] Wilson, Feuillerat, Craig, Coghill, and Nosworthy each argued that contemporary theatrical and printing practices required routine revisions before and after performance from company dramatists such as Shakespeare. Doran's careful study of the first Quarto and the Folio texts of *King Lear* convinced her that political censorship was the cause of the authorial revisions between them; her remarkable theories have continued to influence editors of the play. Honigmann, keeping "windward of the disintegrators," was more cautious in seeing Shakespeare as a later reviser of his original works and suggested that he revised his plays only during their original composition and before they were performed. Therefore, these variant versions, one with Shakespeare's "first thoughts" and the other with his "second thoughts," resulted in what Honigmann described as "textual instability."[82]

However, the discussions of revision in *The Division of the Kingdoms* and Steven Urkowitz's *Shakespeare's Revision of King Lear* have prompted the reopening of the critical debate on Shakespearian revision and have once again forcibly involved the entire community of Shakespearian scholars. In the specific case of *King Lear,* the new revisionists reject W. W. Greg's concept of the single copy-text as the basis of an edition and refuse to term some variants, as E. K. Chambers did, "eccentricities and dislocations." These critics see the 1608 Quarto 1 and 1623 Folio texts as "two versions of the play, each consciously and distinctly fashioned."[83] In recognizing some variants as evidence of deliberate revision and each version as a separate artistic vision carefully crafted by Shakespeare, Gary Taylor, Michael Warren, Stanley Wells, Steven Urkowitz, and the others follow the course pioneered by Edmond Malone, rather than that established by Alexander Pope.

Critical response to both books on *King Lear* has been, as is consistent with the history of revision theories, divided. In their reviews of *The Division of the Kingdoms,* both E. A. J. Honigmann and T. H. Howard-Hill cited the volume as an important turning point for Shakespearian editors and critics, yet while Honigmann endorsed the probability of authorial revision, Howard-Hill argued that unless it can be proven that the Folio *King Lear* was set from Quarto copy, there is little bibliographic evidence for authorial revision rather than nonauthorial redaction.[84] Philip Edwards objected that two main issues, Shakespearian revision and the recovery of a Shakespearian text from the available prints, have not been separated.[85] However, the separation of these two issues has been for three and a half centuries the main crux in revision arguments, and it is no closer to being resolved than when Pope undertook to do so. Traditional editors such as Kenneth Muir have similarly rejected the "new and proselytizing orthodoxy" of these "textual Reformers," who cite authorial revision as the reason to print dual texts rather than the standard conflated editions.[86] Yet the new revisionists, although united in their desire for a rereading and rewriting of *King Lear,* have subsequently offered differing approaches toward and agendas for the textual and literary consequences of authorial revision in order to constitute their individual goals. For example, both Randall McLeod and Michael Warren have argued against editing Shakespeare in any form, and Steven Urkowitz has urged a reconsideration of "bad" quartos as legitimate stages in Shakespeare's composing and revising process rather than the illegitimate result of a pirate's process.[87] John Kerrigan, Gary Taylor, and Stanley Wells have also offered individual rationales for reediting and reinterpreting the revising Shakespeare.[88]

The crisis caused by the question of revision and the type of texts revision produces continues to preoccupy editors, critics, and literary and theatrical audiences engaged in any and all aspects of Shakespearian study, with the result that newspapers now report its influence on the commercial book trade as well as on the commercial theatre. For example, for several weeks in 1985 the "Letters" column of the *Times Literary Supplement* was dominated by a study of the limitations and limitlessness of Shakespearian revision. Stanley Wells responded to Terence Hawkes's review of A. L. Rowse's new, modernized edition of Shakespeare's plays by editorially tracing an author's composition process, concluding that Shakespeare "wrote in full awareness that in performance the script as first conceived would take on new meanings which themselves might impel him to modify his first conception of both words and action."[89] In response to Wells's letter, Eric Sams asserted that "Shakespeare is at last authoritatively acknowledged as a regular and indeed radical reviser of his own work."[90]

However, as Sidney Thomas demonstrated in his article, "Shakespeare's Supposed Revision of *King Lear,*" not all critics have acknowledged that Shakespeare revised, nor has the debate moved off the page or the stage since 1985. Thomas returned to the cruxes and consequences discussed by Shakespeare's first editors when he argued that "what the theory of Shakespearian revision asks us to accept is an assumption that Shakespeare set out to rework his play, presumably to correct or eliminate problems that had surfaced in rehearsal or performance, and then left untouched some of the most glaring and disturbing puzzles of the plays."[91] Thomas implies that Shakespeare made revisions at one particular moment, then forever left the play alone, unwittingly creating more "puzzles" than he had just solved. Yet, as so many other editors have argued, Shakespeare, throughout the time and space of his twenty-year writing career, may have unpuzzlingly regarded his plays as theatrical property which he could reclaim and revise.

In an attack on revisionists similar to that made by Thomas, Harold Jenkins incontrovertibly stated in the Introduction to his 1982 edition of *Hamlet* that "there has been too much irresponsible conjecture about Shakespeare's supposed revisions of supposed earlier attempts. My conception of Shakespeare is of a supremely inventive poet who had no call to rework his previous plays when he could always move on to a new one."[92] Jenkins's tenacious refusal to even consider that Shakespeare may have revised some plays, and his conception of Shakespeare as a poet with no calling to revise (so similar to Nicholas Rowe's in 1709) is rooted in a critical theory editorially derived from the First Folio which has transfixed so many for close to four hundred years.

Thus the Folio continues to exert an authority that is not easily challenged, although its meaning and form have been reinterpreted. In their recent edition, *William Shakespeare: Complete Works,* and its *Textual Companion,* Wells and Taylor support the authority of the Folio texts in establishing the canon of Shakespeare: "When the Folio speaks, we must echo it; but when the Folio is silent, its silence cannot be so confidently interpreted or obeyed."[93] The editors produce not a "genetic" but a traditional edition that primarily uses the Folio texts as copy-texts. Taylor defines individual editorial reconstructions as

> texts prepared by one or more editors, who attempt to correct errors of transmission in the earliest available documents, and who present the results of those individual decisions in modern typography, in old or modern spelling, with or without commentary, with or without textual apparatus.

Taylor concludes, "Our own edition is of this kind."[94] Although the editors convincingly document and discuss extensive authorial revision in several of Shakespeare's plays dating after 1596, particularly *2 Henry IV, Hamlet, Troilus and Cressida, Othello,* and *King Lear,*[95] they refuse to present a conflated edition only in the case of *King Lear,* printing instead edited texts of both the Quarto and the Folio. These editorial procedures, although dictated by printing exigencies,[96] appear to ignore Wells's dissatisfaction, stated elsewhere, with editors who attempt to produce a "single standard text" of plays which exist in two substantive texts.[97] Regardless of the influence of this edition, its encyclopedic *Textual Companion,* centered on theories of authorial revision, will serve as the new standard textual reference work, supplanting rather than supplementing Greg's standard textual companion, *The Shakespeare First Folio.*

David Bevington finds the editing of the Oxford *Complete Works,* based on the assumption that Shakespeare was an "ardent reviser," often so "disfiguring" and "confusing" that the resulting "indeterminate Shakespeare" disturbs the approaches of editors, scholars, teachers, and readers to the texts.[98] Yet the textual problems in editing Shakespeare, first encountered by Alexander Pope and soon taken up by Edmond Malone and succeeding editors and critics, remain central, disturbing, and inescapable for all Shakespearian scholars and literary and theatrical audiences.[99] Editors can no longer "determine" the least disturbing Shakespeare possible, but must recognize, like his readers, that the revising Shakespeare built indeterminacy into his texts, upsetting the strictly formulaic and traditional methods used to make him "determinate." These arguments for revision have forever changed the ways in which theatrical directors, actors, and audiences interpret and respond to Shakespeare's texts. When a Royal Shakespeare Company director speaks, and chooses to present a production of the "revised" Folio text of *King Lear,* a world of audiences watches and listens.

# Revision in the Manuscripts of Shakespeare's Contemporaries

The manuscripts of Shakespeare's plays are no longer extant, yet the extant manuscripts and printed texts of the plays of his contemporaries, many of whom wrote for the Chamberlain's or King's Men, reveal the common authorial practices of dramatists of the period. For centuries, scholars have scrupulously studied the characteristics of these literary and theatrical, private and professional documents and records and have formulated standardized theories about the composition, theatrical, and printing histories of plays by such dramatists as Ben Jonson, John Marston, Thomas Dekker, Thomas Heywood, Francis Beaumont, John Fletcher, and Thomas Middleton. Yet these same scholars have never comprehensively catalogued the irrefutable evidence of *authorial revision* in the manuscripts as well as printed texts of these and other dramatists, nor have they been courageous enough to battle the fundamental, non-revising Shakespeare orthodoxy by offering, as I do, this overwhelming evidence to support theories of Shakespearian revision.

So many extant manuscripts prove that professional dramatists writing during the Elizabethan and Jacobean age shared specific patterns of composition, including the deliberate introduction of indifferent and substantive variants into the multiple texts of their plays, that scholars can no longer avoid or dismiss their testimony. Although contemporary holographic manuscripts of poems by other Renaissance authors also survive, they can by their nature reveal very little about Shakespeare's or others' authorial practices as dramatists; poetry, which is not subjected to the theatrical process, does not share all of the variables of transmission available for a dramatic manuscript. Enough evidence exists to demonstrate that many of the substantive variants in dramatic manuscripts are due to deliberate authorial revision; this revision (contrary to the arguments of scholars like Greg, who tried to reduce the authority of revisions by claiming that they usually resulted from censorship or some other external force) was often performed willingly by the author in order to reshape the work for his own artistic reasons. Shakespeare, a professional dramatist writing for the same acting company and theatres as many of these revising dramatists, must have shared his contemporaries' practices of authorial revision.

I have used four criteria for this particular study of authorial revision. First, I examine only those extant manuscripts (holograph and/or scribal) with revisions (holograph and/or scribal) and early printed texts with substantive revisions between editions which can reasonably be thought to have been made by or with the knowledge of the original author. As the average theatrical manuscript of this period may have passed through the hands of many correctors,[1] revisions made by correctors who appear to have worked without the author's consent are not discussed in detail.

Second, I assume that any type of substantive change to any portion of a play-text can be classified as a revision, because the term "revision" can encompass the entire range of terms used in labeling changes: corrections, alterations, additions or insertions, omissions or deletions, cuts, amendments, augmentations, and stop-press variants. The distinction that T. H. Howard-Hill, for example, draws between "revision" as "a literary act of rewriting" and "redaction" as "preparation of a text for publication, or another use"[2] is one that only a scholar and not an author would make; extant manuscripts show that a literary act of rewriting in the case of some extant manuscripts was made for the preparation of a text for "another use."

Third, I acknowledge the many stages during which revisions may have been made by the author: the writing out of the foul papers; the transcription of fair papers and/or promptbooks; the adaptation of the playhouse text any time before and/or after performances to suit censorship, theatrical, and/or artistic requirements; the updating of any form of the text for revivals, the preparation of any form of the text for publication or private ownership; the correction of the text during printing; and later changes at any of these stages.

Finally, I do not assume that an author always revised a play in order to "improve" it. A dramatist may have changed his play simply because the current version was not, for any combination of reasons, suitable, thus producing another version which he may or may not have seen as an improvement on his original work. Asserting that a new version constitutes "improvement" without evidence of the author's concurrence (in a preface, for example) requires making judgments that are much too difficult to support. A revision can be said to produce an alternate, rather than an improved, version of a play.[3]

## Revising Dramatists

A large number of English Renaissance manuscripts provide internal evidence of authorial revision and reveal that a dramatist's foul papers and often the fair copy transcription made from them were not un-blotted, uncorrected, or unchanged pieces that remained in only one state, but rather were fluid, ever-revisable works. Extant manuscripts show various kinds of revisions, made in many ways, including interlineations, marginal additions (in left, right, bottom and top margins), and slips or sheets interleaved, glued onto, or pinned into the existing sheets. The marginal additions as well as those written out on separate sheets and their places of insertion in the original text are usually marked with a variety of corresponding symbols, including crosses, ampersands, circles, stars, asterisks, arrows, and even drawings of pointing index fingers.[4] Many manuscripts also have interlined *currente calamo* changes, which if they are in the author's hand suggest second thoughts and if they are in a scribal hand suggest that the foul papers were difficult to decipher, perhaps due to the author's revisions.[5]

Manuscripts with marginal additions include Anthony Munday's *John a Kent & John a Cumber* (1590); the anonymous *Richard II* or *Thomas of Woodstock* (1590s); John Fletcher and Philip Massinger's *Sir John van Olden Barnavelt* (1619, also with inserted slips); the anonymous *The Two Noble Ladies and the Converted Conjurer* (1622–23); Thomas Heywood's *The Captives* (1624); Massinger's *The Parliament of Love* (1624); the anonymous *The Honest Man's Fortune* (1624); Thomas Dekker's *The Welsh Embassador* (1625); the anonymous *The Faithful Friends* (1625?, also with one inserted slip and scenes summarized by the scribe who lacks the foul papers for them),[6] *The Wasp* (1630s), *Love's Changelings' Change* (1630s), and *The Soddered Citizen* (1630s); Arthur Wilson's *The Inconstant Lady* (1632); Henry Glapthorne's *The Lady Mother* (1635, also with one

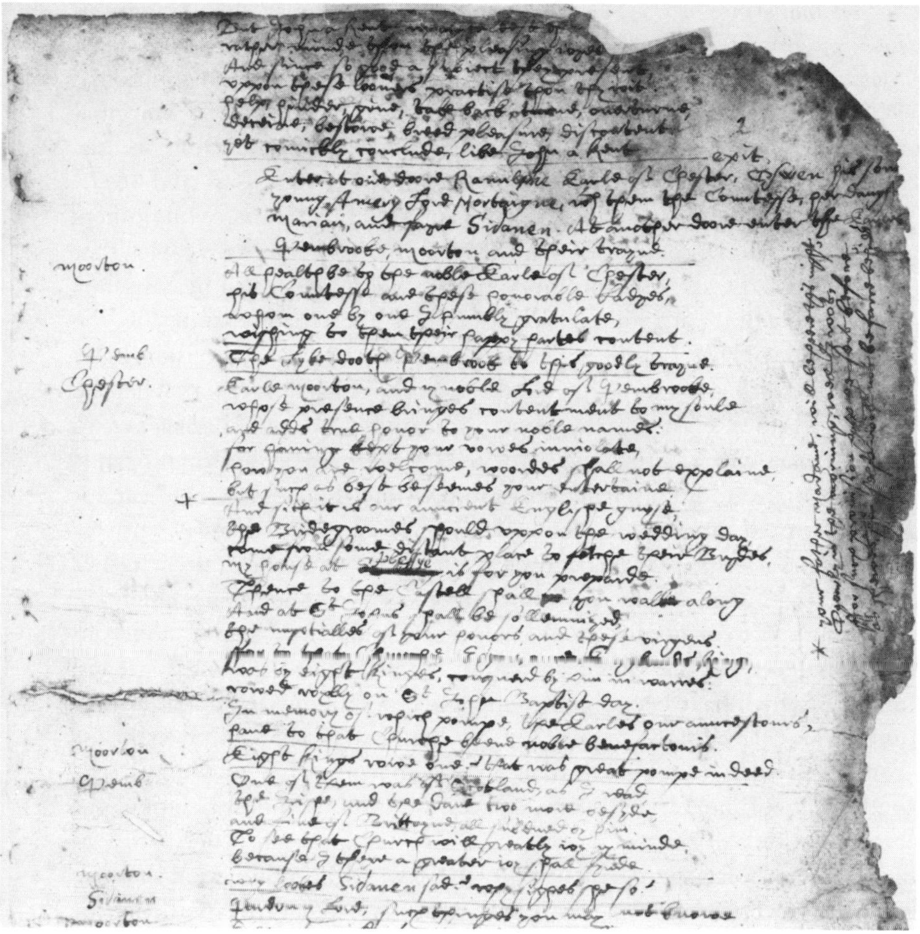

*Figure 1.* Upper half of Folio 2 of Anthony Munday's manuscript of *John a Kent & John a Cumber,* showing interlinear revisions and a marginal addition (with asterisks to mark place of insertion) in his hand. The Huntington Library, San Marino, California (MS. HM 500).

inserted slip); and William Cavendish's *The Country Captain* (1635, also with one inserted slip).

Manuscripts with inserted slips include John Bale's *King Johan* (1538, 1547–1560, also with marginal additions); Munday's and collaborators' *Sir Thomas More* (1593?, also with marginal additions); the anonymous *John of Bordeaux* (1590s) and *The Second Maiden's Tragedy* (1611); Massinger's *Believe as You List* (1630–1631, also with marginal additions); William Mountfort's *The Launching of the Mary* (1633, also with marginal additions); and Francis Jaques's *The Queen of Corsica* (1642), as well as numerous comedies written by William Percy between 1601 and 1647.[7]

Some of these manuscripts may be authors' first drafts, while others clearly served as promptbooks; however, others are foul/fair copies that were intended to serve as promptbooks but were revised so heavily they became illegible at points. For example, the chaotic state of the mansucript of *The Launching of the Mary,* caused by the revision of so many passages, produced this rebuke from Sir Henry Herbert when he relicensed the revised manuscript: "I commande your Bookeeper to present mee wth a faire Copy hereafte[r]."[8] So many extant manuscripts show so many additions, deletions, and revisions that "faire Copy" cannot be constituted as a single, definable type of regularized, neat, entirely legible manuscript;[9] Herbert, in fact, may have wanted a "fairer" rather than a "fair" copy. Manuscript promptbooks have annotations which are not confined to stage directions, properties, and actors' names added in a bookkeeper's hand; they also contain letters, words, passages, scenes, and acts which have been significantly and carefully revised by the author and/or his scribe. Many manuscripts without extant changes nevertheless contain crosses or other symbols in the margins that may mark the author's, book holder's, censor's, or actors' additions and/or deletions for performance. All four of these types of corrections constitute authorial revision for company dramatists involved with the production of their own plays. There are also less obvious but still powerful methods: for example, Robert Turner argues that both act-end notations and repetition brackets (entire or partial duplications of a line at some distance from its incorrect first appearance) found in Elizabethan and Jacobean manuscripts and printed texts often signal authorial revision.[10] And in at least one instance a collation of an extant manuscript with a printed text can reveal authorial revision: the scribe copying out John Fletcher's play *Bonduca* informs readers that his manuscript has been transcribed from incomplete "fowle papers," and the variants between this text and the

1647 Beaumont and Fletcher Folio text suggest that the latter text was printed from Fletcher's revised fair copy which served as the "booke where by it was first Acted from."[11]

In addition to this type of internal evidence in manuscripts, other types of evidence of revision, both authorial and nonauthorial, can be found in authors' comments in prefaces and printers' statements (sometimes, but not always, exaggerated or false) on the title pages of printed editions of plays. A few dramatists advised readers in prefaces that the printed versions varied significantly from the stage versions. King's Men company dramatists Beaumont and Fletcher apparently allowed theatrical revisions, as the printers' preface to the 1647 Folio edition of their plays explained that "when these *Comedies* and *Tragedies* were presented on the Stage, the *Actours* omitted some *Scenes* and Passages (with the *Authours* consent) as occasion led them."

However, Richard Brome, Thomas Heywood, and other dramatists appeared to have been disturbed enough about theatrical interferences that they warned readers that in performance their plays had received some nonauthorial revisions from actors or other dramatists. Brome, in the preface to the 1640 first Quarto of *The Antipodes*, complained that actors had changed his original text: "You shal find in this Booke more than was presented upon the *Stage,* and left out of the *Presentation,* for superfluous length (as some of the *Players* pretended) I thoght good al should be inserted according to the allowed *Original.*" One of Heywood's prefaces did not specifically attack actors or dramatists for revising a play for performance but berated those who had printed memorial reconstructions. In the Preface to the 1608 Quarto of *The Rape of Lucrece,* Heywood noted that his lack of interest in committing his plays to the press had encouraged pirated editions so "corrupt and mangled, (copied only by the eare) that I haue bene as vnable to know them, as ashamde to chalenge them." He promised to furnish the play in this edition in its "natiue habit." Heywood's statement here makes clear that he, like Brome, would not allow his reading or viewing public to accept a version of his play that was not his own.

While an author's preface discussing revision seems trustworthy, title page advertisements, often posted in booksellers' windows to promote sales, may seem less so; yet they still imply that revised editions of plays were commercially profitable. A Quarto of at least one of the dramatists who had warned of nonauthorial revisions in some of his plays clearly advertised authorial revision: the title page of the 1632 Quarto 2 of *The*

*Foure Prentises of London* states that it was *"written and newly reuised* by THOMAS HEYWOOD." Ben Jonson also insisted on distinguishing between the authorial and the nonauthorial revisions of his plays: the title page of the 1600 Quarto 1 of Jonson's *Every Man out of His Humor* advertises, "As it was first composed by the Author B. I. / Containing more than hath been Publickely Spoken or Acted," whereas the title page of the 1604 Quarto 1 of *His Part of King James his Royall Entertainment* advertises, "With other Additions."[12] Two other Quartos which advertise revision by the author on the title page are John Marston's *The Malcontent* (1604) and George Chapman's *Bussy D'Ambois* (1641).

However, some title-page advertisements do not specifically name who has performed the revisions in the plays. Some of the many Quartos (excluding those by Shakespeare) which state on their title pages that they have been "newly set forth," "corrected," "amended," "augmented," "enlarged," "added to," "revived and polished," and thus revised, either with or without mention of the author's name, include Richard Edwards's *Damon and Pythias* (1571); Robert Wilmot's *Tancred and Gismund* (1591); the anonymous *A Knack to Know a Knave* (1594) and *Locrine* (1595); Thomas Kyd's *The Spanish Tragedy* (1602); John Marston's *Parasitaster* (1606); Barnabe Barnes's *The Devil's Charter* (1607); Samuel Daniel's *Cleopatra* (1607); Wentworth Smith's *The Hector of Germany* (1615); the anonymous *Mucedorus* (1598, 1610); Christopher Marlowe's *Dr. Faustus* (1619), Beaumont and Fletcher's *The Maid's Tragedy* (1622) and *Philaster* (1622); Thomas Middleton and William Rowley's *A Fair Quarrell* (1622); Fletcher's *The Faithful Shepherdess* (1629, 1634); and Heywood's *The Rape of Lucrece* (1638).[13]

These title-page statements suggest that many plays were revised again and again and that printers were aware that the advertisement of such revisions would attract buyers who wanted to own the latest version of a popular play. However, printers' greed may in some cases have led to fraud; as Timothy Murray explains, "the publicity of the printed play's fidelity to the current stage version was so important to sales that many unrevised plays were falsely advertised as newly corrected."[14] Although the title-page claims in the later Quartos of *The Spanish Tragedy* that the play had been "newly corrected, amended and enlarged with new additions," for example, may have been false, it is significant that the play's various printers distinguished among "corrections," "amendments," and "enlargements" in advertising the revisions, as if the paying public wanted to know precisely what kind of changes had been made to new editions.

Fredson Bowers has questioned whether such advertisements by printers were made not only to encourage more sales but to lower costs by circumventing printing regulations. Bowers cites a rash of examples of authorial revision between the first and subsequent editions of Dekker's *The Magnificent Entertainment,* and *The Whole Magnificent Entertainment* (1604) and *The Honest Whore,* (1604, 1604–05, 1605), and between Marston's *The Malcontent* (1604) and *Parasitaster* (1606), all printed by the same printing house over a short period of time. Explaining that the Stationers' Company laws restricted editions of books from any one setting of type to 1,250–1,500 copies, Bowers contends that printers who attempted to get around the law by using standing type in order to save money either reprinted the subsequent editions from mostly standing type with a few formes hastily reset (hence producing "revisions") or rushed a faulty first edition into print so that customers would be forced to purchase the subsequent editions advertised with "corrections."[15] Bowers questions therefore whether Dekker and Marston revised these entertainments and plays to suit their own artistic and theatrical needs or to ensure greater sales when these works were reprinted.

A few printers, as Bowers suggests, may have been resourceful enough to claim authorial revision in order to skirt printing regulations. Other printers, however, were more concerned with being charged with fraud by falsely advertising authorial revision. The printers of Beaumont and Fletcher's 1647 Folio hastily added in a postscript to the volume: "We forgot to tell the *Reader,* that some *Prologues* and *Epilogues* (here inserted) were not written by the *Authours* of this *Volume;* but made by others on the *Revivall* of several Playes." Their apology for omitting these statements from the original preface, which had *already* advised that the plays had been theatrically abridged, demonstrates that the printers felt some pressure to advertise their edition correctly.

Extant records of Elizabethan and Jacobean acting companies, as well as authors' and printers' remarks, provide significant external evidence of the practice of revision, particularly of revision made for the revival of a play. Philip Henslowe recorded payments to Ben Jonson, Henry Chettle, Thomas Dekker, William Byrd, Samuel Rowley, Thomas Heywood, Thomas Middleton, and "the 4 poetes" to mend, alter or add to old plays for the Admiral's Men.[16] Acting companies, like printers, were sometimes motivated by financial gain to pass off an existing play as a new one, as they found it less expensive and more lucrative to revise old and often extremely popular or fashionable plays rather than purchase new ones. Revisions may have been required to update a play because many factors, including an acting company's personnel or theatre, the political or social climate, and audience taste, had changed since its original composition.[17] Revision of a play specifically for revival met with the approval of at least one Master of the Revels, for Sir Henry Herbert gave permission for additions to be made to an old play in order, as he noted, "to give it out for a new one."[18]

Such internal and external evidence of revision leads G. E. Bentley to conclude that most plays first printed more than ten years after composition and kept in active repertory by the company which owned them received later revisions by the author or a company dramatist. Bentley further asserts that because refurbishing plays for revival was the standard practice in the London theatres from 1590–1642, all attached professional dramatists routinely revised their own or others' plays.[19] A play may have been revised to update it for a later revival, but it may have also been revised by the author at any point after its composition for any single or any combination of reasons. Albert Feuillerat cites manuscript and theatrical records of the period to argue that plays were revised at several stages: during original rehearsals, for later performances, or for revival, so that plays were in a "continual state of transformation." Feuillerat argues that revisions of a dramatist's original text were frequent and often changed the very nature of the play.[20] Anne Lancashire's study of the heavily revised manuscript of the anonymous play *The Second Maiden's Tragedy* similarly convinces her that "authorial revision seems to have been usual in autograph MSS, and in scribal MSS where extra, major revision (e.g. addition-slips, extensive censorship changes) took place."[21]

Professional dramatists who had already acquired a financial interest in their acting companies, a popular following, or some other form of control, made or supervised routine playhouse and printing revisions in their plays. The fact that Jonson, Heywood, and others felt it necessary to explain to readers on title pages and in prefaces that their plays had often been performed, revived, and printed in altered versions demonstrates that they were concerned about distinguishing between their own revisions and those revisions made by others, including actors and printers. Other authors may have been even less tolerant of changes to their plays if they were still involved in the production or performance of them. John Freehafer argues that George Chapman must have been responsible for the revisions made in 1622–1624 to his play, *Bussy*

*D'Ambois,* first printed in 1607, because "no living author of Chapman's time is known to have allowed anyone else to revise one of his plays or to write a prologue for one of them. The revisions and new prologues in plays by Kyd, Marlowe, Beaumont, Fletcher, William Rowley, and Henry Shirley were added after those writers had died."[22]

Among those dramatists who retained control of and revised their own plays after their original composition are Jonson, Heywood, Dekker, Beaumont, Fletcher, and Massinger as well as Chapman; the certain evidence of careful and coherent authorial revision by these dramatists is so extensive that only a brief discussion is possible here.

Jonson has been recognized by his recent editors as being extremely concerned both with reworking his plays after performance and with having them correctly set in print, even reading the proof sheets himself. Joseph Loewenstein claims Jonson disabled "the proprietary intrusion of acting companies" in order to revise drastically many of his plays for the Folio, "sometimes changing settings, always relocating them from stage to page."[23] As John Kerrigan summarizes of Jonson:

> All his early plays, from *Every Man in his Humour* (1598) to *Catiline* (1611), were overhauled before the publication of his *Works* in 1616 — most, if not all, for the sake of their appearance in that volume. Generally speaking, the later the play the lighter Jonson's revision.[24]

Kerrigan and others see Jonson's insistence on having his plays correctly printed without others' additions and with his own latest revisions as atypical of Jacobean dramatists.

Yet Jonson's insistence seems atypical only because he left substantial evidence in the form of numerous comments about and examples of the author's process of revision on title pages and in prefaces and texts. Like Jonson, Thomas Heywood informed the public of the true form of his plays when they reached print and disclaimed revisions made to them by others. Although he complained of nonauthorial revision in *The Rape of Lucrece,* Heywood was responsible for some revisions found in the first and later Quartos of the play.[25] Heywood claimed that the early pirated editions of *If You Know Not Me You Know Nobody* (Part 1) contained nonauthorial changes, but he may also have revised this play himself.[26] The title page of the Quarto of *Love's Mistress* (1640), in addition to *The Foure Prentises of London* (1632), advertises corrections and new revisions by the author. Heywood's most ambitious attempt at revision appears to have been *The Escapes of Jupiter* (printed 1611), a play he fashioned from two separate plays, *The Golden Age* and *The Silver Age,* which he had written ten years earlier.[27] Heywood, a prolific dramatist and collaborator, apparently was comfortable with the idea of reworking existing plays, including his own.

Thomas Dekker similarly appears to have been a frequent and practiced reviser of his plays and also, as Henslowe records, of his predecessors' or collaborators' plays. Modern editors have recognized probable authorial revision in *The Magnificent Entertainment, The Honest Whore, The Shoemaker's Holiday, Satiromastix, Northward Ho, The Whore of Babylon, The Wonder of a Kingdom, The Sun's Darling,* and *The Welsh Embassador;* this last play was evidently recast by Dekker from his earlier play, *The Noble Spanish Soldier.*[28]

Beaumont, Fletcher, and Massinger also revised their plays, whether they were written singly or collaboratively; persuasive evidence of revision during and immediately after composition and after some period of time appears in several plays in the Beaumont and Fletcher canon, including *The Maid's Tragedy, A Wife for a Month, Philaster, The Woman Hater, A King and No King, The Masque of the Inner Temple and Gray's Inn, Cupid's Revenge, The Noble Gentleman, Bonduca, The Tragedy of Valentinian,* and *The Two Noble Kinsmen.*[29] In addition to reworking his own plays, including *The Bondman,*[30] Massinger revised a number of plays written collaboratively with Fletcher alone or also with Beaumont and later revised other plays after Beaumont's and Fletcher's deaths in 1616 and 1625; Thomas Middleton, William Rowley, and James Shirley may also have revised Fletcher's plays after his death.[31]

The specific instances of and occasions for revision in plays by Chapman, Jonson, Heywood, Dekker, Beaumont, Fletcher, and Massinger have been used to develop general theories about revision during the period by other professional dramatists who have left no evidence of their composition practices. Critics and editors have for many years assumed from the evidence provided by manuscripts, printed editions, and theatrical records that most, if not all, Elizabethan and Jacobean dramatists routinely made or consented to revisions in their plays. However, many scholars have refused to make this same assumption about Shakespeare because there is no specific holographic evidence to support theories of authorial revision in his plays. Although W. W. Greg dismissed revision as a regular practice by Shakespeare, he had no such hesitation in discussing the composition practices of Shakespeare's contemporaries. In examining the derivation of Thomas Heywood's *The*

*Escapes of Jupiter* from his plays *The Silver Age* and *The Golden Age,* Greg stated, "*The Escapes of Jupiter* adds one more to the indubitable instances of revision to be taken into account by those who seek to minimize the practice."[32]

Yet Greg and other scholars have minimized the practice of authorial revision by Elizabethan and Jacobean dramatists in an effort to challenge the practice of authorial revision by Shakespeare, perhaps because they believe that placing Shakespeare in the same category with lesser, revising dramatists would somehow denigrate his reputation. E. K. Chambers, who so effectively rejected theories of authorial revision in Shakespeare, also attempted in the same lecture on disintegration to rebut theories of authorial revision in plays by his contemporaries. Chambers found that any theory which entails "the progressive revision of lost versions" forces us to arrive at

> the notion of the long-lived manuscript in the tiring-house wardrobe, period-ically taken out for a revival and as often worked upon by fresh hands, abridged and expanded, recast to fit the capabilities of new performers, bright-ened with current topical allusions, written up to date to suit new tastes in poetic diction.

Chambers dismissed this idea of "continuous copy," claiming that revival did not demand revision, and the few plays, including *The Book of Sir Thomas More* and *The Spanish Tragedy,* which show continuous revision are exceptional examples of a rarely used practice.[33] R. C. Bald accepted Chambers's dismissal of continuous copy, yet in the process he provided examples of at least two other plays with revisions which could be included in this exceptional group.[34] A more recent article agreed with Chambers's sixty-year-old argument: Roslyn Knutson strenuously argued that "the assumption that revision accompanied revival cannot be supported" because "revision for the occasion of revival was neither commonplace nor economically necessary."[35] However, Knutson's argument here is invalidated by a great deal of external and internal evidence in this period.

The two plays cited by Chambers, the collaborative *The Book of Sir Thomas More,* originally written in the early 1590s and revised within the next ten years,[36] and *The Spanish Tragedy,* written by Kyd between 1582 and 1592[37] but published anonymously, should not, as they very frequently have, stand as primary examples of the ways in which *all* plays were revised, precisely because they contain mainly nonauthorial revisions. The handling of these two plays proves to be exceptional not because, as E. K. Chambers argued, they *were* revised, but because they present no clear evidence of revision performed by or with the permission of the original author. For example, the manuscript of *Sir Thomas More,* written primarily in the hand of Anthony Munday with markings of offensive passages in the hand of the Master of the Revels, Edmund Tilney, contains additions to the text written in at least five other hands on inserted sheets or slips. Munday may have been responsible for early revisions made to suit the censor's demands, but the bulk of the revisions were probably not supervised by Munday.[38]

The complicated printing history of *The Spanish Tragedy* also makes clear why this play cannot serve as an archetypal case of revision. The title pages of the 1592 Octavo, probably a memorial report, and the subsequent Quartos reprinted in 1594 and 1599 advertise that they have been "newly corrected and amended of such grosse faults as passed" in the first or former impressions (suggesting a nonextant earlier Quarto or Octavo, either brought forth illegally by the same printer and confiscated, or by a rival printer who had legal title to the play).[39] The title pages of the 1602 and later Quartos claim that they have been "newly corrected, amended, and enlarged with new additions of the Painters part, and others, as it hath of late been diuers times acted."

Although the play appears to have been revised at a number of stages throughout the years, perhaps first by Kyd before his death in 1594, and later by the company dramatists who prepared the enormously popular play for revivals by different companies, no clear internal or external evidence points to Kyd as the play's primary reviser. Philip Edwards argues that elements of two versions still stand in the first edition (which may have been produced to supersede an earlier pirated one), suggesting perhaps that the play had been at some time "revised to make it shorter and more suitable for the public stage." Yet he dismisses the 1602 advertising claims of revision, calling the 1602 Quarto basically a "slavish reprint" of the 1599 edition with the addition of five new passages, including the Painter scene, which enlarge upon the mad grief of Hieronymo.[40] Because Henslowe's *Diary* records two payments to Jonson in 1601 and 1602 for two sets of additions to "Geronymo" (the subtitle given to *The Spanish Tragedy* on the 1615 Quarto title page is "Hieronimo is mad againe"), Jonson may have been the play's reviser for two different revivals, one of which probably produced the 1602 Quarto 3 text. However, these revisions may have been replacements only made to mod-ernize the play and produce for publication a composite version that had not been acted,[41] and do not derive any authority from Kyd.

In spite of the evidence presented by *The Spanish Tragedy* and *Sir Thomas More,* there is still enough evidence left by Jonson, Beaumont, Fletcher, Dekker, Heywood, and other dramatists to accept E. A. J. Honigmann's assertion that "the contemporary evidence that play texts in the Elizabethan period were commonly revised, and were revised in many different ways, is overwhelming and irrefutable."[42] E. K. Chambers's concept of "continuous copy" does present numerous prob-lems because it implies that only one type of revision was practiced, that of a certain kind of nonauthorial, continual tampering with an existing play. The evidence which can be drawn from title pages, prefaces, and particularly extant theatrical documents (including holographic manu-scripts) proves that although some plays were subjected to nonauthorial tampering, many were deliberately revised by their original authors.

The extent as well as the type or form of an author's revisions varied from one author to another and from one play to another, even varying between plays by the same author. Therefore, setting strict limits for the amount of revision that an author made to his own play, as, for example, John Kerrigan does in separating adapters from revisers, also implies that dramatists practiced one kind of revision. Kerrigan concludes that when an adapter overhauled another author's play, he "cut, inserted and sub-stituted sizeable pieces of text without altering the details of his pre-cursor's dialogue," and authors who revised their own plays tended "to tinker, introducing small additions, small cuts and indifferent single-word substitutions."[43] Although adapters may not have acted like au-thors, authors could and did act like adapters. Many extant manuscripts and printed texts of this period demonstrate that there were no solid categories of authorial revision, and adapters cannot always be so neatly distinguished from revisers. Dramatists could make major or minor changes to their own plays.

Some dramatists may have wanted or needed to both overhaul and tinker with their plays for any number of reasons. For example, John Bale overhauled his own play, *King Johan,* by cutting, inserting, and substituting sizeable pieces of text without significantly altering the existing dialogue; he also tinkered with other lines when revising it several years after its original composition. Unlike Bale, Ben Jonson both overhauled and tinkered with not one but most of his plays. In discussing Jonson's revisions between the 1601 Quarto 1 and 1616 Folio versions of *Every Man in His Humor,* Henry Holland Carter lists the varied and sometimes contradictory categories of minor and major changes made to the later edition:

> 1) localization of scene in England; 2) condensation; 3) expansion; 4) change of abstract expressions to concrete; 5) more direct and simple expressions; 6) less simple expressions; 7) more vigorous or forceful expressions; 8) insertion of words of more specific reference to persons; 9) insertion of qualifying adjectives or adverbs; 10) introduction of figures, and improvement in existing figures; 11) better sentence-structure; 12) readings more appropriate to context; 13) syntactical changes; 14) elision; 15) change from solemn forms; 16) change in oaths; 17) changes without clear reason or improvement.[44]

J. W. Lever, a more recent editor of the play, argues that these subtle and "painstaking" revisions "reshaped almost every aspect of the play."[45]

This kind of "painstaking revision" is significantly different from the changes resulting from what Honigmann described in 1965 as "textual instability." He argued that an author's second draft may show substantive and indifferent "second thoughts" variants when compared with his first draft. These two "unstable" drafts represent

> not so much a fastidious author's determined attempts to improve passages that fail to satisfy as an author so unconceited with himself and so fluent that little verbal changes, not necessarily always for the better, ran quite freely from his pen when the process of copying refired his mind.[46]

The crux of the problem in determining deliberate authorial revision arises, as Honigmann implies, when separating instances of textual "instability" from instances of painstaking revision made by an author who was not satisfied with his original work. The differences become clear with an in-depth study of one play in print, Marston's *The Malcontent;* one masque in manuscript, Jonson's *The Gypsies Metamorphosed;* and two plays in manuscript, Bale's *King Johan* and Middleton's *A Game at Chesse.* The extant manuscripts and printed texts of these plays clearly illustrate the varying types and extents of and occasions and reasons for later authorial revision of a finished work. These authors changed single words or entire scenes and substituted, added to, deleted, or in some way altered large and small passages. Through these processes of revision they reshaped the plays' structures, settings, plots, themes, and characters, thus "giving out an old play for a new one."

## Four Case Studies

John Marston, John Bale, Ben Jonson, and Thomas Middleton were all motivated by theatrical considerations, political and social demands, and their own artistic reasons to deliberately revise *The Malcontent, King Johan, The Gypsies Metamorphosed,* and *A Game at Chesse.* In his discussion of Heywood's *The Escapes of Jupiter,* W. W. Greg concluded that "as a rule the work of revision, if hasty, is competently done and shows adequate knowledge of the needs of the situation and the text of the original."[47] These four dramatists, however, some working hastily, showed more than "adequate" knowledge of and in fact paid extremely careful attention to the needs of the texts. Contrary to the implications of Greg's argument, the author cannot be divorced from his text and labeled a barely competent technician. The later versions of these four texts show the same all-absorbing authorial concern for dramatic unity, coherence, and artistry as the original versions.

### The Malcontent

Because the manuscripts of John Marston's *The Malcontent* are no longer extant, there is no holographic proof of his alterations. Yet the evidence provided by the printed editions indicates how and why Marston deliberately revised major passages to suit new artistic and theatrical requirements for his play. Most of the evidence supporting authorial revision comes from within *The Malcontent* itself. Three Quartos of the play were issued by the same printer in 1604 in slightly different states, the title page of the third claiming it was "augmented by *Marston.* With the Additions played by the Kings Maiesties servants. Written by *Ihon Webster.*" The second Quarto, which apparently added a prologue, an epilogue, and other passages,[48] is a corrected version of the first, while the third, printed from the second, adds an induction with a heading which repeats the title page's note that the additions were made by Webster.

   The conversation between Sly and Condell in the induction in the third Quarto of *The Malcontent* confirms that the play received additions by Webster, and probably Marston's augmentations, because it was now being performed by a company and in a theatre other than those for which it was originally written:

> *Sly.*   I would know how you came by this play?
> *Cun.*   Faith sir the booke was lost, and because twas pittie so good a play should be lost, we found it and play it.
> *Sly.*   I wonder you would play it, another company having interest in it?
> *Cun.*   Why not Maleuole in folio with vs, as Ieronimo in Decimo sexto with them. They taught vs a name for our play, wee call it *One for another.*
> *Sly.*   What are your additions?
> *Cun.*   Sooth not greatly needefull; only as your sallet to your greate feast, to entertaine a little more time, and to abridge the not received custome of musicke in our Theater. (sig. A4)

From this passage we learn from Webster that the King's Men had stolen *The Malcontent* from the boys' company which had stolen *Ieronimo* (either *The Spanish Tragedy* or *The First Part of Ieronimo,* printed 1605) from them, and that the new venue, the public, outdoor Globe theatre, less accustomed to musical interludes, required theatrical changes in moving a play from the private, indoor Blackfriars theatre. Rather than each text representing a single version of the play that was originally or later improved or impaired, the Blackfriars text and the Globe text actually represent separate versions of the play.

Although only the third Quarto advertises Marston's augmentations and Webster's added induction, all three Quartos, according to G. K. Hunter, "show signs of definitive authorial revision or correction from MS."[49] These revisions and corrections were designed to reshape the play and are not characteristic of the second-thought changes which signal mere instability. That Marston revised the play is clear; his precise reasons for revising it are less clear. Some revisions, mostly deletions, suggest that the author and the printer were subjected to or concerned about religious and political censorship.[50] Hunter supports Bowers's conclusions that some slight alterations may also have been due to the printer's attempt to circumvent printing regulations by reprinting Quarto 2 and Quarto 3 from standing type. However, Hunter stresses that conflicts among the interests of many groups, including the King's Men's rights to the play, the censor's restrictions on it, the printer's monetary interest in it, the public's demand for a popular play, and Marston's own artistic concerns, produced several types of and several causes for the authoritative corrections and revisions in each subsequent Quarto.[51]

Marston takes full credit for the printed state of the play. As he asserts in the preface found in the first and subsequent Quartos, "I have my selfe therefore set forth this Comedy; but so, that my inforced absence must much relye vpon the Printer's discretion: but I shal intreat, slight errors in orthography may bee as slightly or'e-passed." This type of authorial concern with the correct printing of his play, considered by so many modern critics to have pertained to Jonson alone, is, rather, typical of court and private theatre dramatists writing after 1600. Marston's statement in the original preface, which was not revised to suit the third Quarto, cannot actually validate the new advertising claims in the third Quarto of augmentation and addition on the title page and the heading to the induction. Yet Marston appears to have had enough control over the printing of all three Quartos that the claims of authorial revision are probably genuine.

What is most significant is that the title page of the third Quarto distinguishes between augmentations (by the author) and additions (by another author), implying that in this case, and possibly others, not all changes to a play-text were classed by the printer and author into one ambiguous category but were carefully separated and delineated. The induction to the play and probably some newly inserted passages appear to constitute Webster's "additions," and minor and major expansions of existing passages and the insertion of new ones in the body of the play appear to encompass Marston's "augmentations." For some reason, the addition of the prologue and epilogue in the second Quarto did not inspire a new title page claiming augmentation or additions by the author or another dramatist; perhaps then the two pieces were written by Marston alone, and the printer felt no need to advertise this fact, or these pieces did not excite as much audience interest as the additions in the third Quarto did.

Hunter sees the extra eleven passages inserted into the third Quarto, including those featuring Passarello, a role written to suit Robert Armin, a clown with the King's Men, as enlargements on existing situations in the earlier form of the play, but assigns only six of the passages to Marston on stylistic grounds, assigning the authorship of the others to Webster or another dramatist. D. J. Lake attributes at least five of the additional passages to Webster on the grounds of linguistic evidence.[52]

If Webster (or another dramatist) contributed the Passarello scenes, he apparently did so with Marston's collaboration or permission. It is also possible that some of the additions represent restored deletions cut from the earlier Quartos, although it seems more likely that because the majority of the major additions, including the comic scenes, occur in the first or last act, they may have been inserted for the Globe performances, as Bernard Harris argues, to "extend the length of the less musical version without undue dislocation of the strongly plotted main structure."[53] Marston's careful corrections and deliberate revisions, possibly including the restoration of passages omitted in the first Quarto because of printing errors or the anticipation of censorship, were made with great concern for a coherent style, plot, and structure as well as the dramatic integrity of both the dramatist and his text.

## King Johan

Although scholars can only hypothesize about Marston's authorial practices by carefully using stylistics as a basis for separating authorial from nonauthorial revisions in his printed texts, the composite manuscript of John Bale's *King Johan,* first printed in 1838, records compelling and indisputable internal evidence of deliberate authorial revision made several years after the original composition of a play. The first part of the manuscript is written on Folio sheets in a scribe's hand, and the latter part, with revisions, on additional Quarto sheets in the author's hand. The original scribe appears to have made some alterations and corrections at the time of copying the manuscript and again sometime afterward. Bale expanded the earlier text, apparently over a period of years, by inserting major speeches on separate leaves and in the margins of the existing leaves, revising minor speeches above the existing lines, altering spelling and punctuation, correcting errors, and, although less concerned with stage business than the first scribe,[54] adding stage directions.

The fragmentary earlier version, written about 1538 and possibly performed in 1539, appears to lack the original concluding portion of the play, as it ends mid-scene and does not present any type of coherent theatrical piece. Thus it does not seem to represent an abridged acting version of the play. The later version, written between 1547 and 1560,[55] fits coherently into the end of the earlier version, modifying some short speeches and canceling three of the earlier leaves in order to do so.

Bale systematically and conscientiously used a variety of distinct sym-

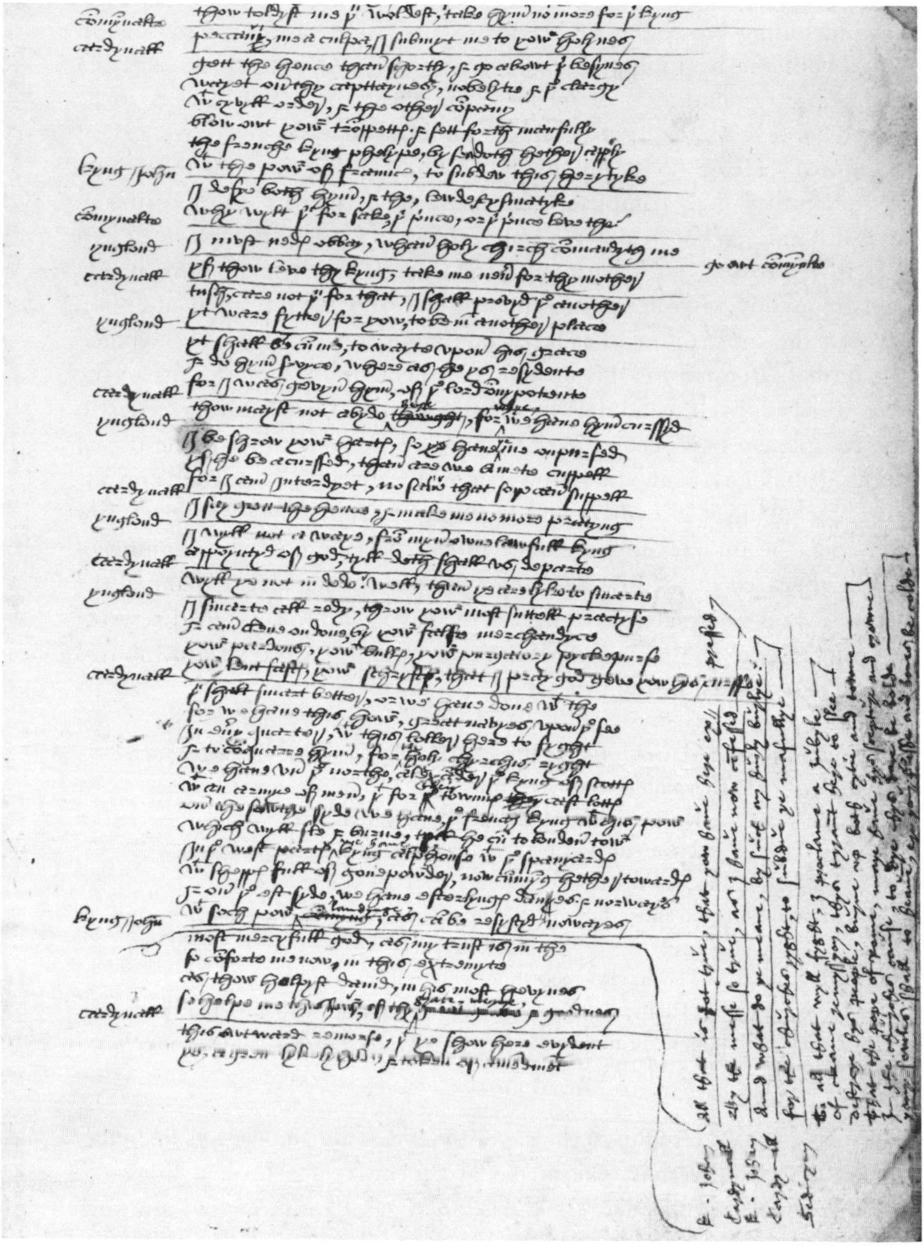

*Figure 2.* Lower half of Folio 20 of scribal portion of John Bale's *King Johan* showing numerous interlinear revisions and major marginal additions in Bale's hand. The Huntington Library, San Marino, California (MS. HM 3).

bols, including crosses, periods enclosed in circles, and ampersands, to mark both the beginning of an addition in the Quarto sheets and the precise, corresponding spot in the Folio sheets in which it was to be placed (a few of the spots marked for insertions do not have extant additions).[56] He economically revised around existing dialogue in the first version rather than completely rewriting it, as in this original line in scribal hand, "W$^t$ soch powr commyng as can be resystyd nowayes," in which he crossed out "commyng" and added "landynge" above it. He also frequently rewrote within the original line, paying great attention to even the most minor details; at one point, for example, he changed the scribal "th'owr" to "this howr," by squeezing in "is" and "h" to the two words as well as adding the final comma. When adding scenes in the completely new second part of the play, he sometimes made use of existing dialogue from the first version by canceling its earlier appearance, recopying it elsewhere and working it around new material. For example, the unbracketed dialogue in this passage on the poisoning of Johan appeared in the first version of the play; when Bale expanded the scene several years later, he canceled the earlier Folio sheet and rewrote the old dialogue, making careful major and minor revisions, shown below in brackets, in the process:

| | |
|---|---|
| *Diss.* | yf ye wold drynke [dronke] all. [vp] yt ware the better for ye |
| | [It woulde slake your thirst and also quycken yo$^r$ brayne |
| | A better drynke is not, in Portyngale nor Spayne |
| | Therfor suppe it of, and make an ende of it quycklye] |
| *K.John.* | nay, thow shalte drynke halfe. Ther is no remedy |
| *Diss.* | good lucke to yow than haue at yt evyn harttely [at it by and |
| | bye] |
| *K.John.* | god seynt the good monke. w$^t$ all my very hart |
| *Diss.* | loo I haue dronk yow halfe now drynke yow owt that part |
| | [I haue brought ye half, ~~now drynke out that~~ conueye me that |
| | for yo$^r$ parte][57] |

Although W. W. Greg used the case of Heywood's *The Escapes of Jupiter* to argue generally that revision "is apt to introduce broken lines and other textual irregularities," Bale has taken great care to avoid any such irregularities in most of the revised sections of the text.[58] Perhaps because Bale rewrote his play several years after its original composition and did not need to work in haste, his later version also shows very few signs of textual instability.

The complete extant version, which has several late topical allusions, could not represent the original unabridged text of the play, although it is possible (as is the case with any text which exists in more than one version) that it adds material that was cut from the earlier version during a revision. Bale adds an epilogue spoken by the Interpretour to conclude the first act and introduce the second act, and an act-division direction of "finit actus primus." These changes and the later final direction, "Thus endeth the .ij. playes of kynge Iohan," give the play a stronger and more coherent two-act structure than the earlier version.[59]

The remarkable textual evidence in this manuscript shows that Bale took great care to revise his play in a focused and coherent way to create a new version of *King Johan,* paying extremely close attention to both the play's style and content. The play appears to have received revisions for occasional performances, including celebrations of the coronation of Edward VI in 1547 and the visit of Elizabeth to Ipswich in 1561.[60] However, rather than simply inserting flattering speeches to suit the current monarch, Bale carefully worked into the text attacks on Catholic rites, relics, and hierarchical clerical orders, giving his characters greater range and thematically and theatrically reshaping the plot to produce greater conflict between the defenders of the new Protestant faith, including Johan, and the Catholic tempter, Sedition. Bale's revisions demonstrate that an author could exert later artistic control over his original work and could revise to suit both occasional performances and the current political and religious climate in a way which would suit his own artistic and aesthetic requirements for the play.

## The Gypsies Metamorphosed

A revised manuscript of Ben Jonson's masque *The Gypsies Metamorphosed* similarly and strikingly records both the explicit types of and specific occasions for revisions made to it; this remarkable document represents not merely the vanity of an author determined to display all of his work but the common practice of the revising dramatist. Unlike Bale, Jonson may have immediately and hastily revised his masque after composing the first draft. The masque was performed first for James I on 3 August 1621, at Burley-on-the-Hill, the country estate of George Villiers, Earl of Buckingham; a second time on 5 August, at Belvoir Castle, home of the Earl of Rutland, Buckingham's father-in-law; and a third time in September at Windsor Castle. It is unusual for a masque to have had three performances, and it was revised not only to suit a new venue and a new audience but apparently to celebrate anniversaries important to James I. The Burley performance celebrated the seventh anniversary of the first meeting of James I and his favorite, Buckingham, while the second appears to have celebrated the twenty-first anniversary of James's escape from the attempt on his life during the Gowrie Plot of 1600.[61] Thus, Jonson had several thematic and topical concerns in mind in revising the masque.

The text was revised slightly for the second performance and substantially for the last performance. Three composite versions of the text, each with its own substantive and accidental variants, exist: the printed 1616 Folio, the Newcastle scribal manuscript, and the Heber-Huntington scribal manuscript containing revisions carefully labeled and written in the margin to suit the two other occasional performances. In addition, the printed version of 1640 exists in two states: one representing the unrevised early Burley performance and another with two additional quires containing some of the most "marked" later revisions, which replaced several leaves.[62] Stephen Orgel sees the Heber-Huntington manuscript as an attempt to distinguish among the texts of the three individual performances and thus as "an intermediate state of the work, and what one wants is a corrected version of Jonson's final text, that of the folio and the Newcastle manuscript."[63] However, Jonson did not seem concerned with presenting only one, final, corrected version of the text, but all the permutations of it; rather than representing only an "intermediate state," the Heber-Huntington manuscript offers significant evidence of three separate states of composition and revision by an author who was accustomed to revising his works.[64]

In addition to making revisions to acknowledge anniversaries important to James I, Jonson included allusions to the stately homes which served as places of performance, and he revised the fortunes told by the gypsies in the masque to include members of the audience. W. W. Greg suggests that other revisions were made for the Windsor performance to provide a sense of "decorum":

> The revision at w 670 to my mind suggests that Jonson made it in submission to authority and with his tongue in his cheek. In tidying up the cuts he may have made a few revisions elsewhere. I do not think there is any doubt that even the latest revisions are Jonson's.[65]

However, all three versions, each presented before the monarch and his courtiers, contain bawdy dialogue and songs, and revision by Jonson of the Windsor version to suit a new "decorum" or to offer a more refined sense of taste just a few days or weeks after the last performance is unlikely.

Greg's argument here derives from the traditional view of authorial and nonauthorial revision: that it was usually undertaken to patch up pieces of text that had been removed due to censorship. Abundant evidence does exist to support the theory that censorship demanded revisions; for example, an extant manuscript in Philip Massinger's hand of his 1630–31 drama, *Believe as You List,* proves that he was forced by Sir Henry Herbert, the Master of the Revels, to remove politically dangerous anti-Spanish matter; he completely revised the play by sub- stituting the story of Antiochus, King of Syria, for that of Sebastian, King of Portugal.[66] However, authors also revised in order to add, or alter in some way, material even when not subjected to censorship.

Greg further argued that the composite texts (the two manuscripts and other printed versions) of *The Gypsies Metamorphosed* do not go back to a Windsor promptbook but "derive more or less directly from the original manuscript upon which successive revisions had been carried out by means of marginal alterations and inserted leaves," so that Jonson could produce as complete a literary record as possible.[67] This type of careful editorial work is consistent with what is known about Jonson's concern with the publication of his work. However, Greg's conclusion here, so similar to Orgel's—that Jonson was not interested in producing three separate versions of his masque, one original and two revised, but the most current, improved version—also ignores the manuscript itself, which testifies that Jonson felt it necessary to record and distinguish among all three versions, each with its own necessary revisions, in order to present three coherent and theatrically whole texts.

The variants in the elegant Heber-Huntington manuscript, which could serve as a presentation copy, range from one-word substitutions to replacements of entire speeches, primarily written in the margin. Most of the pages have been trimmed in an effort to reduce the size of the manuscript after it had been copied out, and only the sheets with marginal additions have not been as severely trimmed (the scribe has rewritten letters which were accidentally trimmed off a line onto the subsequent line). Unlike Bale in *King Johan,* this scribe has not always carefully marked the placement of additions but has written them in the margin in the approximate area into which they should be placed. A new "Prologue at Windsor" is added to replace the prologue "at the Kings entrance at Burly." In the first song, the Burley (and Belvoir?)

texts advise the ladies in the audience to endure the gypsies' fortunes and to "not cause you cut yo<sup>r</sup> laces," while the marginal insertion for the Windsor performance substitutes advice to men to "not cause you quit yo<sup>r</sup> places." The scribe has carefully underlined these particular variants, so there is no confusion about where to insert the addition marked "windsor."

Two stanzas later, the scribe in this manuscript has not replaced the lines "though wee be here at Burly / wee'd be loothe to make a hurly" for the later two performances, although, presumably, the lines would not have been used. At "Beauer," the singular "Gentry Cove" is pluralized. The Windsor additions mostly add allusions to St. George and the Order of the Garter and replace references to members of the Buckingham family, who were now no longer in the audience.[68] For example, the Burley-Belvoir version has a right marginal addition for the original passage reprinted at left below:

| | |
|---|---|
| Heres no Justice *Lippus* | |
| Will seeke for to nip vs | At windsor |
| in *Cramp-ringe* or *Cippus* | |
| and then for to stripp vs | the *George & the garter* |
| and after to whipp vs | into o<sup>r</sup> owne quarter |
| while here we doe tary | or durst I goe farder |
| (his Justice to vary) | in methode & order |
| | theres a purse & a seale |
| But be wise and wary | I haue a great minde to steale |
| and we may both cary— | that when o<sup>r</sup> tricks are done |
| the *Kate* the *Mary* | wee might seale o<sup>r</sup> owne pardon |
| and all the bright aery | all this we may doe |
| away to the Quary | and a greate deale more too |
| If o<sup>r</sup> braue *Ptolomee* | If o<sup>r</sup> braue *Ptolomee* |
| will but say followe mee. | will but say followe mee.[69] |

In this type of revision, the new speech is carefully inserted to fill in the space of the speech that is deleted, so that it can conclude with the existing couplet. By fitting in the passage so neatly, Jonson skillfully avoids creating textual irregularities. In a similarly coherent fashion, Jonson makes other topical substitutions. A later insertion in the masque for the Belvoir performance is a "fithe of August" reference to the anniversary of the Gowrie Plot of 1600 and to "the good man of Beuer / our Buckinghams father," who hosted that performance. This insertion

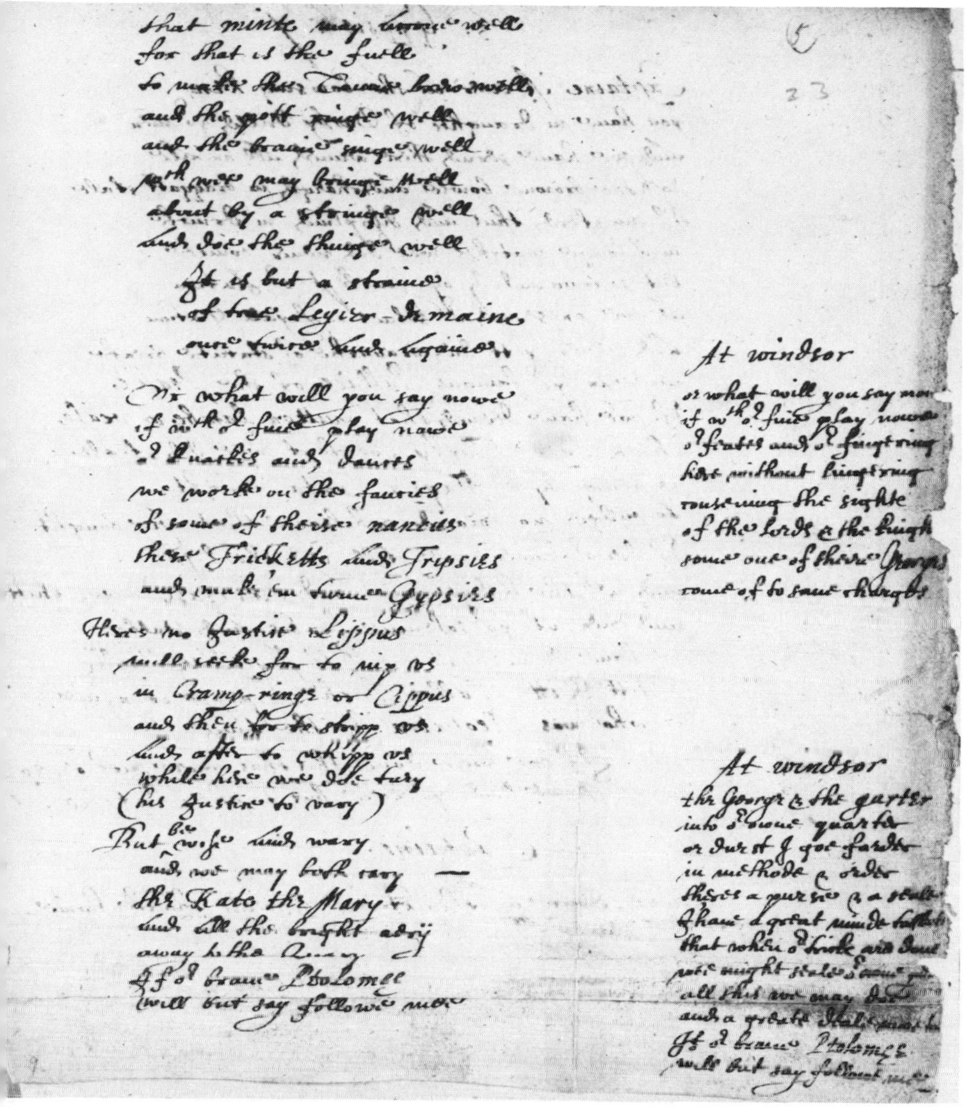

*Figure 3.* Folio 23 of the scribal Heber-Huntington manuscript of Ben Jonson's masque of *The Gypsies Metamorphosed,* showing revisions for performance at Windsor Castle. The Huntington Library, San Marino, California (MS. HM 741).

was probably not used at the Windsor performance, as the Burley salute to the lords and ladies present was also appropriate there.

Significantly, Jonson revised by making use of the existing text and inserting neccesary changes into it, rather than starting over with completely new dialogue to surround revised passages. Jonson revised in the same manner as Massinger who, in *Believe as You List,* "endeavoured to save himself trouble as much as possible."[70] Jonson also moved easily and unawkwardly among the three versions of the text, allowing, for example, satisfactory Burley passages to stand in the Windsor version, even though they had been removed in the Belvoir perfomance. In these ways, Jonson's professional practices of revision resemble those of John Bale: they display concern for theatrical and artistic coherence and unity. Jonson's text, like Bale's, does not show signs of variant first and second thoughts (and thus textual instability), but deliberate and painstaking revisions made to satisfy the author's new artistic and theatrical needs.

## A Game at Chesse

Unlike these manuscripts of Bale and Jonson, the manuscripts of Thomas Middleton's *A Game at Chesse* show signs both of the textual irregularities noted by Greg and of the textual instability discussed by Honigmann. Because the play's performances received so much attention from various commentators of the period, scholars have always had a great deal of evidence of the political, topical, and legal concerns that apparently forced Middleton to produce hastily, carelessly, and surreptitiously written variant versions of his play, including holographic manuscripts, for private audiences. Most editors and critics have regarded these variant versions as "unstable" texts. According to R. C. Bald, more is known about this play than any other pre-Restoration play,[71] yet what is not known, and what has not previously been examined, is whether the variant states of the play's manuscripts provide enough evidence to suggest that Middleton carefully, skillfully, and deliberately revised his play to satisfy his own changing dramatic and literary needs.

Six manuscript versions produced during this period survive: the Trinity College manuscript, entirely in the author's hand; the Bridgewater-Huntington manuscript, in the hand of two unknown scribes with part of the second scene in Act 2 and almost all of Act 5 in the author's hand; the Lansdowne, Malone, and Archdall manuscripts in the hand of the professional scribe, Ralph Crane; and the Rosenbach manuscript in the hand of two unknown scribes with the title page in Middleton's hand.[72] Three Quartos were also printed, probably in 1625, without author's and printers' names; Quarto 2 is basically a reprint of Quarto 1. Major variants occur in all these extant versions of the play, perhaps because the texts had to be hastily reconstructed from other sources, including foul papers, early transcriptions, stage plots, actors' parts, or memory, if the licensed (prompt?) copy of the play had been confiscated by the Privy Council. Only the Rosenbach manuscript and the Quartos, although variant, present "complete" texts, and the other manuscripts are "incomplete" versions. Susan Zimmerman concludes that all the texts show Middleton's influence.[73] Bald and Zimmerman agree that many of the errors and corruptions, such as indifferent variants, are due to Middleton's haste and carelessness in copying.[74]

Middleton's anti-Spanish, anti-Catholic satire, with its attack on the Spanish Ambassador, Gondomar, was, as the first Quarto advertises, "Acted nine days together at the Globe on the banks side." The play's sensational and unprecedented consecutive long run from 6 to 16 August 1624 was officially ended by order of the Privy Council because it represented a modern Christian king on the stage. The original complaint against the play was apparently made by Gondomar. Although summoned, Middleton did not appear before the Council, but the King's Men did present their licensed copy of the play, which they claimed they had performed exactly as approved by the Master of the Revels, Sir Henry Herbert. After the Globe Theatre was closed, the players petitioned the King for leniency and were lightly reprimanded and warned not to act the play again. The warrant for Middleton's arrest was withdrawn after his son Edward appeared before the Privy Council. The royal furor about the play soon quieted, and apparently neither Thomas Middleton nor Sir Henry Herbert was penalized for his part in writing or approving the play.[75]

In *A Game at Chesse,* Middleton had violated all five of the restrictions which would provoke censorship from the Master of the Revels: critical comments on the policies or conduct of the government, unfavorable presentations of friendly foreign powers or their sovereigns, great nobles or subjects, comment on religious controversy, profanity (after 1606), and personal satire of influential people.[76] Yet Sir Henry Herbert had licensed the play. Middleton, as an experienced dramatist, was aware of the risks he had taken at each stage of the controversy, especially in defying the Privy Council's summons, arrest warrant, and warnings not to circulate copies of the banned play.[77] In the Malone manuscript dedication to William Hammond in 1625, for example, Middleton ac-

knowledged the play's prohibition: "This, Which nor Stage, nor Stationers Stall can showe, / (The Common Eye maye wish for, but ne're
knowe)."[78]

Middleton's actions in originally writing and later transcribing the play
and Herbert's in licensing it may have been calculated rather than
reckless. Because the play was licensed on 12 June 1624 but was not
publicly performed for two months, John Dover Wilson suggests that it
may have been performed at court during this period at the instigation
of Buckingham and Prince Charles, who favored war with Spain (and
who served as the play's models for the White Duke and White Knight
who capture the Black Knight, Gondomar, and checkmate the Black
King, Philip IV of Spain). Wilson concludes that the play was performed
publicly only while James was away from court and unable to respond
quickly to the anticipated complaint by Gondomar. The play was allowed
several performances before royal action could be taken, and the company could transcribe its prompt-copy before its inevitable confiscation.[79]

If Middleton did receive some type of protection against prosecution
for his play, it is doubtful that, at any stage either before or after
performance, he wrote or commissioned hasty, careless, and sloppy transcriptions derived from incomplete sources because he lacked the official
prompt-copy, as Bald and Zimmerman have charged. One transcript, the
Archdall (which lacks the prologue and epilogue), carries the date 13
August 1624, while another, the Malone (which carefully and coherently
cuts 770 lines of the complete play[80]), contains a dedicatory page dated
1 January 1625, written perhaps at the same time as the manuscript, but
probably added to it later. Middleton may have had ample time, as he
did in the case of the Malone manuscript, to add to or recopy the other
transcripts of the play, perhaps from the original prompt-copy, for private
ownership if he was dissatisfied with their existing state. The Archdall
has corrections in at least four hands, including the author's,[81] and
Bridgewater also shows correction, probably in Middleton's hand, so
Middleton and his scribes paid very careful attention to the state of the
transcribed copies. Middleton apparently did not have to rush the transcription of his private manuscripts by carelessly or deliberately omitting
substantial sections of the play.

Although Wilson claims that the case of *A Game at Chesse* is "so
peculiar that it is risky to argue from it to ordinary theatrical practice"
and faults Bald for seeing the transcriptions of it as typical practice,[82]
these transcripts almost certainly reveal ordinary authorial practice. Evidence provided by the earliest manuscript, the Archdall, convinced both

Bald and Zimmerman that Middleton had revised the play sometime either before or after its licensing or before its first performance.[83] The Archdall manuscript, dated 13 August, when the play was still in performance, does not contain the characters of the Fat Bishop, modeled on the Archbishop of Spalatro, and his pawn, which are found in the later versions. The Archdall instead has the role of the Black Bishop (which is greatly reduced in the versions which replace him with the Fat Bishop). This earlier version also contains less development of the character of the White King's pawn, modeled on Middlesex, the Lord Treasurer, who was being impeached at the time the play was being written.[84]

There seems no doubt that Middleton revised the early version of the play to work in the current scandals and misfortunes of Spalatro and Middlesex and produced the versions later than the Archdall manuscript. Yet replacing characters after the play's original composition may not have been the only type of revision that Middleton performed. The existence of at least eight substantively variant versions of *A Game at Chesse* (six manuscripts and the first and third Quartos) signal not merely textual "instability" but deliberate authorial change, hence, revision. Several of the texts, including those transcribed by the author, lack entire scenes found in other versions, and Middleton, who participated in most of the transcriptions, does not seem to have been disturbed that several substantively variant versions of the play existed.[85]

A collation of the two manuscripts, Trinity and Bridgewater, which are wholly or partly autograph elucidates the type of variants found in the other manuscripts and presents evidence that Middleton transcribed and approved of alternate versions of *A Game at Chesse*. Trinity, entirely holograph, contains no corrections,[86] and Bridgewater, although only partially holograph but completed by Middleton, contains hundreds of pencil corrections which were apparently made later than the ink *currente calamo* corrections.[87] The penciled corrector ruled off speech headings, added numerous punctuation marks (an average of five per page), made a few interlinear revisions, and rewrote a few unclear words. Some if not all of these penciled corrections appear to be in Middleton's hand; they appear in the scribal portions of the text (the first four acts) as well as in the holographic section of 2.2; the entirely holograph Act 5 contains no pencil corrections.[88] Many of the ink and pencil variants between the holographic portions of the Trinity and Bridgewater manuscripts are single word or line substitutions, transpositions, or deletions/additions which are characteristic of the variants due to authorial second thoughts and of textual instability.[89]

Both Trinity and Bridgewater lack a scene but each version of the text is coherent without the omitted scene. Trinity omits all of 4.5, a scene of sixty-nine lines in which the White King rescues the White Queen from the Fat Bishop. Bald, who did not have access to the actual manuscript, argued that Bridgewater omits much of 2.2, two hundred and thirty-two lines on the confrontation of the White and Black Houses, because the scribe did not leave enough pages in the manuscript for Middleton to completely add the portion of the text that he was to copy; when confronted by the single page left to transcribe the several hundred lines of text, Middleton heavily edited his copy by trimming a long speech of the Fat Bishop's, conflating two speeches by the Black Knight and assigning them to the Black Bishop (probably in error), and omitting the rest of the scene. Middleton also canceled the scribe's stage direction of "Enter" for the Fat Bishop, which began the next scene, 3.1, so that the stage direction became a speech heading and this separate scene became a continuation of the edited scene.

Yet, the actual, physical state of the manuscript contradicts Bald's hypothesis. Rather than being forced to squeeze his material onto one remaining side of a sheet, Middleton removed an entire extra sheet and *chose* to revise his material by condensing it. The page on which Middleton continued the scribe's transcription is the verso of a single quarter-sheet which is bound between the half sheets which form Folio pages. (The title-page sheet and this sheet are the only single sheets in the manuscript.) Middleton in fact continued the transcription which the scribe had ended mid-line on the first line of the page. As the fifth act contains no penciled corrections, it appears that Middleton proofread only the first four acts, which had been assembled and were probably still unbound. The manuscript evidence suggests that the sheet with this scene was loose, probably because, as George R. Price claims,[90] Middleton ripped the extra sheet out when confronted with too little space to transcribe the entire scene; thus the extant quarter-sheet was originally a half sheet until Middleton divided it. Middleton need not have ripped out this portion of the half sheet; he could also have inserted extra sheets to continue the transcription in the still unbound manuscript, but he did not do so. He may then have been satisfied with the existing transcription of 2.2 after having copied it and after having proofread it or he may have wanted to produce this scene exactly as it appears. He made only minor grammatical changes to this holograph section.

Although the Bridgewater scene was carefully and coherently edited, Middleton did not add an extra leaf or sheet in order to present the "full" version of the scene. It appears that he (or someone he supervised) so meticulously proofread and corrected the Bridgewater manuscript that he added four hundred penciled corrections to the first four acts, including the page of 2.2 which he transcribed. If Middleton was responsible for these corrections, as the handwriting suggests, he was curiously undisturbed by the variant scene, especially if he was preparing this manuscript for private sale or publication, as the detailed corrections suggest.

Many of the omitted lines in 2.2 in the Bridgewater manuscript concern the actions of the Fat Bishop, the Black Bishop's Pawn, and the Black Bishop. Because the Black Bishop originally served in the role taken over by the Fat Bishop in the later manuscript and printed versions, Middleton may have revised rather than edited this scene in Bridgewater. Even if Middleton changed the scene because he was forced to cut lines due to a lack of space, he still *revised* it. Perhaps Trinity's missing scene did not exist or was being revised when Middleton transcribed that manuscript. Whatever the reasons for the lack of these scenes in Trinity and Bridgewater, Middleton produced both manuscripts, and perhaps the other versions, in forms which met his artistic or literary demands for the play. Thus Middleton's texts display not only the first and second thought variants which Honigmann describes as types of *currente calamo* changes contributing to textual instability, but later deliberate revisions made to satisfy his changing visions of the play.

The manuscripts of *A Game at Chesse* prove that a Renaissance dramatist, writing for the same acting company for which Shakespeare wrote, could produce variant, alternate, and reliable versions of his own play. If, as Bald argued, the features of these and other manuscripts owned by the King's Men do not indicate assembling but represent a 1623–24 scribal practice used in copying out certain texts intended for the reader and not for the theatre,[91] Middleton's authorial practices may not have been unusual but consistent with the practices of the King's Men dramatists and scribes during this period—a period in which some of the manuscripts used in the printing of Shakespeare's First Folio were also probably copied or recopied.

Several critical assumptions about authorial practice during the Renaissance can be made from the the evidence provided by Marston's *The Malcontent,* Bale's *King Johan,* Jonson's *The Gypsies Metamorphosed,* Middleton's *A Game at Chesse,* and the plays of other dramatists. Professional dramatists who continued to exert some theatrical or artistic control participated in or supervised changes made to their plays and disclaimed, whenever possible, nonauthorial changes. Dramatists tended to revise economically; that is, they worked around existing dialogue in order to add to or alter passages, rather than deleting large chunks and completely rewriting their texts, but if necessary they overhauled an entire play. In the process of revising, dramatists sometimes produced separate and coherent multiple versions of their plays suited to private or public theatrical or literary audiences.

Several important conclusions about the types of and reasons for authorial revision of a play during this period can also be drawn. Types of authorial revisions included changes in or addition or deletion of characters *(King Johan, Believe as You List, The Malcontent, A Game at Chesse)*, themes *(King Johan, The Gypsies Metamorphosed, A Game at Chesse)*, plot *(Believe as You List, King Johan, A Game at Chesse)*, structure *(The Malcontent, King Johan, A Game at Chesse)*, and setting *(Believe as You List)*. Reasons for authorial revisions included: external or self-imposed censorship *(Believe as You List, The Malcontent, A Game at Chesse)*; the different needs of publication or private transcription *(The Malcontent, A Game at Chesse)*, or of occasional performance or revival *(King Johan, The Gypsies Metamorphosed, Bussy D'Ambois, A Game at Chesse)*; the personal or artistic demands of the author *(The Malcontent, King Johan, The Gypsies Metamorphosed, A Game at Chesse)*; and changes in acting company, venue, or audience *(The Malcontent, King Johan, and The Gypsies Metamorphosed)*, ownership of the play *(Bussy D'Ambois, The Malcontent)*, or political climate *(King Johan, A Game at Chesse)*.

R. C. Bald confidently stated in 1929 that

> those who have been engaged on the study of Shakespearian texts are beginning to find that the method of inferring the nature of the original manuscripts from the printed quarto or folio has its limitations, and that valuable aid can be obtained from the study of the extant manuscripts of plays of the other writers of the period.[92]

Yet, in the case of authorial revision, this valuable aid, so long neglected or dismissed, is only now being obtained in this study.

## ༉ 3 ༉

# Occasions and Occurrences of Revision in Shakespeare's Plays

I n arguing for revision by Shakespeare, Stanley Wells makes an important and necessary distinction in dividing changes made to a play into two categories: those arising from external circumstances, such as religious or political censorship, nonauthorial theatrical interpolation or adaptation, and nonauthorial literary revision; and those arising from internal circumstances to suit the dramatist's artistic demands, such as first and second-thought variants during composition, additions made after performance, and extensive revisions resulting in two separate texts of a play, as in the cases of *Hamlet, Troilus and Cressida, Othello,* and *King Lear.*[1] Wells's distinction is one that many editors from Nicholas Rowe to Harold Jenkins have been unwilling to make because they want to canonize only external causes as the sources for Shakespeare's own revisions.

Editors and critics have offered a multitude of occasions and occurrences of such "forced" revisions, to use Bowers's term,[2] and I will briefly survey these recent critical discussions of authorial revisions due to the external causes within one text or between two or more texts of a play. Yet I will also extend this critical discussion by recognizing Wells's other category of authorial revisions and by presenting studies of plays with authorial second-thought or later revisions within or between specific texts due to Shakespeare's own artistic concerns or demands.

## Censorship

A collation of Folio texts with their counterpart Quarto texts readily locates changes due to religious censorship in some of the texts of

Shakespeare's plays. Although the Act of 1606 against profanity applied to stage performances and not to printed texts,[3] several Folio texts, including *Titus Andronicus, Richard III, The Merry Wives of Windsor, 1 Henry IV, Twelfth Night,* and *Othello,* show an expurgation of oaths, or the substitution of a secular oath for the religious oath printed in the Quarto. For example, Falstaff's most frequently used epithet in *1 Henry IV,* "By the Lord," appears in Quarto 1 but has been systematically removed from the Folio text, and his and others' oaths to "God" in the Quarto have been altered to "heauen" in the Folio. It is possible that numerous other Folio texts of plays without an earlier edition display other less apparent signs of expurgation.

In addition to the censorship of profanity, Shakespeare's plays were subjected to the four other political and religious restrictions which could provoke censorship from the Master of the Revels, including representation of the monarch and satire of influential nobles. Shakespeare apparently crossed often into this dangerous territory, particularly in his history plays, by in several plays alluding to and in one play portraying the deposition of Richard II, thus reminding Elizabeth of the recent threats to her throne (particularly the rebellion of the Earl of Essex), and by borrowing the name of the Protestant martyr, Sir John Oldcastle, for his comic character in at least one play. The deposition scene, 4.1, of *Richard II* was not published in the first three Quartos in 1597, 1598, and 1608, although the scene may have been staged beginning with the first performance of the play.[4] The scene, apparently reported or memorially reconstructed, was first printed in the 1608 Quarto 4, whose title page advertised the play "with new additions of the Parliament Sceane, and the deposing of King Richard."

Dramatic material alluding to Richard II may have forced cuts or substitutions in Shakespeare's subsequent history plays; at least half of the eight passages in the Folio of *2 Henry IV* which do not appear in the 1600 Quarto 1 may have been cut from the latter text because they alluded to the Bolingbroke-Percy rebellion and the subsequent abdication of Richard.[5] Quarto 1A of the play lacks the first scene in Act 3, in which the dying Henry IV reflects on his role in the deposition of Richard, possibly because the Chamberlain's Men attempted to bypass the censor,[6] or because the scene was temporarily pulled from the stage, or for some other reason. The scene was printed later in the year in the second issue of Quarto 1.

Political references offensive to the person or the policies of the reigning monarch may also have been removed by order of the censor

from the Quarto or Octavo 1 of *2 Henry VI, 3 Henry VI,* and *Henry V,*
and the Folio of *Macbeth,* among other texts.[7] Madeleine Doran and W.
W. Greg argue that censorship forced the substitution of the civil war
within the kingdom in the Folio text of *King Lear* for the foreign war
with France in Quarto 1,[8] although Gary Taylor finds evidence of
censorship in the Folio text not in the removal of the French material
but in the removal of the Fool's satiric comments on royalty.[9] Annabel
Patterson suggests that Shakespeare exercised self-censorship in some
plays but not in others; for example, *Richard II* acquired topical significance *after* its composition, while *King Lear* commented on the current
problems of a new monarch intent on union of his kingdoms, so that
both the Quarto and Folio texts of *King Lear* during their compositions
were shaped by Shakespeare's understanding of the "hermeneutics of
censorship."[10]

Shakespeare's representation of Oldcastle in the original version of *1
Henry IV,* and probably *2 Henry IV,* was to bring him the continuing
displeasure of and objections from Oldcastle's descendants, the Brooke
family, particularly William Brooke (Lord Cobham), the Lord Chamberlain (although not the patron of Shakespeare's company) from mid-
1596 to early 1597.[11] Evidence in the first Quartos shows that Shakespeare
was forced to revise the first play after it had been performed but before
it was printed and the second play after its composition, and probably
after its early performances, by altering Oldcastle's name to Falstaff and
by changing the names of two other characters apparently named for
historical figures (Harvey, changed to Bardolph, and Russell, changed to
Peto). There are still traces of the original names or marks of their
excision remaining in the Quarto 1 texts of both plays: in 1.2 of *1 Henry
IV,* Hal calls Falstaff "my old lad of the castle"; the apparent substitution
of "Falstaff" for "Oldcastle" disturbs the meter in 2.2; the name appears
as a speech prefix in 1.2 of *2 Henry IV,* as do the names Harvey and
Russell in 1.2 and 2.4 of *1 Henry IV* and Russell in 2.2 *2 Henry IV.* An
addition at the end of the epilogue of *2 Henry IV* reminds the audience
that "Old-castle died Martyre, and this is not the man." At least *1 Henry
IV* and probably *2 Henry IV* had been performed in 1596–97 but withdrawn for revision after protests from the Brooke, Harvey, and Russell
families, certainly before the composition in early 1597 of *The Merry
Wives of Windsor,* when the "fat knight" had already become "Falstaff."
The *Henry IV* plays reappeared on stage later with the offending names
changed and the apologetic epilogue to *2 Henry IV* appended. *1 Henry*

*IV* was printed early in 1598, probably to publicize the alterations and appease the displeased families.

Continued pressure by the Brooke family may have resulted in the excision of Falstaff's character in *Henry V* (the epilogue of *2 Henry IV* had promised that "our humble author will continue the story, with Sir John in it"),[12] as well as the change in character name from "Brooke" in the Quartos to "Broome" in the Folio of *The Merry Wives of Windsor*.[13] Shakespeare's company may have made similar changes to a touring version of *Hamlet*. G. R. Hibbard concludes from the evidence of the title page that the 1603 Quarto 1 reflects the text as it was performed at Oxford University, for which performances the names of Polonius and Reynaldo were changed to Corambis and Montano to avoid offending two men associated with the University.[14] However, the change of character names may have arisen from other theatrical exigencies.[15]

But whether the censorship was absolute or slight, direct or indirect, externally or self-imposed, Shakespeare would have had to adjust the surrounding text of a play when an offensive passage had been removed. He may have made minor one-line insertions or added whole passages to fill in for cuts and also reworked other uncensored portions of the text when reexamining the current condition of his play, especially if the loss of the censored material shifted structure, setting, plot, theme, or character. Shakespeare exerted a form of artistic control over his plays even when altering them at the prompting of an external cause.

## Acting Conditions

Changes in the acting company performing a play, such as changes in company size or personnel, also "forced" revisions. The title pages of several Quartos of Shakespeare's plays identify, probably reliably, at least one of the companies which acted them. Performance by the Lord Chamberlain's Men is noted on the title pages of the 1599 Quarto 2 of *Romeo and Juliet*, the 1600 Quartos 1 of *2 Henry IV, Henry V, The Merchant of Venice, A Midsummer Night's Dream, Much Ado About Nothing*, and the 1602 Quarto 1 of *The Merry Wives of Windsor*,[16] and performance by the King's Men, the name used by the Chamberlain's Men beginning in 1603, is noted on the title pages of the 1603 Quarto 1 of *Hamlet*, the 1608 Quarto 1 of *King Lear*, the 1609 Quartos 1 of *Pericles* and *Troilus and Cressida*, the 1622 Quarto 1 of *Othello*, the 1631 Quarto

2 of *Love's Labor's Lost,* and the 1631 Quarto 1 of *The Taming of the Shrew.* A comparison of early and later Quarto title pages also shows that at least four Chamberlain's Men plays, *Richard II, Richard III, Romeo and Juliet,* and *Titus Andronicus,* were still active ten years later in the repertory of the King's Men.

Revisions were apparently made in the texts of a few plays to reduce the number of actors needed or to allow some to double minor parts. Bowers argues that the character of Poins drops out of 2.4 in Quarto 1 of *1 Henry IV* because the actor who played him was needed to double another role, so that Peto becomes a surrogate Poins figure to Prince Hal later in that scene.[17] Bowers's theory is plausible although not irrefutable; Shakespeare may simply have abandoned his original intention of focusing on Poins in this scene. Doubling may have also caused a change of intention on Shakespeare's part in *Julius Caesar* and *The Tempest.* The addition of the role of the "lean" Caius Ligarius in *Julius Caesar* after the play had been written out may have necessitated doubling this role with Cassius, causing a major revision and expansion in one scene and some minor revision in another.[18] Ariel's long delay in appearing to Prospero, who has summoned him after the masque in 4.1, and the addition of several intervening lines of dialogue may have been necessary to allow the actor portraying Ariel to make a costume change if he doubled another role in the masque.[19] Some anomalies in the Folio text of *The Two Gentlemen of Verona* may also reflect later cuts to suit a new cast.[20]

At least two plays show a reassignment of songs to other characters when a boy who had previously acted a singing role grew into an adult or left the company. The singing boy who originally played Viola in *Twelfth Night* may not have been available for a later revival, and the song before the Duke, as printed in the Folio, was transferred to Feste, played perhaps by Robert Armin.[21] Similarly, the "Willow" song may have been cut from Quarto 1 of *Othello* when a singing boy was not available to play Desdemona,[22] and although the character of Rosalind in *As You Like It* does not sing, discrepancies in dialogue about her height in the Folio text may signal that some lines were changed for a later revival to suit a boy taller than the original one.[23]

More substantial revisions may have been required for plays which had been acted by other companies before Shakespeare's attachment to the Chamberlain's Men. The 1594 Quarto 1 title page of *Titus Andronicus* advertises that it had been "plaide by the Right Honourable the Earle of

*Darbie,* Earle of *Pembrooke,* and Earle of *Sussex* their Seruants" and the 1600 Quarto 2 title page adds to this list "the Lorde Chamberlaine theyr Seruants," leading some to suggest that Shakespeare worked for Pembroke's Men before they broke up in 1593 and that he overhauled the play first for the later performances of Sussex's Men and again for his new company, the Chamberlain's Men.[24] The closing of the London theatres during outbreaks of the plague throughout the 1590s, particularly from 1592–1594, forced acting companies to tour the provinces with adapted or abridged plays suitable for makeshift stages and a reduced number of actors. Some of Shakespeare's plays were apparently abridged for the touring Pembroke's Men and later, when the company went bankrupt, sold to printers who published them in these shortened and often mangled Quarto editions, which were often far removed from the versions in the dramatist's foul papers.[25] For example, Greg argues that since the Chamberlain's Men acquired *Titus Andronicus* after it had been in print for some years and had already been performed by three preceding companies, it is doubtful that they had access to the author's foul papers,[26] used to print Quarto 1; they probably acted the play from the original prompt book with its cuts restored or from a newly transcribed and perhaps greatly derivative one. A play-text that passed through the hands of several acting companies could exist in multiple copies and versions, some or none of which derived from the original author.

The anonymous Quarto of *The Taming of a Shrew,* which may be a reported version of or a source play for Shakespeare's *The Taming of the Shrew,* also advertises that it had been performed by Pembroke's Men and may preserve some material of Shakespeare's that was later changed for the Chamberlain's Men's performances.[27] *A Shrew* contains both the prologue and epilogue material with Christopher Sly, while *The Shrew* lacks this epilogue, suggesting that the first version of the play was written for a larger company, possibly the Queen's Men, and then cut to suit a smaller company[28] in which the actors who performed the Sly material doubled other roles rather than remaining on stage to watch the entire play.[29] The title page of *The True Tragedy of Richard, Duke of York* also names it a Pembroke's Men play, and the company probably owned *The First Part of the Contention;* the Octavo and Quarto are reported versions of *3 Henry VI* and *2 Henry VI* which may nonetheless preserve an accurate record of Shakespeare's plays as written to suit Pembroke's Men.[30] The first Quartos of *Richard III* and *Romeo and Juliet* and a nonextant version of *1 Henry VI* may also have been abridged acting versions used by Pembroke's Men.[31]

Clues on the title pages and within the texts of the plays also suggest that plays were adapted for performance at different venues or for different types of audiences. The text of a play could be made suitable for private performances at court or in stately homes before monarchs and nobles, for public provincial tours outside London on makeshift stages, for public performances at outdoor theatres like the Theatre, the Curtain, or the Globe (used by the Chamberlain's Men beginning in 1599) or for indoor theatres like Blackfriars (acquired by the King's Men in 1608). Some Quarto title pages provide evidence of at least one place of performance. Globe performances are noted in the 1608 Quarto 4 of *Richard II*, the 1609 Quartos 1 of *Pericles* and *Troilus and Cressida* (first issue only) and Quarto 3 of *Romeo and Juliet*. (None of the title pages of the Quartos lists Blackfriars as the only place of performance.) Any of these plays may have been performed at other venues or theatres and for other types of audiences than those specifically noted.

In a few cases, the title pages provide evidence that a play has moved from one venue and type of audience to another, possibly requiring alterations and revisions. The reported 1602 Quarto 1 title page of *The Merry Wives of Windsor* states that the play has been performed "before the Queene and else-where." The nonspecific venue and audience of "else-where" appear again on the similarly reported Quarto 1 title page of *Hamlet*, which advertises the play "as it hath beene diuerse times acted by his Highnesse seruants in the Cittie of London: as also in the two Vniuersities of Cambridge and Oxford, and else-where"; both plays may have had public performances in an outdoor theatre. The title pages of the 1622 Quarto 1 of *Othello*, the 1631 Quarto 1 of *The Taming of the Shrew*, and the 1631 Quarto 2 of *Love's Labor's Lost* advertise that these plays had been performed both at the Globe and at Blackfriars. The title page of the 1608 Quarto 1 of *King Lear*, with the text as performed for "*the Kings Maiestie at Whitehall vpon S.* Stephans *night in Christmas Hollidayes* By his Maiesties seruants playing vsually at the Gloabe," evidently attempted shrewdly to advertise both a royal command performance and continuing public performances.

*Troilus and Cressida* may have also been publicly and privately performed. The strongest piece of evidence comes from alternate title pages for the two different states of the 1609 Quarto 1: in the first state, the play is advertised "as it was acted by the Kings Maiesties seruants at the Globe." In the second state, this notice is canceled, and the description "Excellently expressing the beginning of their loues, with the conceited wooing of Pandarus Prince of Licia" is substituted; an epistle describing the play as "new," "a Comedy," and "neuer stal'd with the Stage, neuer clapper-clawd with the palmes of the vulger" is also added. The alternate title pages suggest that the printer erred in first advertising the play as being publicly performed or that he later falsely claimed it had not been acted, but it appears the play did have private performances.

In addition to title-page evidence, there appear to be signs of revisions for change of venue within the plays, either in stage directions or in alternative endings containing added or revised masques or epilogues. The curious stage direction, "They sleepe all the Act," at the end of Act 3 in the Folio text of *A Midsummer Night's Dream* may signal act divisions characteristic of Blackfriars performances.[32] The 1600 Quarto 1 and 1623 Folio texts may preserve alternate endings to the play: the fairy masque for private performance and Puck's epilogue for public performance.[33] Masques may have also been reworked in or added to *As You Like It*, *Cymbeline*, *The Tempest*,[34] and other plays in order to update them for later audiences now accustomed to spectacle in the theatre or to make them suitable for an occasional performance.

The Folio text of *The Merry Wives of Windsor*, like the manuscript of Ben Jonson's masque *The Gypsies Metamorphosed* represents an occasional performance at Windsor to celebrate a Garter feast. The appearance of allusions to Windsor Castle and the Order of the Garter in the masque in Act 5 in the Folio but not in the reported 1602 Quarto text suggests a private and alternative ending to the play, which at some point had also been performed publicly. Shakespeare may have originally written *The Merry Wives of Windsor* for a Garter feast, probably the installation of Lord Hunsdon (the Lord Chamberlain and Shakespeare's patron) in 1597, or added the Folio Garter passages for a 1604 performance to celebrate the 1603 installation of the Prince of Wales and others into the Order.

Scholars have cited Simon Forman's incomplete descriptions of two plays in 1611 to argue for the later additions of musical and dance passages printed in the Folio texts. It seems unlikely that Forman saw but simply failed to note the dance of the satyrs in 4.4 of *The Winter's Tale* and the Hecate scene in 3.5 of *Macbeth* in his otherwise extremely detailed and precise summaries of the scenes of both plays; in the case of *Macbeth* Forman almost certainly saw a version of the play before two songs and a dance originally written by Thomas Middleton for *The Witch*, a play in the King's Men repertory, were added to it. The dance of the satyrs may then have also been added sometime after the original performances of *The Winter's Tale*.

## Involvement of Other Authors

Some of Shakespeare's plays may also show signs of his revision of the work of his predecessors or of his collaborators. The probable appearance of Shakespeare's hand in the manuscript of *The Book of Sir Thomas More* has convinced some scholars that Shakespeare was accustomed to adding to or taking over an existing work. Due to the lingering influence of F. G. Fleay and J. M. Robertson in the early twentieth century, critics such as John Dover Wilson continued to see preexisting plays as the basis of many of Shakespeare's plays, and modern editors have agreed with Wilson in certain cases. Henslowe's listing of *Titus Andronicus* as "ne" in 1593 for Sussex's Men in his *Diary* may have marked the play as new, newly licensed, or newly revised at that time,[35] so it is possible that Shakespeare took over an old play.[36]

However, it is difficult to distinguish among source plays from which Shakespeare borrowed characters, plots, or dialogue, preexisting plays which he adapted through revision, and new plays on which he collaborated with other authors. For example, J. M. Nosworthy argues that the close resemblances between *The Merry Wives of Windsor* and Henry Porter's play, *The Two Angry Women of Abingdon,* suggest that Shakespeare's play was a reworking of Porter's,[37] but Shakespeare may have borrowed rather than adapted. Many critics agree that the three parts of *Henry VI* were the result of Shakespeare's partial or entire reworking of collaborative plays (Henslowe listed "Harey the vj" as "ne" in 1592).[38] *The Troublesome raigne of John King of England* may have served as source play or the prerevised basis for the Folio text of Shakespeare's *King John*.[39] The large number of variants between the first and second Quartos of *Hamlet* has convinced some critics that at least one of the versions represents the text of the *Ur-Hamlet* after it had been reworked by Shakespeare.[40] The stylistic differences within the text of *Pericles* may stem from Shakespeare's revision of an old text or from his collaboration with another author.[41] Shakespeare evidently collaborated with John Fletcher on *Henry VIII* and *The Two Noble Kinsmen*[42] and possibly with Middleton on *Timon of Athens*.[43] Some scholars have much more controversially argued that the printed texts of Shakespeare's plays hold traces of later revision by other authors. J. W. Lever rejected Dover Wilson's argument for nonauthorial additions to the text of *Measure for Measure,* first printed in the Folio, by claiming that Wilson's theories depended upon "subjective estimates of what is or is not good enough for Shakespeare to have written."[44] John Jowett, however, has argued that Thomas Middleton may have rewritten a portion of 1.2 and another author may have revised the end of Act 3 in order to adapt the play for later performances by the King's Men.[45] Middleton probably did not revise portions of *Macbeth* but he or a member of the King's Men may simply have added his songs and one dance from *The Witch*.[46] Henry Chettle may have contributed some material to the memorially reconstructed Quarto 1 text of *Romeo and Juliet*.[47]

## Varieties of Authorial Revision

The last of the external causes that Wells lists, literary revision, appears to have affected primarily the Folio texts which show signs of heavy and consistent editing. John Jowett and Gary Taylor convincingly distinguish between the types of alterations made by an editor and author:

> An editor might add stage directions which he believed to be necessary, or modernize obsolete or obscure spellings, or provide act and scene divisions, or remove profanities; he might even, according to some textual scholars, regularize speech prefixes, or substitute commonplace words for rare or arcane ones. But why should he deliberately and randomly insert words of 'nearly equivalent meaning' to substitute for those in his printed and manuscript sources?[48]

Several of the manuscripts or earlier printed editions which served as printer's copy for the Folio were annotated; errors, gaps, and inconsistencies in plays such as *Julius Caesar* and *Romeo and Juliet* were apparently corrected, and other texts were regularized and modernized. The copies used to print *The Taming of the Shrew* and *Titus Andronicus* and other plays show no alteration of obvious errors; thus some plays received little or no editing before being printed in the 1623 First Folio collection.[49]

Although many of Shakespeare's plays probably received both authorial and nonauthorial revisions as a result of external causes, enough evidence exists on title pages of Quartos and within and between the various printed texts of his plays to argue also that Shakespeare made revisions to his plays for his own artistic reasons. The 1599 Quarto 2 of *1 Henry IV* simply advertises that it has been "newly corrected," but others advertise or imply alterations and additions as well as correction. The 1598 Quarto 1 of *Love's Labor's Lost* advertises that it has been "newly corrected and augmented," and the 1599 Quarto 2 of *Romeo and Juliet* that it has been "*newly corrected, augmented, and amended.*" The 1608 Quarto 4 of *Richard II* advertises "new additions," the 1602 Quarto 3 of *Richard III* advertises the play as "newly augmented," and the 1602 Quarto 2 of *Hamlet* advertises that it has been "newly imprinted and enlarged to almost as much againe as it was, according to the true and perfect Coppie." The word "corrected" on the Quarto title pages may have been used by the various printers to signify that these editions were printed to supersede reported (and in some cases nonextant) Quartos. Yet there is enough evidence within the texts of these plays to indicate that printers used the terms "augmented," "amended," and "enlarged" to advertise the recent authorial alteration of existing passages and additions of new ones, and it is possible that such advertisements were made with Shakespeare's consent. As E. A. J. Honigmann has argued, "the good quartos could not have been sneaked into the world again and again without his knowledge, and the replacement of bad quartos by good ones points to the author's concern for his reputation rather than to the players' for theirs."[50] This concern would imply that Shakespeare did not lose interest in his plays after their performance or printing.[51]

Other possible internal indicators of revision are changes in speech headings within or between scenes, mislined verse due to marginal additions, awkward verbal transitions within or between characters' speeches, and duplications (also called doublets or repetition brackets). For example, speech-prefix changes in Quarto 4 *Richard II* and Folio *Julius Caesar, Titus Andronicus, A Midsummer Night's Dream, Richard III,* and *Troilus and Cressida* may frame passages that were revised or added to the plays.[52] Marginal additions are probably incorporated into the

Quarto texts of *Titus Andronicus, Romeo and Juliet, A Midsummer Night's Dream, Hamlet, Othello,* and *King Lear* and duplications in the Quarto/Folio texts of *Titus Andronicus, A Midsummer Night's Dream, Love's Labor's Lost, Julius Caesar, Romeo and Juliet,* and *Othello.* In addition to second-thought signs of revision during composition there are numerous significant variants due to later revision between Quartos and Folios of these plays and others, including Quarto 1A and 1B of *2 Henry IV* and Quarto 1 and Folio *King Lear.* Authors can share patterns of composition, and theatrical and printing exigencies can introduce similar types of changes into texts, yet these substantive variants serve as signs of authorial revision because they repeatedly and consistently show identical patterns of "stylistic evidence, image-clustering, source references, linguistic preferences, and bibliographic dependence"[53] deriving from one single author, Shakespeare himself. Evidence that Shakespeare revised his plays can no longer be ignored or reconstituted into the externally forced category of revisions; the overwhelming evidence of authorial revision must be recognized and thus canonized and constituted into the texts so that they, rather than their editors, reveal the authorial process.

*Two case studies:* Romeo and Juliet *and* Love's Labor's Lost

The Quarto and Folio texts of *Romeo and Juliet* and *Love's Labor's Lost* can serve as models by which to evaluate second-thought and later revisions that proceed from the author himself in several of his other plays. Although its authority has been largely dismissed by modern scholars, the reported 1597 Quarto 1 of *Romeo and Juliet* contains a number of cuts that may have been due to abridgment for a small acting company, cuts probably made by Shakespeare himself. Although I recognize that reported or "bad" texts, in many cases, hold evidence of prerevised or postrevised Shakespearian material, I also recognize that such material has been surreptitiously printed.[54] The title page of the 1599 Quarto 2 advertises, like that of Quarto 1 of *Love's Labor's Lost* from the same printer, that the play has been "*newly corrected, augmented, and amended,*" probably in an effort to separate it from the earlier edition. The Quarto 2 text contains a number of authorial second-thought revisions (suggesting that it was largely printed from foul papers with coexistent first and second versions) and occasionally misinserted corrections and marginal additions, such as in the Queen Mab speech in 1.4 (sig. C2), which is printed as prose.

Some of the duplications disturb the meter and the sense of the passages in which they are found, but both versions are printed side by side in the later Quarto and Folio texts without correction. One remarkable example which reveals Shakespeare's composition practice appears in Romeo's final speech at the end of 2.2 (sig. D4ᵛ; TLN 999–1009), when he marvels:

> The grey eyde morne smiles on the frowning night,
> Checkring the Easterne Clouds with streaks of light,
> And darknesse fleckted like a drunkard reeles,
> From forth daies pathway, made by *Tytans* wheeles.
> Hence will I to my ghostly Friers close cell,
> His helpe to craue, and my deare hap to tell.

The Friar begins the next scene, 2.3, with the same lines:

> The grey-eyed morne smiles on the frowning night,
> Checking the Easterne clowdes with streaks of light:
> And fleckeld darknesse like a drunkard reeles,
> From forth daies path, and *Titans* burning wheeles.

Although it is not entirely certain for which character the speech was first written, in the process of transferring it from one to the other Shakespeare appears to have introduced, as Honigmann has argued generally of Shakespeare's plays,[55] minor second-thought variants. "Flecked" and "darkness" have been transposed in the third line, and in the fourth line a few words have been altered in order to modify "Titans wheels" with "burning" and intensify the metaphor in the Friar's, and probably the second, version. What is most noticeable is that Shakespeare either did not cancel one of the passages, perhaps because he intended to make corrections after completion of his foul papers but never did so, or he marked cancellations in such a way that the compositor did not recognize the marks.[56] A third possibility, that he intended both characters to speak the same lines in succession, is unlikely, since he slightly altered the imagery.

One duplication in Quarto 2 appears to have been corrected in the Folio, which was reprinted from Quarto 3 (1619) and Quarto 4 (1622),[57] perhaps by the printing-house annotator who made other corrections in it.[58] Romeo's speech in 3.3 on hearing of his banishment appears below as printed in Quarto 2 (sig. G4):

> This may flyes do, when I from this must flie,
> And sayest thou yet, that exile is not death?
> But *Romeo* may not, he is banished.
> Flies may do this, but I from this must flie:
> They are freemen, but I am banished.

While Quarto 3 and Quarto 4 reprint this passage as it appears in Quarto 2, the Folio (TLN 1843–1845) reprints it without the last two lines. Because there is no evidence that Shakespeare made the correction, modern editors emend, and thus recanonize, the passage by removing either the first line or the last two lines.[59] It is possible that Shakespeare was aware that his first thought, "Flies may do this . . . I am banished," had been printed alongside his second thought, "This may flyes do . . . he is banished," or that, as Randall McLeod argues in general about the duplications, Shakespeare intended all of the lines to stand, so that no cancellation of a "version" was needed.[60]

Among the several other passages in Quarto 2 which W. W. Greg notes as preserving the first versions, with the subsequent second versions following, are those in Romeo's speech in 2.2 (sig. D2), "It is my Lady, ô it is my loue, ô that she knew she wer"; in Lady Capulet's speech in 3.1 (sig. F4$^v$), "O Prince, O Cozen, husband, O the bloud is spild"; in Juliet's speech in 3.2 (sigs. G1$^v$, G2$^v$), "And by their owne bewties, or if loue be blind," and "Rauenous douefeatherd rauen, woluishrauening lamb"; in the Friar's speech in 4.1 (sig. I3$^v$), "Then as the manner of our countrie is . . . Be borne to buriall in thy kindred's graue"; and in Romeo's speech in 5.3 (sig. L3), "Depart againe, come lye thou in my arme . . . Thy drugs are quicke. Thus with a kisse I die."[61] However, none of these passages or the two noted above appears as a duplication in the reported Quarto 1. In *each* instance, Quarto 1 *corrects* the duplicated passage by presenting only one of the two versions; for example, the "grey eyed morne" speech is given to the Friar alone. Of the five line "flies/banished" passage, Quarto 1 presents only the line, "But *Romeo* may not, he is banished."

There are at least three possibilities to account for the omission of duplications in Quarto 1 and their appearance in Quarto 2: the duplications were written out in the foul papers but corrected or cut in the abridged acting text, and thus the reporter never heard them; the reporter himself cut the duplications after hearing them performed on stage or recognizing them in the acting text which he obtained; or Shakespeare added the second versions sometime after the abridged performance which the Quarto 1 reporter transcribed, suggesting that the second versions in each duplicated passage were not written out during original composition but added some months or years later.[62] The second of these possibilities can easily be dismissed, as the reporter did not elsewhere bother to correct his faulty text and it is unlikely that many of these duplications were used in performance.

The title page of Quarto 1 notes that the play had been publicly acted by "the right Honourable the L. of *Hunsdon* his Seruants," so it must have been reported during the period from mid-1596 to early 1597 when Shakespeare's company used this name.[63] The play may have undergone revisions (as in the duplicated passages) before being printed in 1599, perhaps at the same time that Shakespeare rewrote and expanded the Queen Mab speech by marginally adding to it, so that the printer set it as prose rather than as verse in Quarto 2 (the original speech is printed in verse in Quarto 1). Most of the recent editors of the play favor the theory that Quarto 2 was printed mostly from foul papers and partly from Quarto 1, rather than the theory that Quarto 2 was printed mostly from Quarto 1 and partly from foul paper insertions,[64] and it is possible that Shakespeare wrote out the second versions of the duplicated passages on separate sheets and inserted them into his foul papers, later serving as Quarto 2 copy. If so, Shakespeare made revisions to his foul papers rather than to the promptbook being used for performance.

If Shakespeare revised *Romeo and Juliet* after a gap of some years, the title page advertisement of Quarto 2 possesses more authority than previously granted it by modern scholars.[65] Quarto 2 was "corrected" of the errors printed in the reported Quarto 1, and also "augmented" and "amended" by Shakespeare, each term specifying carefully delineated revisions: addition of a new passage and alteration of an existing one. However, if revision occurred during or immediately after composition, then the Lord Hunsdon's Men acted the play from a transcript of the foul papers which had carefully eliminated duplications; in this case Quarto 2 reproduces the play as it was originally composed in 1596 but not as it was originally performed. Yet this last possibility seems unlikely, and the Queen Mab speech, which is clearly enlarged in Quarto 2 and apparently postdates rather than predates the version printed in Quarto 1, would still have to have been revised after the report of the Quarto 1 text.[66]

Either of these two sets of circumstances produced the Quarto 1 and 2 texts of *Romeo and Juliet:*

1. Shakespeare rewrote the "duplicated" passages during composition; his foul papers were very carefully edited and corrected and then transcribed for the prompt-copy; this prompt-copy or another copy was abridged for performances by Hunsdon's Men, and subsequently reported and printed in Quarto 1 in 1597; Shakespeare reworked the Queen Mab speech in the margins of the passage in his foul papers, perhaps when the play ceased to be acted in an abridged version by the Chamberlain's Men, and this revision (and possibly others) may or may not have been added to the prompt-copy; and the uncorrected and unedited foul papers were released to the printer in 1599 for an edition that would supersede the reported one.

2. Shakespeare composed the play and his first version was transcribed and perhaps abridged for performances by Hunsdon's Men, and subsequently reported and printed in Quarto 1 in 1597; Shakespeare revised several passages in his foul papers, including the "duplicated" passages and the Queen Mab speech, perhaps when the play ceased to be acted in an abridged version by the Chamberlain's Men; a new prompt-copy was transcribed from the revised foul papers, either with or without the old versions of the revisions canceled; once the new version had been successfully recopied, the uncorrected and unedited foul papers were released to the printer in 1599 for an edition that would supersede the reported one.

The second scenario presents a more plausible series of events, as the restoration of abridged passages to the prompt-copy after 1597 would have required some authorial reworking of the foul papers, and the recopying of the newly reworked foul papers into a prompt-copy could easily explain why the Chamberlain's Men released their original version to a printer in 1599. Because the evidence of later revision in *Romeo and Juliet* depends on the authority of the reported Quarto 1, the play may serve as a tenuous model for other revised plays. However, many of the methods and patterns of revision in this play appear to a greater extent and with a clearer purpose in a play written during roughly the same period, *Love's Labor's Lost.*

The 1598 Quarto 1 of *Love's Labor's Lost* presents compelling evidence of second-thought revisions within the text. The title page advertises the text "as it was presented before her Highnes this last Christmas. Newly corrected and augmented *By W. Shakespere.*" The play may have had other occasional performances and may have been written between 1593 and 1594 for a private performance and then revised for the later court performance or for public performances.[67] However, evidence within the Quarto and Folio texts demonstrates that the play's main revisions, in the speeches of Berowne, were made during or shortly after the original composition.

Two sets of duplicated passages appear in the Quarto and are reprinted in the Folio in dialogue spoken by Berowne. In the first seven lines of his major speech in 4.3, Berowne attempts to convince the love-stricken King Ferdinand, Dumaine, and Longaville to reconsider their three vows "to fast, study, and to see no woman." Berowne promptly declares fasting to be "treason gainst the kingly state of youth," and then proceeds to explain how study cannot be performed except in the company of women. In the beginning portion of the first version (sig. F2$^v$; TLN 1646–1668), Berowne offers this doctrine:

> And where that you haue vowd to studie (Lordes)
> In that each of you haue forsworne his Booke.
> Can you still dreame and poare and thereon looke.
> For when would you, my Lord, or you, or you,
> Haue found the ground of Studies excellence
> Without the beautie of a woman's face?
> From womens eyes this doctrine I deriue:
> They are the Ground, the Bookes, the Achadems,
> From whence doth spring the true *Promethean* fire.

Berowne continues to insist on the contradiction of the second and third vows of the men, and concludes the twenty-three line speech with the lines, "Then when our selues we see in Ladies eyes, / With our selues. / Do we not likewise see our learning there?"; this last line appears to conclude the speech. However, a second and repetitive speech assigned to Berowne follows immediately. In an expanded and evidently substituted passage of forty-eight lines (sigs. F2$^v$-F3; TLN 1669–1716) on the absurdity of the vows to study and avoid women, framed with material from the first version, Berowne analyzes the power of women's eyes on the lover's eyes, ears, tongue, and feeling:

> O we haue made a Vow to studie, Lordes,
> And in that Vow we haue forsworne our Bookes:
> For when would you (my Leedge) or you, or you?
> In leaden contemplation haue found out
> Such fierie Numbers as the prompting eyes,
> Of beautis tutors haue inritcht you with:
> Other slow Artes intirely keepe the braine.

Berowne presents as his conclusion of this passage the opening frame of the earlier version:

> From womens eyes this doctrine I deriue.
> They sparcle still the right promethean fier,
> They are the Bookes, the Artes, the Achademes,
> That shew, containe, and nourish all the worlde.
> Else none at all in ought proues excellent.

Berowne's following plea to the men to forswear their oath to avoid the company of women was probably added in the second version as the new conclusion (or it stood as the original conclusion to the first passage). Shakespeare either wrote out the second version during the original composition or he added it sometime later on an extra sheet of paper (forty-eight lines would fill one page of foolscap)[68] and marked the first passage for deletion. Evidence from extant manuscripts during this period shows that an author often marked deletions solely with a small cross or vertical bar in the margin without excising any portion of the text itself; the compositor, setting from a manuscript written some years earlier and later marked up in various ways, could easily have missed such slight cancellation marks and printed both passages.

In revising, Shakespeare extended the metaphor on the power of women's eyes by inserting the added lines economically inside the same frame used in the first draft, working in much the same way as John Bale and Ben Jonson in *King Johan* and *The Gypsies Metamorphosed.* Shakespeare inserted the new passage into the opening seven lines and interpolated some of the original lines into the new ones, revising them subtly. This duplication, which cannot merely result from corruption by bookkeepers or printers or another external force, proceeds from the author's composing and recomposing process. This process also demonstrates, as in the case of *Romeo and Juliet,* the contextual, stylistic, and linguistic resemblances between the first and second versions of the passage, marking them both as authorial. A comparison of a few lines

of the first and second versions elucidates the indifferent and substantive
variants arising from this type of deliberate authorial revision:

> From womens eyes this doctrine I deriue:
> They are the Ground, the Bookes, the Achadems,
> From whence doth spring the true *Promethean* fire.

> From womens eyes this doctrine I deriue.
> They sparcle still the right promethean fier,
> They are the Bookes, the Artes, the Achademes,
> That shew, containe, and nourish all the worlde.

Editors and critics have debated for centuries whether the second version
of the long speech is an "improvement" on the first; what is undebatable
and much more important is that the later and more poetically lush
version, with its metaphor on the power a beloved's eyes transmits to
the lover, intensifies the audience's view of Berowne as the play's elo-
quent and persuasive spokesperson for Platonic ideals of love.[69]

Yet no editorial or critical attention has been paid to how another
substantive variant in the duplicated passages entirely reshapes the character of Berowne. At the beginning of the first version of the duplicated
passage, Berowne reminds the King and the two courtiers:

> And where that you haue vowd to studie (Lordes)
> In that each of you haue forsworne his Booke,

but in the second version, Berowne reminds himself and his companions:

> O we haue made a Vow to studie, Lordes,
> And in that Vow we haue forsworne our Bookes.

This variant from "you" in the first version, which implies that Berowne
did not agree to these contradictory vows, to "we" in the second version,
which implies that Berowne had joined the others, becomes essential in
the context of establishing Berowne's character. In the opening scene of
the Quarto, Berowne listens first to the King proclaim that his three
courtiers would obey his edict and his statutes, and secondly to Longaville
and Dumaine swear obedience, but he strongly protests that "not to see
Ladyes, study, fast, not sleepe" were "barraine taskes, too hard to keepe."
After much complaint, Berowne reluctantly agrees to follow the edict
but remains throughout the play more than willing to break these
troublesome oaths. Had Shakespeare forgotten when he wrote the first
version of the duplication that he had already made Berowne swear to

study in 1.1, and then corrected his error by including him with the others in the second version of the duplication? Or had Shakespeare intended a different role for the original Berowne, the man who boasts to his King in 4.3 that he has not in the end obeyed the royal edict?

Another duplication-expansion which similarly and strikingly alters the character of Berowne occurs in his exchange in 5.2 with Rosaline. After the Princess receives the news of her father's death, which requires her to leave the court of Navarre, she asks the King to spend one year in "austere insociable life." In brief speeches, Rosaline, Katherine, and Maria similarly set tasks for Berowne, Dumaine, and Longaville for the coming year. Although Berowne has just asked Rosaline "And what to me my Loue? and what to me?" and has already been told (sigs. K1-K1ᵛ; TLN 2777–2830):

> You must be purged to, your sinnes are rackt.
> You are attaint with faultes and periurie:
> Therefore if you my fauour meane to get,
> A tweluemonth shall you spende and neuer rest,
> But seeke the weery beddes of people sicke,

he asks Rosaline again, after Longaville has received his charge from Maria, "Impose some seruice on me for thy Loue." Rosaline responds:

> Oft haue I heard of you my Lord *Berowne*,
> Before I saw you: and the worldes large tongue
> Proclaymes you for a man repleat with mockes,
> Full of comparisons and wounding floutes:
> Which you on all estetes will execute,
> That lie within the mercie of your wit
> To weede this wormewood from your fructfull braine,
> And therewithall to winne me, yf you please,
> Without the which I am not to be won:
> You shall this tweluemonth terme from day to day,
> Visite the speachlesse sicke, and still conuerse,
> With groning wretches: and your taske shall be,
> With all the fierce endeuour of your wit,
> To enforce the pained impotent to smile.

Berowne answers her by scoffing at the power of mirth to move a soul in agony, but Rosaline, in a passage of twelve lines, rebukes him for his idle jesting and scorning and asks for his "reformation."

The second version of this passage, probably canceling the first (although both were printed by the compositor, as in 4.3), serves several crucial dramatic functions. In the first version, Shakespeare presents Berowne and Rosaline as the second of four couples who set and receive tasks, but in the second version, he isolates them as the last of the four couples, giving them dramatic centrality as the hero and heroine who conclude the play. In the first version, Berowne, like the other men, does not question the sentence he has been given by his beloved; however, in the second, he jests with Rosaline's words and her command to serve the sick, allowing her to turn his very words upon him. Most important, in the second version Berowne's character is better drawn as a "man repleat with mockes," who speaks wittily but does not always understand the power of his witty words, but who, with Rosaline's help, will soon be reformed. Thus, in the second versions of the duplications in 4.3 and 5.2 Shakespeare rethought and redrew his concept of Berowne's character. Rather than being fairly indistinguishable from Longaville and Dumaine, and his King for that matter, Berowne takes center stage as the man reluctant to forswear the study of women who indeed learns the greatest lesson about himself in the company of a woman whom he studies and who studies him. In revising Berowne, Shakespeare revised his hero, his play, and his own artistic role, function, and method. In other words, Shakespeare revised himself.

Other loose ends in the play, particularly in the long second scene of Act 5, suggest that Shakespeare was reworking several aspects of *Love's Labor's Lost* during its original composition. The two unnamed lords who accompany Boyet throughout most of the play drop out after Act 4 and do not return. Costard's brief mention at the end of 4.1 (sig. D4) of Armado (accompanied by his page) bearing the fan of a lady and kissing his own hand may indicate that Armado's escapades were seen on stage in an earlier draft or simply that Shakespeare had intended to dramatize them but changed his mind. He may also have intended the Princess to have received a document, rather than the news of her father's death, from the messenger to substantiate her claim that her father's debt to the King of Navarre was repaid, as suggested by her offer of thanks to the King for "my great sute, so easely obtainde" (sig. I3$^v$).[70] And the casting of the Nine Worthies for the pageant in 5.2 (sigs. H4$^v$-I3) before the King and his court does not correspond to that made by Holofernes in 5.1 (sig. G1).

The text may preserve alternative endings which were sorted out in foul papers or written at different periods; the play may have originally ended with Berowne's lament that "Iacke hath not Gill" and that a twelve-month wait is "too long for a Play" (sig. K1ᵛ), so that the reentrance of Armado and the other comic characters who present the songs of Winter and Spring were later additions to please an audience now accustomed to music in the theatre. The comic characters are at the center of other textual problems: they appear in speech prefixes throughout the play in either their character names or in general terms, so that, for example, Costard sometimes appears as "Clown" and Holofernes as "Pedant." Shakespeare may not have given them names and their comic fortes, which they could display in the Nine Worthies pageant, until late into the play's composition.[71]

These duplications, inconsistencies, and changes of plan and intention in character, plot, and speech prefixes may simply be signs that the Quarto text was printed from foul papers or from a previous quarto set from them.[72] It is impossible to determine whether alterations were made within the foul papers during the original composition, added immediately afterward, or added at some later time as second-thought revisions to the original foul papers or on inserted sheets of paper. Yet the collation of the Quarto text and the Folio text printed from it offers more extraordinary evidence of Shakespeare's early rather than later reworking of the play.

A much-studied textual crux is the "Rosaline-Katherine tangle," the variant speech prefixes for the character engaged in word play with Berowne in 1.2. Early in the scene in the Quarto text, the newly arrived Princess listens as each of her ladies favorably describes a lord in Ferdinand's court: "1. *Lady*" describes Longaville, whom she has met at a wedding; "2. *Lady*" mentions that she saw Dumaine at the home of Duke Alansoes (Alencon); and "3. *Lady*" adds that she saw Berowne in Dumaine's company at Alencon's. The Princess replies, "Are they all in loue? / That euery one her owne hath garnished" (sig. C1). After the King enters with these courtiers and greets the Princess, Berowne asks a masked Katherine (so designated in the speech prefix rather than as a numbered "*Lady*"), "Did not I dance with you in *Brabant* once?" prompting this exchange (sig. C1ᵛ-C2ᵛ):

> *Kather.*  Did not I dance with you in *Brabant* once?
> *Ber.*  I know you did.
> *Kath.*  How needles was it then to aske the question?
> *Ber.*  You must not be so quicke.

| | |
|---|---|
| *Kath.* | Tis long of you that spur me with such questions. |
| *Ber.* | Your wit's too hot, it speedes too fast, twill tire. |
| *Kath.* | Not till it leaue the rider in the mire. |
| *Ber.* | What time a day? |
| *Kath.* | The houre that fooles should aske. |
| *Ber.* | Now faire befall your maske. |
| *Kath.* | Faire fall the face it couers. |
| *Ber.* | And send you manie louers. |
| *Kath.* | Amen, so you be none. |
| *Ber.* | Nay then will I be gon. |

After a long exchange among the King, the Princess, and Boyet on the subject of the Princess's suit, the King exits, apparently taking the silent Longaville and Dumaine with him. Berowne immediately speaks to the lady designated "*Ros.*" in the speech heading, telling her "Ladie, I will commend you to my none hart (sig. C2$^v$)." The two characters continue the passage with puns on Berowne's groaning heart, concluding:

| | |
|---|---|
| *Ber.* | Now God saue thy life! |
| *Ros.* | And yours, from long liuing! |
| *Ber.* | I cannot stay thankes-giuing. |

The duel of wits over, Berowne exits the stage. Dumaine points to a lady and Boyet identifies her as Rosaline, heir of "Alanson," while Longaville points to another lady and is told she is the heir of Faulconbridge. Berowne returns to ask Boyet the identity of the woman "in the capp" and receives the answer, "Katherin." As the ladies were designated as "1," "2," and "3" when they earlier described the lords with whom they wanted to be paired, the name of the lady to be matched with Berowne does not become clear until this point in the play. Shakespeare may have even intended to pair Dumaine with Rosaline and Berowne with Katherine but later changed his mind.

John Kerrigan hypothesizes that after Shakespeare realized during composition that he had paired Rosaline rather than Katherine to Berowne in the rest of the play he canceled the Berowne-Katherine passage by interleaving a separate sheet with the Berowne-Rosaline replacement passage; however, the printer printed both passages, the first where it stood in foul papers and the second where it was interleaved, with Shakespeare forgetting to change Katherine's name to Rosaline in Boyet's identification of the lady in the cap.[73] Yet, it does not seem unusual that Berowne, chafing at his vow to avoid women, would speak to Katherine, particularly since he apparently met her in the company of Rosaline at the home of the Duke of Alencon, and then approach Rosaline. If both of Berowne's passages, with Katherine and with Rosaline, stand in this scene, Berowne appears, as he did in the earlier versions of the two duplicated passages, as a flirtatious and faithless dissenter from the monkish court of Navarre.[74]

In fact, the theory that Shakespeare first intended both passages to stand as characterizing his early concept of Berowne and later eliminated the duplication in reperceiving his main character and the scene is further demonstrated when the Quarto is compared to the Folio text. In the Folio, Rosaline and, as a consequence, Berowne are clearly set apart from the two other ladies and the two other courtiers. Rather than being called "3. *Lady*" in the speech prefix in 1.2, which would be consistent with the other speech prefixes of "1. *Lady*" and "2. *Lady*" who describe Longaville and Dumaine, the third lady is named "*Rossa.*" in the speech prefix, and it is she who describes Berowne. Thus it is not surprising that the Quarto's exchange between Berowne and Katherine is given to Berowne and Rosaline in the Folio (TLN 609–623), so that it is this pair who once danced together at Brabant. Although the speech prefixes for Katherine have been changed to Rosaline, there are no other revisions in the passage or in the following lines, except in the speech prefix for the character who offers his "owne heart" to Rosaline: in the Folio (TLN 677–690), Boyet, the Princess's courtier, jests about his groaning heart; in the Quarto, these lines are given to Berowne. The Quarto/Folio variants suggest that in the Folio version Shakespeare wanted to establish Berowne and Rosaline as the play's main couple, as he did in the revised duplicated passages in the Quarto, and thus clearly set Rosaline apart from the other ladies of the court by making her Berowne's partner and only equal. Therefore, the couple spars verbally early and only once with each other, requiring Rosaline's second sparring partner, who is decidedly inferior to her first, to change to Boyet.[75]

Rather than reflecting later alterations, these Folio speech prefix changes were probably made at the same time as the second versions of the duplicated passages, and like these were not noticed by the printer.[76] The Folio text does not correct but lets stand the versions of the duplicated passages, and introduces only a few substantive differences other than in these speech prefixes, most notably in the Nine Worthies pageant. As most of the Folio speech prefix variants are directly related to changes to Berowne's character within the Quarto text itself, the Folio

does not present new alterations but prints the original revisions, including the Katherine-Rosaline speech prefix changes, as Shakespeare
made them within foul or fair papers.[77] What is evident is that the
Katherine-Rosaline "tangle" must be seen in the context of the two other
tangled duplications in 4.3 and 5.2; all three derive from Shakespeare's
reconception of the character of Berowne. While Kerrigan sees the
character and plot inconsistencies in the Quarto as Shakespeare "at work"
writing and revising the play,[78] particular, specific, and deliberately
crafted revisions in the texts of *Love's Labor's Lost* show Shakespeare
reshaping and redefining the role of Berowne, whom he decided to
establish as the play's central spokesperson for love, from faithless to
faithful, a man wittily replete with mocks who reforms and revises
himself through the power of his beloved's eyes and through the power
of his revising poet, Shakespeare.

The remarkably similar transmissions of the texts of *Romeo and Juliet*
and *Love's Labor's Lost* have important implications for the transmissions
of the texts of other Shakespearian plays. Shakespeare often revised
during the course of composition so that his foul papers were full of
loose ends, false starts, inconsistencies, deletions, and additions. The two
plays examined here suggest that when he revised after some period of
time had elapsed, he made his alterations if not in the promptbook then
in the foul papers, either interlinearly, in the margins, or on inserted
sheets. In some cases he made them as he wrote out a fair copy, and the
prompt-copy could derive from this intermediate transcript. He did not
appear to cancel noticeably the rejected words, lines, and passages in his
papers. If revisions were added to the prompt-copy, sometimes they were
written out on separate sheets which were interleaved and sometimes a
new prompt-copy was transcribed.

This discussion of revision has established that artistic demands as well
as external forces and exigencies provoked changes to an existing Shakespearian play, but I also argue that such changes were made by the author
rather than by other dramatists, bookkeepers, actors, or editors. The type
of foul paper duplications which appear in *Romeo and Juliet* and *Love's
Labor's Lost* must be authorial not only because they derive from foul-
paper copy but because they are identical in content, style, and linguistic
preference to earlier versions. Thus, later revisions also identical in sense,
style, and linguistic preference which appear within the same text or
between two or more texts of a play and were made in the course of
updating or transcribing foul papers are also authorial.

Other, nonauthorial changes, such as those resulting from the printing process, also made their way into the texts, but the "corruption" of nonauthorial forces can no longer be regarded as the chief reviser of Shakespeare's plays. As dramatist and actor-sharer in the Chamberlain's/King's Men, Shakespeare exerted an artistic and financial control over his text and the presentation of it that would not allow changes made without his consent, participation, or collaboration. Therefore, even when required to alter a play because of external censorship, Shakespeare could meet his own demands and rethink his play by revising for theatrical and artistic coherence and unity.

# ❧ 4 ❧

# Revising Shakespeare
# Before and After 1596

In his duplications, additions, and speech-prefix changes in *Romeo and Juliet* and *Love's Labor's Lost,* Shakespeare reveals his composition and revision practices in two plays written early in his career. However, textual critics have recently argued that "as a class, the heavily revised plays all date from after *1 Henry IV* (1596), when Shakespeare was securely established as the leading dramatist of the capital's leading company," and that such extensive revision was a "luxury."[1] I will examine the revisions in two other plays written before 1596, *Titus Andronicus* and *A Midsummer Night's Dream,* as well as three plays written after 1596, *Julius Caesar, The Merry Wives of Windsor,* and *Macbeth,* in order to argue that Shakespeare's methods and patterns of revision cannot be canonized and constituted into a pre- and post-1596 category. Revision in Shakespeare's plays was neither luxurious nor measured, although it is measurable, not in terms of its meaning but of its form; early *and* late in his career, Shakespeare, by revising even one element (such as a single character or theme) reconstructed every other interlocking element in the play. That Shakespeare was constantly thinking ahead to his later plays and simultaneously rethinking his earlier plays becomes evident in my conclusions about *1 Henry VI, 2 Henry VI, 3 Henry VI, Richard III, Richard II, 1 Henry IV, 2 Henry IV,* and *Henry V,* whose original compositions and later revisions span most of the years in which Shakespeare was writing. Throughout his career, Shakespeare's revisions, extensive in meaning and in form and extending to every aspect of the text, continued to expand and reconstitute the very canon of his plays and his role as the canonical dramatist.

## *Titus Andronicus*

The 1594 Quarto 1 and 1600 Quarto 2 texts of *Titus Andronicus* present clear evidence both of the nonauthorial revision recognized by so many editors and critics as the chief revising agent in the plays and of the authorial revision, recognized by some editors and critics but not acknowleged as being extensive in method, that appears in *Romeo and Juliet* and *Love's Labor's Lost*. The nonauthorial revision does indeed derive from the printing process: Quarto 2 was set from a copy of Quarto 1 with damaged leaves in the I and K gatherings; when confronted with unreadable copy, the compositor made his own conjectural emendations in these sheets and added a four-line conclusion to the text. All of his alterations, made in a process evidently unsupervised by Shakespeare, were reprinted in the Quarto 3 and Folio editions.[2]

Yet the recognition of authorial revision in *Titus Andronicus* has also depended on critical arguments for an intervening external cause rather than an inherent authorial one. Because the Quarto 1 and 2 title pages advertise that the play had been performed by at least three companies, Derby's (Lord Strange's), Sussex's, and Pembroke's Men by 1594 and by the Lord Chamberlain's Men by 1600, many have argued that Shakespeare reworked *Titus Andronicus* to suit the casting of the different companies. Although John Dover Wilson follows eighteenth-century editors and the later disintegrator, J. M. Robertson, in claiming that the play was not originally written by Shakespeare (largely because portions of the play seemed inferior or inconsistent),[3] most modern scholars believe the play to have been entirely written by Shakespeare by 1590 and revised for performance in 1594,[4] at which time it was entered in Henslowe's *Diary* as "ne" for Sussex's Men.

Evidence exists within the Quarto 1 text of authorial second-thought revisions and changes of intention that affected the structural and thematic content of the entire play. In his expository speech at the beginning of Act 1 (sig. A3$^v$) on the election of Titus, Bassianus remarks:

> Fiue times he hath returnd
> Bleeding to Rome, bearing his valiant sonnes,
> In Coffins from the field, and at this day,
> To the Monument of that *Andronicy*
> Done sacrifice of expiation,
> And slaine the Noblest prisoner of the Gothes.

> And now at last laden with honours spoiles,
> Returnes the good *Andronicus* to Rome.

After the entrance of Titus and his sons and the captive Tamora, the Queen of the Goths, and her sons Chiron and Demetrius, Titus's son Lucius demands that "the prowdest prisoner of the *Gothes*" be turned over to the family so that they may "hew his limbs and on a pile / *Ad manus fratrum,* sacrifice his flesh" (sig. A4ᵛ), to revenge their brothers' deaths. Tamora pleads for the life of her eldest son, but Titus allows his sons, as the stage direction states, to exit with "Alarbus." The sons soon return, boasting of having lopped off Alarbus's limbs and burned his entrails. Shakespeare apparently had forgotten that Bassianus had already described the revenge murder of Alarbus when he portrayed the episode on stage, or perhaps he reconsidered the effect of describing Titus's murder of Alarbus and added the action of the murder, now assigning it to Lucius and his brothers.

More important than the revision here is Shakespeare's recognition of its impact. He, or possibly a theatrical or publishing-house annotator, was certainly aware of the inconsistency in these Alarbus episodes, as the three and a half contradictory lines in Bassianus's speech do not appear in the later Quartos or Folio. However, as in the case of the duplications in Quarto 2 of *Romeo and Juliet* and Quarto 1 of *Love's Labor's Lost,* other inconsistencies in the Quarto 1 text of *Titus Andronicus* were similarly not corrected; these include apparently inserted passages in 1.1 on the death and burial of Mutius, Titus's son, which conclude with Marcus's abrupt and awkward transition to the subject of Tamora: "My Lord to step out of these dririe dumps" (sigs. B3ᵛ, B4ᵛ-C1). Two duplications appear in Titus's dialogue in 4.3 and 5.2 (sigs. H2, I3ᵛ), probably as a result of marginal additions: in the first, Titus twice instructs the Clown how to deliver his message to the Emperor, and in the second, the last two, original, lines in this passage,

| | |
|---|---|
| *Tamora* | These are my ministers and come with me. |
| *Titus* | Are them thy ministers, what are they calld? |
| *Tamora* | Rape and Murder, therefore called so, |

were replaced by Titus's sixteen-line speech addressing Tamora's ministers, Rape (Chiron) and Murder (Demetrius), immediately preceding the passage. These textual changes suggest that Shakespeare added the characters of Alarbus and Mutius and reworked the character of Titus during or shortly after the composition of the play.[5]

Shakespeare may also have reworked the role of Aaron the Moor during this same period;[6] in the Quarto 1, he seems as uncertain about how to proceed with Aaron in Act 1 as he is about Alarbus and Mutius. Aaron enters with Tamora and her sons but is mute in the long single scene of Act 1, and his Machiavellian character only begins to build in Act 2. Shakespeare probably added on an inserted sheet the portion of Aaron's dialogue with the Goth and Lucius in 5.1 (sigs. I2-I2$^v$) which is typeset in Quarto 1 with centered speech prefixes, setting it off from the rest of the scene.[7] Prior to this passage, Aaron fully confesses his role in directing and abetting Chiron and Demetrius in the rape and murders of Titus's children. Aaron continues in the passage with the centered speech prefixes to narrate sensationally all of his crimes and to assert that he feels guilt and shame not for performing them but for failing to perform so many other heinous deeds. He further shocks his audience by describing one crime he has been able to commit frequently: unearthing and mutilating corpses so that they can serve as reminders of grief to the families. Aaron, still unremorseful, concludes "Nothing grieues me hartelie indeed, / But that I cannot doe ten thousand more." Lucius and the other listeners then decide that death by hanging is too sweet for such a devil and bring him down off the ladder which they use as a gallows. Through this masterfully coherent expansion of his character, Aaron revises himself to become yet more horrific, more dangerous, and more central to the play's meaning and form.

Further signs of this added, central sensationalism in the play appear in the striking textual anomaly of the printing of one scene, 3.2 (TLN 1451–1539), in the Folio which does not appear in Quarto 1, 2, or 3. In this scene of eighty-five lines, Titus, Marcus, Lavinia, and Lucius's son eat at a banquet, and Titus, in the madness caused by his grief at the mutilation of himself and his daughter Lavinia, reprimands his brother Marcus for killing a fly. The omission of the scene in the *Titus Andronicus* Quartos, particularly the second and third Quartos of 1600 and 1611, which corrected the Alarbus contradictions, and its appearance in the Folio might imply that the scene was added at a date later than 1611. However, the scene is reminiscent of the "Painter" scene on the madness of Hieronymo after the death of his son, which was added before 1602 to *The Spanish Tragedy* for an audience which enjoyed watching madness deriving from parental grief on stage; thus the similar "fly-killing" scene in *Titus Andronicus* probably dates from the 1590s rather than the 1610s.

Eugene Waith argues that Shakespeare wrote out the scene on one separate leaf when revising the play for Sussex's Men in 1593–94, and the leaf was inserted into the promptbook, never reaching the printer, who set his copy from uncorrected foul papers.[8] Yet Shakespeare most likely wrote out this additional scene in foul or fair papers at the same time he wrote out the other additions to the play, including Aaron's dialogue in 5.1. After Aaron boasts that he has committed myriad horrible crimes, he advises his terrified audience, "I haue done a thousand dreadfull things, / As willingly as one would kill a flie" (sig. I2$^v$). These lines echo in 3.2 (TLN 1505–1532), when Marcus protests, "Alas (my Lord) I haue but kild a flie," and Titus laments for fourteen lines the "poore harmelesse Fly," finally concluding,

> Yet I thinke we are not brought so low
> But that betweene us, we can kill a Fly,
> That comes in likenesse of a Cole-blacke Moore.

This verbal echo brilliantly and circularly connects the later, revised lines and character of Aaron and the later, revised lines and characters of Titus and Marcus, suggesting that Shakespeare added Aaron's sensational speech in 5.1, which was printed in the 1594 Quarto 1, at the same time as or shortly before the sensational "fly-killing" scene of Act 3; the "fly-killing" scene could have been misleaved in the foul papers or overlooked by the printer (as may have occurred in the printing of 2 *Henry IV*). If Shakespeare wrote out a new fair copy of the entire play in 1593 for Sussex's Men, rather than adding one leaf to the old prompt-book, he could have added 3.2 in the process of transcription (as in the case of *Romeo and Juliet*), which would explain why 3.2 does not have the centered speech prefixes of the added Aaron passage written out on an inserted sheet; he could have made the Aaron revisions earlier in an insertion in his foul papers, producing at least two separate, reliable, revised texts of the play: his foul papers and his fair copy. These revisions proceed not from any identifiable external pressure exerted on Shakespeare, but from his own, certain involvement in the dramatic process.

Other Quarto/Folio variants, particularly in the stage directions, appear to represent both printing-house impositions and changes in staging after the play had been performed,[9] perhaps to suit the later performances by the King's Men advertised on the 1611 Quarto 3 title page. The Folio printers' oversight in retaining the non-Shakespearian four-line conclusion added in Quarto 2 signals that they used this Quarto to typeset the play, perhaps because the promptbook was not available. Shakespeare evidently made most of his revisions, including the duplications printed in Quarto 1, corrections printed in Quartos 2 and 3, and additions printed in Folio, which revise and re-present the characters of Titus, Marcus, Aaron, Alarbus, and Mutius, as well as the interlocking elements of the play in which these characters play central roles, sometime between the play's composition around 1590 and its first printing in 1594.

## A Midsummer Night's Dream

The 1600 Quarto 1 of *A Midsummer Night's Dream* expertly shows traces of expert Shakespearian revision within foul papers during composition as well as pre- and post-promptbook alterations which stunningly and continually alter the play's forms and meanings. The title page notes that *A Midsummer Night's Dream* had been "sundry times *publickely acted*." If the play was also performed privately (as some scholars have argued[10]) the Quarto text holds traces of revision for change in venue and audience. For example, Puck's concern in the epilogue to offer the audience "amends" four times in a short speech of sixteen lines seems addressed to a regular public theatre audience rather than an occasional private one which would not be able to return and judge if the company had indeed mended their theatrical portrayals in this play[11] or in some earlier, displeasing play.

More significant and more extensive revision than the addition of an epilogue appears in Act 5, beginning with Theseus's speech which opens the first scene (sigs. G2$^v$-G3). After Hippolyta remarks of the two couples who have been found sleeping in the woods, "Tis strange, my *Theseus*, that these louers speake of," Theseus responds:

> More straunge then true. I neuer may beleeue
> These antique fables, nor these Fairy toyes.
> Louers, and mad men haue such seething braines,
> Such shaping phantasies, that apprehend more,
> Then coole reason euer comprehends.

In this blank verse speech, Theseus simply and surely connects the seething brains and shaping fantasies of louers and madmen. As he continues, however, he adds the poet to his list of those who possess an imagination which transforms and revises cool reason. The verse in this part of the speech is badly mislined (I have inserted slashes in the places where lines should end):

> / The lunatick,
> The louer, and the Poet / are of imagination all compact /
> One sees more diuels, then vast hell can holde:
> That is the mad man. The louer, all as frantick,
> Sees *Helens* beauty in a brow of *Aegypt*.
> The Poets eye, in a fine frenzy, rolling, / doth glance
> From heauen to earth, from earth to heauen. / And as
> Imagination bodies forth / the formes of things
> Vnknowne: the poets penne / turnes them to shapes,
> And giues to ayery nothing, / a locall habitation,
> And a name. / Such trickes hath strong imagination,
> That if it would but apprehend some joy,
> It comprehends some bringer of that joy.
> Or in the night, imagining some feare,
> How easie is a bush suppos'd a Beare?

All of the hypermetric lines in this speech concern the poet; the one and a half lines on the poet's kinship to the lunatic and the lover, "The lunatick . . . all compact," and the six lines on the poet's eye and pen, "The Poets eye . . . And a name," are apparently later marginal insertions, so that Shakespeare originally wrote:

> Louers, and mad men haue such seething braines,
> Such shaping phantasies, that apprehend
> More then coole reason euer comprehends.
> One sees more diuels, then vast hell can holde:
> That is the mad man. The louer, all as frantick,
> Sees *Helens* beauty in a brow of *Aegypt*.
> Such trickes hath strong imagination. . .

Shakespeare evidently wrote out the additions in the margins of his manuscript, and the compositor reproduced them in print exactly in the places he saw them in the foul papers, or a transcript of it, which he used for copy. The marginal additions may have been made sometime afterward to suit a revival of the play, as John Dover Wilson argues.[12]

However, these revisions appear to have been made during the composition of the play, rather than several years later.[13] Theseus returns to the theme of the power of the poet to transform through imagination later in the scene when Hippolyta complains that the mechanicals' play is "the silliest stuffe, that euer I heard" (sig. H1ᵛ). Theseus responds, "The best, in this kinde, are but shadowes: and the worst are no worse, if imagination amend them." Hippolyta's retort, "It must be your imagination, then; & not theirs," provokes a response from Theseus which brings the power of the poet to all who witness his work: "If we imagine no worse of them, then they of themselves, they may passe for excellent men." There is no textual evidence to support a claim that this exchange between Theseus and Hippolyta, which continues the themes set up in the later version of Theseus's speech on the lunatic/lover/poet, was added at a later date. If the exchange appears as it was originally written, the marginal additions to Theseus's early speech may have been completed before this later part of Act 5 was originally composed, but it is equally possible that Shakespeare expanded this theme of the later passage by making additions in the earlier passage.[14] Shakespeare revised Theseus's first speech in Act 5 to include the poet with those who, like lovers and lunatics, must use imagination to make sense of their world, providing an ironic comment on his own profession for an audience watching actors who will soon act as audience to another group of actors. Yet he also multiplied rather than reduced or replaced his play's meaning and form and his own function as the poet in making such revisions;[15] he consciously and self-consciously multiplied the power of the revising poet.

Shakespeare's second-thought, marginal, self-revising additions do not end in this one speech at the beginning of 5.1, for after Hippolyta briefly comments again on the strangeness of the lovers' story, Theseus greets the entering lovers and calls for entertainment in another hypermetric passage (sig. G3):

> *The.* Here come the louers, full of ioy and mirth.
> Ioy, gentle friends, ioy and fresh daies
> Of loue / accompany your hearts.
> *Lys.* More then to vs, / waite in your royall walkes,
> your boorde, your bedde.
> *The.* Come now; what maskes, what daunces shall wee haue,
> To weare away this long age of three hours, / betweene
> Or after supper, & bed-time? / Where is our vsuall manager
> Of mirth? / What Reuels are in hand? Is there no play,
> To ease the anguish of a torturing hower? / Call *Philostrate*

The passage probably originally appeared as follows:

> *The.* Here come the louers, full of ioy and mirth.
> Come now: what maskes, what daunces shall wee haue,
> To ease the anguish of a torturing hower?

Sometime later Shakespeare added the other extensive lines on the power
that imagination has to while away the hours. A few portions of the
succeeding dialogue, including Philostrate's account of the mechanicals'
rehearsal and ending with Theseus's choice of *Pyramus and Thisby* as the
marriage entertainment, are also badly mislined, evidently because
Shakespeare had painstakingly, if not luxuriously, enlarged this entire
passage.

   The Folio text of *A Midsummer Night's Dream* contains some minor
changes in stage directions which may have been made to suit performances at Blackfriars, and one striking change in 5.1: the role of Philostrate, courtier to Theseus, is taken in the Quarto by Egeus, on stage to
celebrate the wedding of his daughter Hermia. (Philostrate's name is
retained in the Folio in only one of the speech prefixes assigned to him
in the Quarto, perhaps because that particular speech-prefix was not
changed as all the others were to *Ege*.) Shakespeare may have made the
speech-prefix change for this courtier either to minimize or eliminate the
focus on Philostrate and place it instead on Egeus, or to omit one role
in the play, or for both reasons.[16] Other textual alterations demonstrate
that Shakespeare reworked the opening of Act 5 during the original
composition of the play. Although the Folio prints some of the lines of
Theseus's lover/lunatic/poet speech and his brief exchange with Lysander
in correctly lined verse, it adds other textual discrepancies arising from
probable marginal additions to Theseus's next major speech about the
types of entertainment available.[17] The Quarto version appears below,
with Folio changes in brackets (sigs. G3-G3ᵛ; TLN 1841–1857):

| | |
|---|---|
| *The.*[*Lis.*] | The battell with the *centaures* to be sung, |
| | By an *Athenian* Eunuche, to the Harpe? |
| [*The.*] | Weele none of that. That haue I tolde my loue |
| | In glory of my kinsman *Hercules*. |
| [*Lis.*] | The ryot of the tipsie *Bachanals*, |
| | Tearing the *Thracian* singer, in their rage? |
| [*The.*] | That is an olde deuise: and it was plaid, |
| | When I from *Thebes* came last a conqueror. |
| [*Lis.*] | The thrise three Muses, mourning for the death |
| | Of learning, late deceast, in beggery? |
| [*The.*] | That is some *Satire* keene and criticall, |
| | Not sorting with a nuptiall ceremony. |
| [*Lis.*] | A tedious briefe Scene of young *Pyramus* |
| | And his loue *Thisby;* very tragicall mirth? |
| [*The.*] | Merry, and tragicall? Tedious and briefe? |

The last three lines, "That is hot Ise, / And wondrous stange snow. How shall we find the concord / Of this discord?" are assigned to Theseus in both the Quarto and Folio but are printed as prose in the Folio. It is possible that these Folio changes in speech headings for Lysander in Theseus's speech reflect revisions in the play for some post-Quarto text performance.

However, the division of Theseus's long speech in the Folio into several two-line exchanges in which Lysander describes each entertainment and Theseus comments on it resembles, and thus was probably made at the same time as, the marginal additions in the Quarto, particularly the passage in which Lysander remarks on what waits on Theseus's royal walks, board, and bed. Shakespeare appointed Lysander as the spokesman for the four lovers in the second marginal addition in the Quarto, and he apparently repeated this function for Lysander in this later passage as printed in the Folio. If all three sets of additions were made at the same time, it is conceivable that the Quarto 1 compositor misread the marginal speech prefixes for Lysander in the third addition in the same way that he misread the other marginal insertions, especially if, as Robert Turner claims, he was setting type from a heavily revised manuscript.[18] The Folio would then have been printed from a later transcript which had corrected the placement of all three sets of additions. Other technical, theatrically based changes, such as the addition of stage directions to suit Blackfriars or another theatre, were apparently made some years after the play's original composition. Yet, the revisions in the last act of *A Midsummer Night's Dream*, which serve to reestablish and revise the character of Theseus, who had been absent from the stage for three acts, and to assert his centrality as the poet who makes sense of all that has occurred in the previous four acts by endowing his world with imagination, proceed from the play's chief revising poet, Shakespeare himself.

## *Julius Caesar*

The "unusually clean" condition of the Folio text of *Julius Caesar*, named by W. W. Greg as the "best-printed play in the collection," suggests that the text of this play, written a few years after *A Midsummer Night's Dream* and probably after 1596, was set from a carefully prepared and edited original or later prompt-copy.[19] Close attention to the literary rather than the theatrical state of the text appears in one probable revision: Ben

Jonson's reproach to Shakespeare for his original ungrammatical line in 3.1, "Caesar did never wrong, but with just cause,"[20] evidently encouraged Shakespeare or an annotator to revise the line; it appears in the Folio text as "*Caesar* doth no wrong, nor without cause." Although "clean" as a literary text, as a theatrical text, the Folio is decidedly muddy, as it contains numerous duplications, loose ends, and speech-prefix inconsistencies deriving from authorial revision, which present serious problems in theatrical staging.

A much-studied duplication, which has prompted discussion of authorial revision by John Dover Wilson and T. S. Dorsch among others,[21] appears in 4.3 (TLN 2134–2149, 2183–2192) in Brutus's reaction to hearing the news of Portia's death. After Brutus and Cassius have bitterly quarreled over problems with their army, Brutus tells Cassius the real cause of his anger and his grief:

> *Bru.*                                 *Portia* is dead.
> *Cas.*  Ha? *Portia?*
> *Bru.*  She is dead.
> *Cas.*  How scap'd I killing, when I crost you so?
>         O insupportable, and touching losse!
>         Vpon what sicknesse?
> *Bru.*  Impatient of my absence,,
>         And greefe, that yong *Octauius* with *Mark Antony*
>         Haue made themselues so strong: For with her death
>         That tydings came. With this she fell distract,,
>         And (her Attendants absent) swallow'd fire.
> *Cas.*  And dy'd so?
> *Bru.*  Euen so.
> *Cas.*  O ye immortall Gods!
> *Bru.*  Speak no more of her.

After Messala has entered with Titinius a few lines later, Cassius laments, "*Portia,* art thou gone?" and Brutus replies, "No more I pray you," and begins discussing the letters he has lately received about Octavius and Mark Antony's march on Philippi, which brought the "tydings" of Portia's suicide. However, thirty lines after Brutus first mentions Portia's death and a few lines after he discusses his newly received letters, Brutus tells Messala, who has also received letters about the advance of Octavius and Mark Antony on Philippi, that he has had no letters from or about Portia. Brutus presses Messala for news of her:

| | |
|---|---|
| *Messa.* | Had you your Letters from your wife, my Lord? |
| *Bru.* | No *Messala.* |
| *Messa.* | Nor nothing in your Letters writ of her? |
| *Bru.* | Nothing *Messala.* |
| *Messa.* | That me thinkes is strange. |
| *Bru.* | Why aske you? |
| | Heare you ought of her, in yours? |
| *Messa.* | No my Lord. |
| *Bru.* | Now as you are a Roman tell me true. |
| *Messa.* | Then like a Roman, beare the truth I tell, |
| | For certaine she is dead, and by strange manner. |
| *Bru.* | Why farewell *Portia:* We must die *Messala:* |
| | With meditating that she must dye once, |
| | I haue the patience to endure it now. |
| *Messa.* | Euen so great men, great losses shold indure. |
| *Cassi.* | I haue as much of this in Art as you, |
| | But yet my Nature could not beare it so. |
| *Bru.* | Well, to our worke aliue. |

It is clear that there are two different passages here, the first presenting a Brutus who has for some time subsumed the knowledge and pain of his wife's death in his preparations for battle but who finally breaks down, and the second presenting a man who reacts with little display of grief upon receiving the news of his wife's death as the audience watches. Critics agree that the Brutus-Cassius version offers a more griefstricken Brutus, and the Brutus-Messala version a stoic one, and some have argued for this reason that both versions should be retained. Yet, these critics have not noticed how the role of Cassius has also been subtly altered between the passages. In the second version, after Brutus changes the subject to the work "aliue," Cassius does not publicly display his grief at Portia's death; in the first version, Brutus must twice ask the grieving and shaken Cassius to "speak no more of her."

What appears to be the first version of this duplication is actually Shakespeare's later addition to replace or amplify the original Brutus-Messala version in an attempt to give more dramatic depth to the scene and to the characters of Brutus and Cassius. The speech prefix for Cassius appears in the first version of the duplication as *Cas.*, yet it appears as *Cassi.* throughout the rest of the play, and on the strength of this evidence, Brents Stirling argues that Shakespeare added the Brutus-Cassius passage on Portia's death to the theatrical fair copy of the play, rather than to the foul papers during composition, intending the two contradictory passages to stand in the text.

However, the way in which Brutus twice lies to Messala and then baits him into revealing the tragic news of Portia's death, of which Brutus is already aware, is not consistent with Brutus's character in its original or its revised form and presents a serious problem in the theatrical portrayal of his role. Similarly, the contradictory contents of the letters sent to Brutus present another theatrical contradiction. In the Brutus-Messala version of the duplication, the letters are centered on the military struggle, as they warn that Octavius and Mark Antony come down upon the conspirators "with a mighty power, / Bending their Expedition toward Philippi"; these letters also add news of the execution of Cicero and the other senators, although the exact number of senators killed differs in Brutus's and Messala's letters, and only Messala's letters report the death of Portia. In the second version, the Brutus-Cassius passage, the letters reveal to Brutus a personal tragedy in vaguely acknowledging the public concerns, for the focus is on Portia, who fell distracted and swallowed fire because of her grief that Octavius and Mark Antony "haue made themselues so strong." Shakespeare was clearly reworking the first passage in the duplication, as he seemed uncertain about what exactly the letters of Brutus and Messala would report, and he continued to rework the first passage in the second passage, shifting the focus as well as the content of the letters.

As in *Romeo and Juliet, Love's Labor's Lost,* and *Titus Andronicus,* Shakespeare failed to cancel noticeably the original version, the Messala-Brutus passage, of the duplication, or if he did intend both to stand, he did not noticeably resolve the problem with the letters. The existence of such an unresolved duplication in the "clean" prompt-copy used to print the Folio text presents other problems of theatrical staging. If Shakespeare made the addition in foul papers, he could have written out the new passage on an inserted sheet if not in the papers themselves; he could also have made the addition to the existing prompt-copy, either his or a scribe's fair copy. The coexistence of such duplicate and contradictory layers of revision is not unusual in foul papers but is unusual in a prompt-copy that shows signs of "careful" preparation. The Folio text of this scene suggests that the transcript used to set the Folio was not the original or final theatrical prompt-copy, but either an intermediate transcript written by Shakespeare or a late transcript designed specifically for a literary audience and possibly assembled from a variety of sources, including authorial foul and fair papers.

Other significant problems in staging resulting from several layers of authorial reworking, evidenced by speech-prefix inconsistencies and changes in character groupings, appear in other scenes, particularly 1.3, 2.1, 2.2, and 3.1, in addition to 4.3, affecting the portrayals of Cassius, Cinna, Metellus, Ligarius, Pindarus, and Titinius, as well as Brutus. Shakespeare apparently intended in the first scene of Act 2, which does not appear as set up in the narrative in 1.3, to present a meeting only of Cassius, Casca, and Brutus but altered it into an abrupt and massed meeting of all the conspirators. Shakespeare may have either wanted to rework the structure of the scene or needed to revise to allow an actor to double the roles of Cassius with Ligarius, whom he had added in revision.[22]

Other changes in structure, plot, and character between 1.3 and 4.3 in *Julius Caesar* clearly suggest that Shakespeare continually reworked the play in the process of writing it, and afterward, in a second layer of revision, reworked other passages that needed to be updated in order to fit them into his first layer of revision.[23] Yet the editorial and critical consensus that *Julius Caesar* demonstrates with certainty that "Shakespeare, having 'completed' a play, could rework parts of it not merely for stage-practical reasons but for artistic and aesthetic ones"[24] is ironically founded upon a "clean" literary Folio text that is at some remove from the final theatrical text. Fredson Bowers argues that the recognition by critics of the stages at which authorial revision was made in *Julius Caesar* led to a

> reassessment of the nature of the Folio printer's copy. Greg's generally accepted assumption that it was Shakespeare's own holograph had to make way for the more probable hypothesis—given the characteristics of the text as well as the theatrically motivated revision—that Jaggard's copy was a scribal transcript used for the early stages of rehearsal, or at least for the early planning of the production, before a promptbook had been written up. An intermediate transcript, in short, containing what might have been Shakespeare's own holograph revisions in three and just possibly in four scenes.[25]

Evidence in the texts of *Romeo and Juliet, Love's Labor's Lost,* and *A Midsummer Night's Dream* supports Bowers's argument that *Julius Caesar* and other plays were revised by the author at some point after the play had been fully composed and transcribed; however, the evidence in these same plays also suggests that some Folio plays, including *Julius Caesar,* were printed from intermediate *authorial* rather than scribal transcripts.[26] Thus, the Folio text of *Julius Caesar,* which presents a number of unresolved problems in theatrical staging, could have been printed, possibly at one remove, from the author's intermediate draft. This draft was still undergoing revision and at some later stage underwent the literary revision, but not the theatrical revision, which produced such an editorially and bibliographically "clean" text. This author's draft shows a clear consciousness of the revising dramatist.

## The Merry Wives of Windsor

The texts of *The Merry Wives of Windsor* present further evidence of authorial revisions made in an intermediate authorial transcript as well as in the foul papers, but more important, they present extremely powerful evidence that Shakespeare considered his plays self-revising works which he could alter and re-alter throughout their theatrical lives, never producing a "final" text. Like the plays attributed to Pembroke's Men, *The Merry Wives of Windsor* exists in a "bad" or reported 1602 Quarto, which may have been deliberately shortened by its reporter[27] and which lacks or transposes numerous passages and omits several scenes found in the Folio, often rendering the text nonsensical. External circumstances, particularly political and religious censorship, were apparently responsible for the renaming of Ford's pseudonym of Brooke in the Quarto to Broome and the expurgation of oaths in the Folio. Although corrupt in some repects, the Quarto evidently represents a condensed version of the play as it was acted publicly, before or after being altered by Shakespeare to suit the private performances indicated in the Folio text.

Shakespeare revised the play's masque and conclusion at least once: either for an occasional performance to celebrate a Garter feast and the installation of a patron or nobleman into the Order or to remove such references for public performance. *The Merry Wives of Windsor,* which was reported to have been written at Queen Elizabeth's command for a play showing Falstaff in love, is by its setting and its nature a suitable entertainment for a Windsor feast. Although much of the last scene, 5.5, varies substantively in the Quarto and Folio, both texts present a fairy masque, with Sir Hugh as a satyr, boys as fairies, and Mistress Quickly as the Fairy Queen. In the Quarto (sig. G2), Mistress Quickly orders her subjects:

> You Fayries that do haunt these shady groues,
> Looke round about the wood if you can espie
> A mortall that doth haunt our sacred round:
> If such a one you can espie, giue him his due,
> And leaue not till you pinch him blacke and blew:
> Giue them their charge *Puck* ere they part away.

However, in the Folio (TLN 2538–2555), Mistress Quickly pays tribute to Windsor Castle and the Order of the Garter in the speech:

> Search Windsor Castle (Elues) within, and out.
> Strew good lucke (Ouphes) on euery sacred room,
> That it may stand till the perpetuall doome,
> In state as wholsome, as in state 'tis fit,
> Worthy the Owner, and the Owner it.
> The seuerall Chaires of Order, looke you scowre
> With iuyce of Balme; and euery precious flowre,
> Each faire Instalment, Coate, and seu'rall Crest,
> With loyall Blazon, euermore be blest.
> And Nightly meadow-Fairies, looke you sing
> Like to the *Garters-Compasse*, in a ring,
> Th'expressure that it heares: Greene let it be,
> Mote fertile-fresh then all the Field to see:
> And, *Hony Soit Qui Mal-y-Pence,* write
> In Emrold-tuffes, Flowres purple, blew, and white,
> Like Saphire-pearle, and rich embroiderie,
> Buckled below faire Knight-hoods bending knee;
> Fairies vse Flowres for their characterie.[28]

There are at least three possible ways to explain the presence of this speech and other Garter allusions in the Folio but not the Quarto text of the play: Shakespeare originally wrote *The Merry Wives of Windsor* for a performance at Windsor before the Queen, as represented by the Folio text, then altered the play for public performance, and the public version was transcribed by a reporter and printed in the Quarto; or the play was first performed publicly and reported, and later altered for a Garter celebration or royal performance, possibly the one before James at White-hall on 4 November 1604;[29] or the play in its early and later private and public performances was acted from the same original, unrevised text but was cut by the reporter when he copied down the Quarto text.

The vague advertisement on the Quarto 1 title page that the play has "bene diuers times Acted by the right Honorable my Lord Chamberlaines seruants. Both before her Maiestie, and else-where" cannot settle the question of whether the play was originally written for private or public performance, but it does suggest that the reporter would not *deliberately* cut the Garter speech for an edition that hoped to attract an audience eager for the play as performed for the Queen. Even if the reporter did not perfectly remember the speech, it is highly unlikely that he would have forgotten *all* of its very specific references to the Order of the Garter.

Therefore, the Garter speech either belongs to the play as it was originally written and performed privately, or it was added in a revision of the public play for later private performances.[30] The Folio text clearly preserves some passages of dialogue suitable for an occasional performance which closely resemble Jonson's additions "at windsor" in 1621 in the remarkably fluid and non-finite manuscript of *The Gypsies Metamorphosed*. The sophistication of the masque, the numerous post-1603 topical allusions,[31] and the expurgation of oaths and the name of Brooke in the Folio text of *The Merry Wives of Windsor* suggest that it represents a text later than the Quarto.

However, Shakespeare may have kept a record of the play as performed for different audiences on different occasions, as Jonson did, in the manuscript which served as printer's copy for the Folio text, so that occasional additions and deletions could be inserted and removed as needed, making the text suitable for early and later performances to celebrate several Garter feasts, including the installation of Lord Hunsdon, the Lord Chamberlain and Shakespeare's patron, in 1597 into the Order, as well as as the installation of the Prince of Wales and others in 1603, possibly commemorated in the 1604 performance at Whitehall if not in an earlier one at Windsor.

The Quarto and Folio texts do not simply offer two separate, pre- and postrevision, texts, the "royal" one and the other, with "an alternative ending to the play for use—probably on the public stage—when, perhaps, the special occasion for which the original text was prepared was simply not relevant."[32] Rather, they represent one fluid text capable of being transformed for differing occasions, differing audiences, and differing authorial forms and meanings. The "privatized" text of the play could also be "public-ized" for performance at the commercial, public theatres or provincial stages, either through temporary, occasional additions and deletions or through the continual transmutability of the text in its most basic foundation. Although John Jowett argues that "identifiable signs of revision in F are limited and arise from particular historical exigencies,"[33] Shakespeare produced a non-finite and infinitely self-revising text of *The Merry Wives of Windsor* that expresses neither simple exigency nor a particularly limited historicity.[34]

## Macbeth

As Simon Forman's intricately detailed summary of the 1611 performance of *Macbeth* which he attended makes no mention of the character of Hecate and offers a slightly different rendering of the witches' scenes, many critics have argued that the text as printed in the Folio may have undergone cutting or later revisions, perhaps for presentation before the King of Denmark in 1606 or Princess Elizabeth in 1613. The play would have been frequently revived on stage or at court, as the Scottish matter and the theme of witchcraft would have flattered King James, the author of the 1597 pamphlet, *Daemonologie*. Numerous plot inconsistencies do suggest cutting, alteration, or change of intention, especially in the report of Cawdor's treachery during battle in 1.2, which is unknown to Macbeth, a commander of the troops, in 1.3; in the original plotting of Duncan's murder by Macbeth rather than his wife in Act 1; and in the original staging of the final battle at Dunsinane and the death of Macbeth offstage rather than onstage in Act 5.[35]

However, none of these textual puzzles figures in the Forman account, and all are probably due to different layers of composition and revision. Yet theatrical interpolation or authorial addition after composition and after the performance recorded by Forman is suggested by the presence of Hecate and two stage directions, "*Sing within. Come away, come away, &c.*" and "*Musicke and a Song. Blacke Spirits, &c.*" in 3.5 and 4.1 (TLN 1467, 1572), which allude to songs in two Hecate scenes, 3.3 and 5.3, in Thomas Middleton's play, *The Witch*, probably written (although not printed) between 1609 and 1616, and performed by the King's Men at Blackfriars. The King's Men may have simply recycled the two songs, and perhaps one dance, from Middleton's play, which the author described in his Dedication as "ignorantly-ill-fated," implying theatrical failure,[36] by adding them to Shakespeare's play during a later revival.

Because these cues for two of Middleton's songs were added to the play, John Dover Wilson and Stanley Wells, among others, have argued that Middleton was responsible for whatever later revisions were made to the text of *Macbeth*.[37] It appears that Shakespeare and Middleton did borrow from each other at various points between the original composition and possible later revisions of their two plays; for example, in both 1.2 of *The Witch* and 4.1 of *Macbeth*, witches brew demonic potions in a cauldron, fantastically listing each ingredient. As Middleton's sensational portrayal of Hecate and her several attendant witches probably belongs to the original composition of the play at a date closer to 1616 than 1609, he evidently presented his Hecate in *The Witch* after Shakespeare had presented his in the pre- or post-1611 version of *Macbeth;* thus Middleton borrowed from, rather than revised, Shakespeare's play.

There is little external evidence that Middleton reworked any portion of the text of *Macbeth* for the King's Men, or that he himself added his two songs and in the process revised the Hecate scenes. The internal evidence is based only on dubious linguistic resemblances.[38] Shakespeare's depiction of a tightly controlled and imperious Hecate owes little to the lascivious, gossiping old hag portrayed by Middleton. Shakespeare's Hecate, who in 3.5 (TLN 1433–1439) of *Macbeth* majestically reprimands her subservient witches,

> Sawcy, and ouer-bold, how did you dare
> To Trade, and Trafficke with *Macbeth*
> In Riddles, and Affaires of death;
> And I the Mistris of your Charmes,
> The close contriuer of all harmes,
> Was neuer call'd to beare my part
> Or shew the glory of our Art?

seems little akin to Middleton's Hecate, who in 1.2 of *The Witch* comically reprimands her son, Fire-stone,

> you're a kind Son:
> but 'tis the nature of you all, I see that:
> you had rather hunt after strange women still
> then lye with your owne Mothers: Gett thee gon;
> Sweatt thy six ounces out about the Vessell
> and thou shalt play at Mid-night: the Night-Mare
> shall call thee when it walkes.

It is improbable that Middleton rewrote and redesigned his original portrayal of Hecate in *The Witch* for *Macbeth;* even if Middleton were in a position to revise *Macbeth* after 1611, his assertion, made in the dedication to *The Witch,* that the chief cause for the ill-favored reaction to his play was the fact that "Witches are (ipso facto) by y^e Law condemn'd," suggests that he would not have been eager to add such a figure as Hecate to any other play when she had been so ill received in *The Witch.* Shakespeare's Hecate, apparently, had earlier not produced this same reaction. The rather vague references to the two Middleton songs in the stage directions in *Macbeth* suggest a bookkeeper who was slightly familiar with them rather than their original author, who was completely knowledgeable about them and who would, presumably, have rewritten them out in the body of the text rather than offering quick cues to them in the stage directions.

Thus, Middleton does not appear to have authored the Hecate passages in *Macbeth,* either before or after 1611, and stylistic differences between *The Witch* and *Macbeth* also suggest that Middleton was not the reviser of the other textually difficult passages in Shakespeare's play. Nor does it seem possible that the Hecate passages were written by "an anonymous writer, not without poetic ability," who made slight cuts elsewhere to "balance" the play, as Kenneth Muir argues.[39] The speeches of Hecate vary slightly in style from the speeches of the other witches in the play, probably to set her off from her attendants, but Hecate's command to her subjects in 3.5 (TLN 1452–1463) to confound Macbeth,

> Great business must be wrought ere Noone.
> Vpon the Corner of the Moone
> There hangs a vap'rous drop, profound,
> Ile catch it ere it come to ground;
> And that distill'd by Magicke sleights,
> Shall raise such Artificiall Sprights,
> As by the strength of their illusion,
> Shall draw him on to his Confusion.
> He shall spurne Fate, scorne Death, and beare
> His hopes 'boue Wisedome, Grace, and Feare:
> And you all know, Security
> Is Mortals cheefest Enemie.

closely echoes in style, diction, imagery, and subject the verse spoken by spirits in several other Shakespearian plays,[40] including *A Midsummer Night's Dream,* in which Puck speaks of the "sprights" and fairies that run "by the triple *Hecates* teame" (sig. H3$^v$) which are majestically commanded by their spirit ruler, Oberon. In such instances, the *Macbeth* Hecate passages show a greater resemblance to other passages written by Shakespeare than to those written by Middleton in *The Witch*. As for cuts in other scenes to accomodate additions, presumably an outside author would have trimmed 3.4 and 3.6 to insert the new scene of 3.5, yet neither scene shows the kind of textual irregularities which might imply cutting.

It is possible that Shakespeare composed the play by 1606 with the Hecate scenes in it and that Simon Forman missed the single reference in the play to Hecate's name in the first line of 3.5 and did not note her presence in *Macbeth* in his otherwise heavily detailed 1611 account. However, it is more likely that Shakespeare himself added 3.5, containing Hecate's long speech, and her five-line speech in 4.1 sometime after the performance attended by Forman. At some later point, the cues for the songs and dance, taken from a King's Men performance of *The Witch,* were added to the promptbook from which the play was printed. If *Macbeth* was revised during or after 1611 to bring it into line with the more spectacular plays currently popular, the "revising hand" belonged, as J. M. Nosworthy has argued, to Shakespeare himself.[41]

## The English History Plays

Shakespeare's revising hand, exercised over a period of several years, appears clearly and brilliantly in the English history plays which presented the revisionist portrayals of the Houses of Lancaster and York. The texts of *Richard II* offer substantial evidence of probably externally imposed revision, as the deposition scene was not printed until 1608 in Quarto 4 (sigs. H1-H4$^v$), taken either from a memorially reconstructed version or from Shakespeare's early draft. The Folio text, set from heavily annotated copy at least partially deriving from authorial papers,[42] either prints the original scene or inserts Shakespeare's later draft of it. Externally imposed censorship also "forced" authorial revisions in the two plays which followed *Richard II*. Gary Taylor's argument, based on a 1634 allusion to Shakespeare "abusing" the historical Oldcastle in his "first shewe of Harrie y$^e$ fift," insists that Shakespeare's revisions of the character names predated the completion of *2 Henry IV* and therefore affected only *1 Henry IV*.[43] However, the appearance of the names

Oldcastle and Russell in the Quarto of *2 Henry IV,* with the later appended apology dissociating Falstaff from Oldcastle, suggests that these names were remnants of the earliest composition of the play rather than slips when Shakespeare was composing. Thus external and internal evidence demonstrates that Shakespeare reworked *1 Henry IV* and *2 Henry IV,* and had *Richard II* reworked in its printing, because of objections raised to his censorious portrayal of the figures of Sir John Oldcastle, Harvey, and Russell, as well as the allusions to the deposition of Richard II and usurpation of Henry IV.

The epilogue to *2 Henry IV* summarizes the problems Shakespeare encountered with both plays as they were originally performed. In the first paragraph of the 1600 Quarto 1 epilogue (sig. L1$^v$), printed from foul papers, the speaker seeks pardon from the audience for any offense, adding, "Be it knowne to you, as it is very well, I was lately here in the end of a displeasing play, to pray your patience for it, and to promise you a better: I meant indeed to pay you with this." The speaker apologizes here for delivering the epilogue in an earlier play, probably the Oldcastle version of *2 Henry IV* (*1 Henry IV* does not contain an epilogue). The speaker kneels in prayer to the Queen in an apparent conclusion to this epilogue. However, the speaker continues to excuse himself in a second paragraph in which he offers to dance, and a third in which he belatedly adds:

> One word more I beseech you, if you bee not too much cloyd with fatte meate, our humble Author will continue the storie with sir Iohn in it, and make you merry with faire Katharine of Fraunce, (where for any thing I knowe) Falstaffe shall die of a sweat, vnlesse already a be killd with your harde opinions; for Olde-castle died Martyre, and this is not the man: my tongue is weary, when my legges are too, I wil bid you good night.

The Folio reprints the epilogue with only one substantive variant: the prayer for the Queen is placed at the end of the third and concluding paragraph rather than the first paragraph, thus correcting the Quarto's misplacement of the prayer which, to avoid royal offense, should have appeared at the end rather than in the middle of the speech. The misplacement in the Quarto suggests that at least the third paragraph, with its dissociation of Oldcastle from the play, and possibly portions of the first paragraph were later additions to the original epilogue, at least partially consisting of the second paragraph, in which the speaker begs the Gentlemen and Gentlewomen to acquit him by allowing him to dance out of their debt. In fact, the second paragraph does not appear to fit coherently between the first and third paragraph, and Shakespeare may have attempted to impose a coherent order on the revised epilogue by adding a first paragraph which begins, "First my feare then my cursie, last my speech." Shakespeare may have written out the first and third paragraph additions to the epilogue on a separate sheet and added them to the foul papers or added them marginally within the foul papers, working them into the existing epilogue, without clearly marking the point of insertion, and it is possible that the compositor inadvertently printed some of the lines out of sequence.

It is certain that political censorship and "displeasure" forced Shakespeare to rework some passages in these plays; it is also certain that he chose to rework other passages for his own artistic reasons. Each of the texts of *2 Henry IV,* the 1600 Quarto 1 (issued in two states, A and B) and the Folio, offers signs of revision. Quarto B (sigs. E3$^v$-E5) adds a scene not printed in the earlier text, Quarto A. The printer of Quarto A omitted the long first scene of Act 3, in which the dying King Henry confesses that the corruption of the body politic and the body natural is due to his role in the deposition of Richard II, perhaps because the Chamberlain's Men feared censorship and did not turn over the scene with the foul papers which served as copy, as John Dover Wilson argues,[44] or because the compositor overlooked the scene which Shakespeare had written as an afterthought on an added leaf and inserted out of sequence into his papers by the compositor, as John Jowett and Gary Taylor argue.[45] The theory that Shakespeare added to his original text explains why eight passages in the Folio text (in 1.1 [TLN 225–238, 248–268], 1.3 [TLN 522–525, 537–556, 588–611], 2.3 [TLN 981–1003], and 4.1 [TLN 1923–1947, 1969–2005]) do not appear in either issue of the Quarto; rather than being cut because of censorship, or to relieve "tedious discussion" in the Quarto,[46] at least four of them may have been added in the Folio primarily to expand the role of the rebels in the same post–foul-paper revision which produced 3.1.[47]

Yet, other possibilities for the variant states of the Quarto and Folio texts must be considered: Shakespeare may have added 3.1 and expanded passages with Northumberland and the other rebels because he had to fill in gaps in the play due to the excision of original Oldcastle-Harvey-Russell or similarly censorable passages (which have not survived transmission). All of these Folio passages consist of whole speeches which could be removed or inserted into the surrounding text without disturbing it. However, while at least three touch on dangerous matter, such as the way to "plucke a Kingdome down" and the role of religion in political "insurrection," and thus may have been censored in the Quarto, the other Folio-only passages narrate offstage action, such as the King's refusal to meet with the Bishop of London, and action previously presented in *Richard II* (Bolingbroke's challenge to Mowbray and Richard's subsequent banishment of both men, Bolingbroke's return, supported by the Percies, and the deposition of Richard), and in *1 Henry IV* (the Percy rebellion, and the valiant life and death of Hotspur).[48]

Shakespeare probably added 3.1, which also narrates action portrayed in *Richard II* and *1 Henry IV* and the other passages before the printing of the Quarto to provide dramatic continuity between *Richard II* and the *Henry IV* plays, already in performance, as well as *Henry V*, which was evidently planned to have "sir Iohn in it." Addition of some of the eight passages at a period after the addition of 3.1 seems unlikely because it would posit two sets of continually reworked manuscripts, the foul papers or a transcription of them and the promptbook (especially if Shakespeare had to rework his foul papers once to accomodate the Oldcastle changes and perhaps one other time to add 3.1). The eight other passages would have to have been added (some may have been reinstated from the original text) to the promptbook, which also suffered extensive expurgation of oaths and minor adjustments to Falstaff's dialogue.

Jowett and Taylor argue that Shakespeare added most of the Folio passages and the entire scene of 3.1 immediately after composition; however, if the *Henry IV* plays were written and performed before 1598,[49] Shakespeare could have made the "artistic" revisions anytime before 1600, the date of the printing of both issues of the *2 Henry IV* Quarto, and probably during the same period in which he made the "forced" revisions.[50] The loss of the deposition scene in *Richard II* (either on stage or in print) because of censorship may have thrown Shakespeare's composition of the rest of the *Henry IV* plays into chaos: he may have originally written *1 Henry IV* and *2 Henry IV* with few references to it, but once the scene was returned to the stage and/or the page, sometime before the printing of the 1600 Quarto B of *2 Henry IV*, he inserted vivid and detailed summaries of it into both parts of *Henry IV*, most notably in 3.1 of *2 Henry IV*. He also made some other, minor, theatrical alterations throughout the years.

It is not surprising then that the 1600 Quarto 1 and Folio texts of

*Henry V* show similar signs of textual confusion arising from possible censorship and subsequent revisions. The Quarto, although reported, appears to derive from an acting version abridged for a smaller cast and containing deliberate authorial revisions, including the substitution of Bourbon for the Dauphin in the latter part of the play.[51] Two scenes, 2.1 and 2.3, which appear in both the Quarto and the Folio but do not correspond to the Chorus's summary of Act 2, show signs of having been inserted into the play, probably during composition. Shakespeare abandoned his original intention, set out in the epilogue of *2 Henry IV,* of continuing the adventures of Falstaff in *Henry V,* either because of the unavailability of the actor Will Kemp, who had previously played him,[52] or because of the lingering opposition of the Brooke family, or because of his own changed perception of the plot. Shakespeare apparently reworked the parts of Pistol, Fluellen, the "internationals," and the soldiers Bates, Court, and Williams in order to fill in for the abandoned Falstaff episodes or to otherwise reshape the comic scenes.[53] The Folio text, printed from foul papers, contains a duplication in 3.5 and two marginal additions in 4.3 and 4.4.[54] The stage and literary popularity of *Richard II, 1 Henry IV, 2 Henry IV,* and *Henry V* (all of these plays except *2 Henry IV* went through numerous editions) during the last decade of the sixteenth century and the first two decades of the seventeenth century strongly suggests that the plays were frequently revived, probably acquiring authorial touch-ups and revisions throughout the years.

Many of the same authorially derived textual tangles occur in the reported and abridged Quartos of *2 Henry VI* and *Richard III* and the Octavo of *3 Henry VI,* as well as the Folio texts of these plays and of *1 Henry VI.* Memorial reconstruction in the 1594 Quarto 1 text of *2 Henry VI,* political censorship in the Folio text, and authorial collaboration in both texts influenced the transmission of the plays, accounting for textual irregularities which have been seen by a few critics as signs of revision. Shakespeare most likely cut his play extensively shortly after its composition to suit Pembroke's Men, and this cut version was further altered by memorial reporting when printed in the Quarto. The Quarto holds traces of the play as originally acted, and the revisions which appear in the Folio, printed from authorial foul or fair papers, were due either to censorship, or Shakespeare's (and his probable collaborators') theatrical changes.[55] This version of *2 Henry VI* was printed apparently without other substantial changes in the Folio.

The 1595 Octavo of *3 Henry VI* also seems to represent a reported version of the play after Shakespeare cut it for Pembroke's Men, substituted Montague for Falconbridge, and later corrected or revised one passage concerning Salisbury.[56] This Octavo and the *2 Henry VI* Quarto may not be merely "an accumulation of 'memorial' accidents but an accurate record of the history plays as they were performed by Pembroke's men," as Scott McMillin argues.[57] The revisions in the Folio texts of *2 Henry VI* and *3 Henry VI*, each printed from authorial foul or fair copies,[58] were not entirely motivated by censorship but by theatrical adjustments in the promptbook,[59] as well as by Shakespeare's deliberate desire to rewrite portions of his original play.[60] The textual problems of the Folio *1 Henry VI*, also printed from authorial papers,[61] similarly result from a variety of causes, including revision of a preexisting play or Shakespeare's original to suit the Chamberlain's Men, collaboration, annotation of the manuscript by a stage adaptor, and compositorial error.[62]

Like the Folio text of *2 Henry IV*, the Folio of *Richard III* contains at least one passage not in the previous Quartos which summarizes action presented in the earlier plays in the *Henry VI* sequence. The reported 1597 Quarto 1 text of *Richard III* is not an absolutely reliable standard to mark revision between the Quarto and the Folio, which was largely printed from a transcript of foul papers,[63] although it probably preserves some original portions of the play. Some of the inconsistencies in characters, plot, and action in the Quarto resulted from Shakespeare's second-thought changes during composition or transcription of a fair copy, while other inconsistencies are clearly due to nonauthorial alteration.[64] Many of the more than two hundred lines unique to the Folio were evidently cut from the original play, probably by Shakespeare himself, in order to eliminate several minor roles in court and battle scenes for performance by a smaller or a touring company or for the dramatic reshaping of these scenes, and these abridgments were then taken down by the reporter of Quarto 1. For example, the Quarto omission of entrances for and the brief exchange between Dorset and Rivers in 2.2, both of which appear in the Folio, signals that the characters were cut from the scene at some point.

W. W. Greg dismisses theories of revision within or between the Quarto 1 and Folio texts of *Richard III* as "inherently improbable,"[65] and Gary Taylor agrees that the variants "do not cluster or coalesce into patterns which imply any discernible strategy of revision" as do those in Shakespeare's later plays in which "the luxury of extensive literary revision seems more likely."[66] However, while some of the variants between the Quarto and Folio may have been cuts made to appease the censor or to suit a smaller acting company, others were added by the author, rather than cut, in a discernibly strategic way. A twelve-line Folio passage in Richard's long wooing speech to Lady Anne in 1.2 (TLN 346–357) narrates important dramatic events, such as Clifford's confrontation with Rutland, which were staged in the *Henry VI* plays, and a few of the other "cuts" also give perspective to the current scenes by alluding to events presented on stage in the preceding plays. Thus, sometime after *Richard III* had been reported, Shakespeare adjusted the play's themes and characters by adding, rather than simply restoring, several of the other single-line or entire speech insertions in Richard's and other characters' speeches which are printed only in the Folio. Shakespeare's revisionist views of Richard III and the other royal members of the Houses of Lancaster and York themselves became part of the self-revising process.

Thus, evidence in Folio *Richard III* and Folio *2 Henry IV* strongly suggests that at some point after the four *Henry VI* plays and the four *Henry IV* plays were completed, Shakespeare reworked portions of the later plays by adding speeches in which characters recall events already presented in the early plays, in order to provide a sense of dramatic and theatrical unity and continuity among all four of the plays in each sequence, perhaps in anticipation of performing the four plays together in repertory. At the same time, Shakespeare reworked parts of the earlier plays by adjusting references to events which would be portrayed in the later plays (although he failed to remove one contradiction: the epilogue's promise in *2 Henry IV* that Falstaff would appear in the play which followed). Other textual irregularities, including those in the early "bad" Quartos/Octavo of *2 Henry VI* and *3 Henry VI* and *Henry V,* also reflect then not only nonauthorial corruption but similarly uncorrected inconsistencies arising from Shakespeare's decision to continue the *Henry IV* and *Henry VI* sequences after having completed one or two early plays.

The "bad" Quartos as well as the "good" Quarto and Folio texts of the history plays reveal Shakespeare's deliberate attempt to provide a type of unified structure and cross-referencing among the plays which act as sequels to a previous play. This substantial, painstaking revision, practiced some years after composition, and perhaps largely after 1596 as Gary Taylor argues, sits alongside revisions during composition as well as obvious theatrical and compositorial alterations, indicating that

Shakespeare used deliberate and conscious methods of altering single plays as well as plays followed by sequels. Thus Shakespeare did not abandon his plays after finishing their original compositions; he "continued the storie" by adjusting and re-adjusting them, viewing and re-viewing them, revising and re-revising them, continually and constantly transforming the history plays into dramatically and theatrically coherent revisionist presentations of the English monarchs.

The evidence in *Romeo and Juliet, Love's Labor's Lost, Titus Andronicus, A Midsummer Night's Dream, Julius Caesar, The Merry Wives of Windsor, Macbeth,* and the four plays in the *Henry VI* and *Henry IV* sequences, demonstrates that Shakespeare reworked his plays when they were in the process of being readied for different companies, different venues, or different audiences, so that when he abridged or restored abridged passages in the play for a particular theatrical reason, he also "tinkered," to use John Kerrigan's term,[67] with other passages which he wished to revise for his own artistic reasons. Often, this tinkering resulted in duplications or inconsistencies, so that as E. A. J. Honigmann has conjectured, "Shakespeare's imagination, thrashing around inside a story as it remodelled it and forever revising its options, multiplied entities needlessly—or rather, permitted traces of rejected possibilities to survive in the text";[68] his patterns and methods of revision remained remarkably similar throughout his career. Shakespeare often made his second-thought and later revisions in his foul papers or in his own transcripts of them. Some variants between texts may stem then from his or the bookkeeper's failure to add particular revisions to the current prompt-book, or even from his later acts of revision which canceled these earlier revisions.

As in the case of his contemporary dramatists who left behind numerous dramatic manuscripts, several critical assumptions about Shakespeare's authorial practice can be made: as a professional dramatist for the Chamberlain's/King's Men Company, Shakespeare continued to exert theatrical and artistic control and participated in or supervised changes made to his plays; he tended to add to or alter existing dialogue rather than completely rewriting his texts, but if necessary he overhauled an entire play; and he sometimes produced separate and coherent multiple versions of his plays.

For Shakespeare, as for his contemporaries, the types of authorial revisions included changes in or addition or deletion of characters (*Romeo and Juliet, Love's Labor's Lost, Titus Andronicus, A Midsummer Night's Dream, Julius Caesar, The Merry Wives of Windsor, Macbeth,* the *Henry IV/VI* plays), themes (*Love's Labor's Lost, A Midsummer Night's Dream, Julius Caesar, Macbeth,* the *Henry IV/VI* plays), plot (*Love's Labor's Lost, Titus Andronicus,* the *Henry IV/VI* plays), structure (*Romeo and Juliet, Love's Labor's Lost, Titus Andronicus, Julius Caesar, Macbeth,* the *Henry IV/VI* plays), and setting (*The Merry Wives of Windsor*). Reasons for authorial revisions included: external or self-imposed censorship (*The Merry Wives of Windsor,* the *Henry IV/VI* plays); the different needs of publication or private transcription (*Julius Caesar* and possibly several other plays), or of occasional performance or revival (*Romeo and Juliet, A Midsummer Night's Dream, The Merry Wives of Windsor, Macbeth,* the *Henry IV/VI* plays); the personal or artistic demands of the author (*Romeo and Juliet, Love's Labor's Lost, Titus Andronicus, A Midsummer Night's Dream, Julius Caesar, The Merry Wives of Windsor, Macbeth,* the *Henry IV/VI* plays); and changes in acting company, venue, or audience (*Romeo and Juliet, Titus Andronicus, A Midsummer Night's Dream, The Merry Wives of Windsor, Macbeth,* the *Henry VI* plays), ownership of the play (*Romeo and Juliet, Titus Andronicus,* the *Henry VI* plays), or political climate (*The Merry Wives of Windsor* and the *Henry IV/VI* plays).

The original compositions and the later revisions of so many of Shakespeare's plays extended throughout a wide period of time, both before and after 1596, and went through extensive, various stages and manuscripts, each "with its own characteristic aesthetic, offering together several finalities,"[69] none of which should be finitely or finally edited away. Neither theatrical nor literary revision was a "luxury" for Shakespeare and his contemporary dramatists but an intrinsic part of the authorial process, indistinct only because it was not a separable or removable element in the dramatic act of composition. The only canonizer and constituter of Shakespeare's texts, in all their infinitely revisable variety, is Shakespeare himself.

# ❧ 5 ❧

# Revising *Hamlet, Troilus and Cressida,* and *Othello*

Shakespeare's authorial revisions in character, theme, plot, structure, and setting, made for changed theatrical or political conditions, censorship, publication, or private transcription (and for his own artistic demands) infuse the canon of his plays, from *Titus Andronicus* to *Macbeth.* Yet critics and editors have for many years disrupted the canon by assigning a relative value to particular plays. Canonically, the later tragedies possess a theoretically assigned textual, literary, and cultural value that cannot be matched by the earlier tragedies or by the comedies, romances, and histories written throughout Shakespeare's career. The iconographic representation of his "major" tragedies, particularly *Hamlet, Othello,* and *King Lear,* as textual relics, literary masterpieces, and cultural symbols defeats any attempt to understand these plays as part of a larger canon or of a particular authorial identity; their elevation and subsequent isolation has demanded that they serve as a separate canon by which to judge Shakespeare's other plays and those of his contemporary dramatists. Yet these tragedies cannot serve merely as superior reference points for the other plays; they must be returned to the revising canon primarily and centrally as textual representations of substantively variant Quarto and Folio editions of a single play. I propose a new constitution of canonicity: *Hamlet, Othello, King Lear,* and *Troilus and Cressida* inferentially derive from the authorial composition and revision process established and pursued from the beginning of Shakespeare's career; referentially, their physical texts assign a revisionist value to the preceding and succeeding play-texts in the canon.

## Hamlet

The transmission of the text of *Hamlet* presents more varied and complex problems than that of any other Shakespearian play because it alone exists in three, rather than two, substantively variant editions: the 1603 Quarto 1, approximately 2150 lines; the 1604 Quarto 2, approximately 3600 lines; and the Folio text, approximately 3500 lines. No other Shakespearian play, as W. W. Greg notes, "has been preserved in such a variety of independent but related texts, and of no other have the bibliographical and textual features of the texts been so minutely studied."[1] In some portions of the play, each text has its own reading, and how many of these three versions of a passage are Shakespearian may be too difficult to determine. Although modern scholars have been willing to argue for theatrical cutting of some parts of each text, discussion of extensive authorial revisions in *Hamlet* has been critically acceptable only since the early 1980s. In fact, in 1934, J. D. Wilson, the most vocal twentieth-century supporter of theories of Shakespearian revision, attributed the omission of many of the Folio passages in the Quarto 2 text to "a careless scribe or compositor."[2] Similarly, G. I. Duthie saw the hand of an "interpolative reviser" in Quarto 1.[3]

Duthie established in 1941 that Quarto 1 was a reported text of an acting version;[4] it may have been abridged for the performances advertised on its title page in the City of London (probably at the Globe in Southwark[5]) and also "in the two Vniuersities of Cambridge and Oxford, and else-where." Many passages appear to have been imperfectly remembered by the reporter(s). For example, memorial alteration is apparent in Claudius's speech in 2.2 (sig. D3) at the first entrance of Rossencraft and Gilderstone:

> Right noble friends, that our deere cosin Hamlet
> Hath lost the very heart of all his sence,
> It is most right, and we most sorry for him:
> Therefore we doe desire, euen as you tender
> Our care to him, and our great loue to you,
> That you will labour but to wring from him
> The cause and ground of his distemperancie.

The presentation of this speech in Quarto 2 and the Folio (sigs. E2^v-E3; TLN 1021–1037) is not merely expanded but more fully developed than the compact speech in Quarto 1 (substantive Folio variants from Quarto 2 are bracketed):

> Welcome deere *Rosencrans* and *Guyldensterne,*
> Moreouer, that we much did long to see you,
> The need we haue to vse you did prouoke
> Our hastie sending, something haue you heard
> Of *Hamlets* transformation, so call it.
> Sith nor th'exterior, nor the inward man
> Resembles that it was, what it should be,
> More then his fathers death, that thus hath put him
> So much from th'vnderstanding of himselfe
> I cannot dreame [deeme *F*] of: I entreate you both
> That beeing of so young dayes brought vp with him,
> And sith so nabored to his youth and hauior,
> That you vouchsafe your rest heere in our Court
> Some little time, so by your companies
> To draw him on to pleasures, and to gather
> So much as from occasion you may gleane,
> Whether ought to vs vnknowne afflicts him thus, [line deleted in *F*]
> That opend lyes within our remedie.

The two passages share very little common diction and no imagery, and because the Quarto 1 passage paraphrases what the Quarto 2/Folio passage presents, it appears to be a memorial report rather than the first version of a speech which was later revised. The majority of variants between Quarto 1 and Quarto 2/Folio are of this type, although in some scenes whole passages have been omitted and may reflect cuts made for a smaller or touring company performing the play.

Memorial reporting and/or theatrical abridgment may have produced the alteration in character names and in the placement of scenes between Quarto 1 and Quarto 2/Folio. G. R. Hibbard argues that the names of the characters of Polonius and Reynaldo were changed to Corambis and Montano in Quarto 1 for performances at Oxford to avoid unfavorable references to Pullen (*Polenius* in Latin), the founder of the University, and John Reynolds, the current president of Corpus Christi College and author of a 1599 antitheatrical tract.[6] But the names may have originally appeared as Corambis and Montano in the abridged text, as they do in one probable source for the play, and been altered later for some other reason (as probably happened with the "King," who is never called

"Claudius" in Quarto 1). Hamlet's "To be or not to be" soliloquy and
the "nunnery scene" immediately precede the "fish-monger" passage in
Act 2 in Quarto 1 rather than appearing in Act 3 as they do in Quarto
2/Folio, so that Hamlet's separate "mad" confrontations with Ophelia
and with Polonius-Corambis have been condensed into one scene,
significantly altering the play's structure.

    However, neither memorial error nor theatrical demands appear to be
the cause of several significant and stunning variants in characterization,
plot, structure, and theme between the reported Quarto and Quarto
2/Folio. The most striking change in characterization in Quarto 1 appears in the role of Gertrude in the last three acts of the play. In 3.4, the
"closet scene," "Gertred," distressed by Hamlet's revelation to her that
the King murdered her husband, declares her innocence and agrees to
help Hamlet in whatever "stratagem" he devises for exposing the mur-
derer (in a passage apparently borrowed from *The Spanish Tragedy*[7]). In
this scene in Quarto 2 and the Folio, Hamlet does not reveal that
Claudius murdered his father, but instead accuses his mother of incest
and extracts her promise not to repeat what they have discussed.[8] Also,
in place of the scene, 4.6, in Quarto 2/Folio in which sailors give Horatio
a letter from Hamlet detailing his escape with the pirates from
Rosencrantz and Guildenstern, Quarto 1 presents a scene in which
Horatio tells Gertred that Hamlet escaped from Rossencraft and
Gilderstone after reading the King's letters to the English King calling
for his death, and Gertred vows to continue to deceive her husband in
order to save her son. There are also three other major variants in plot
in the last two acts: in Quarto 1, Laertes does not attempt rebellion
against the King after Corambis's murder; the King, rather than Laertes,
plots to poison the sword Laertes will use in his fencing match with
Hamlet; and Hamlet is not told of the arrival of Fortinbras and the
ambassadors from England before he dies.

    There are enough correspondences, such as Gertrude's collaboration
with Hamlet, between Quarto 1 and the sources for the Hamlet story,
as well as between Quarto 1 and the later German manuscript of *Der
Bestrafte Brudermord,* probably derived from an English touring
company's text of some version of *Hamlet,* to suggest that Quarto 1
represented a version of the play as acted. However, because of its close
resemblances in some portions of the text to the corresponding passages
in Quarto 2 and the Folio, Quarto 1 is apparently not directly descended

from the version of *Hamlet* performed by the Chamberlain's Men at Newington Butts in 1594 or from the *Ur-Hamlet*. If Shakespeare's *Hamlet,* probably written by 1601, is a reworking of an earlier play, Quarto 1 may in part represent Shakespeare's first attempt and the other two texts his subsequent attempts to revise a preexisting play. In any case, it appears that "the variations in the text of *Hamlet* are not alternative versions of a single original text but representations of different stages in the play's development."[9]

Yet, Quarto 1 may not represent the first version of the play, but a later one. This reported text does not contain the inconsistencies which are characteristic of foul papers, and it was derived at some remove from the original foul papers, perhaps from an abridged promptbook or a transcript made from them. It is possible, as J. M. Nosworthy argues, that Quarto 1 is "a memorial reconstruction of an official abridgment of the Folio version, with cuts, amendments and replacements for which Shakespeare was himself responsible."[10] The Folio itself is also at some remove from the foul papers and from Quarto 2, which was evidently printed from them (with some consultation of Quarto 1). As the Folio text skillfully eliminates many of the duplications, loose ends, and false starts which appear in Quarto 2, it may be derived from an authorial transcript of foul papers; if so, the evolution of the play was similar to that of *Romeo and Juliet,* in which duplications do not appear in the reported text but appear in the text printed shortly afterward from foul papers. However, the Folio text of *Romeo and Juliet* does not generally vary substantively from Quarto 2 in the way that the Folio text of *Hamlet* does, and the three substantively variant texts of *Hamlet* demonstrate that this play underwent a further stage of revision than *Romeo and Juliet.*

An examination of the variants between the Quarto 2 and Folio texts establishes the role of Quarto 1 in the transmission of the text and illustrates which texts represent the first, intermediate, and later versions of *Hamlet.* The title page of Quarto 2, which states that the play had been "newly imprinted and enlarged to almost as much againe as it was, according to the true and perfect Coppie," probably, like the Quarto 2 title page of *Romeo and Juliet,* advertised that it both superseded an earlier reported text and contained new revisions. Quarto 2 has enough textual irregularities within it to suggest that Shakespeare reworked the play during or shortly after composition. Many of these inconsistencies, including duplications, were skillfully eliminated in the Folio text. For example, an apparent duplication appears in the Player Queen's speech in 3.2 in Quarto 2 (sig. H2):

> For women feare too much, euen as they loue,
> And womens feare and loue hold quantitie,
> Eyther none, in neither ought, or in extremitie.

In the Folio (TLN 2036–2037), the entire first line and the words "eyther none" in the third line have been deleted, eliminating the partial duplication. Philip Edwards argues that duplications in this and other passages indicate that the manuscript used to print Quarto 2 must have presented the compositor with problems of bad handwriting and unclearly marked deletions and insertions.[11]

Another unnoticed deletion mark in the printer's copy for Quarto 2 probably appeared in 4.1 (sig. K1ᵛ) in one of Claudius's speeches to Gertrude after Hamlet has murdered Polonius:

> Come *Gertrard,* wee'le call vp our wisest friends,
> And let them know both what we meane to doe
> And whats vntimely doone,
> Whose wisper ore the worlds dyameter,
> As leuell as the Cannon to his blanck,
> Transports his poysoned shot, may misse our Name,
> And hit the woundlesse ayre, ô come away,
> My soule is full of discord and dismay.

The passage has been carefully cut in the Folio (TLN 2626–2629):

> Come *Gertrude,* wee'l call vp our wisest friends,
> To let them know both what we meane to do,
> And what's ultimately done. Oh come away,
> My soule is full of discord and dismay.

J. D. Wilson conjectures that Shakespeare intended to delete the Quarto-only lines in his foul papers, beginning with a mark which scored out whatever half-line followed "And whats vntimely doone" in Quarto 2, but the compositor deleted only the half-line and let stand the rest of the passage.[12] Numerous other half-lines appear throughout the Quarto 2 text but not in the Folio, and some may also represent the beginning of a long deletion which was only partially noticed by the compositor, although some may conceivably be abandoned but not deleted false starts.

Quarto 2 also contains numerous other compositional false starts and inconsistencies which are reprinted in the Folio but not in Quarto 1. For example, in Quarto 2 and Folio (sig. D3; TLN 744–776), the Ghost, in narrating his murder to Hamlet, remarks, "Briefe let me be," yet he continues the speech for thirty-three lines. In Quarto 1 (sig. C4), the remark has been moved to his previous short speech (which also appears in Quarto 2 and Folio) in which he does briefly summarize the murder in five lines. At the end of 2.1 (sig. E2ᵛ), after Ophelia has reported Hamlet's strange behavior to her father, he tells her, "Come, goe we to the King. . . Come," but she does not appear with him when he enters the court in the next scene. However, in Quarto 1, Corambis takes Ophelia with him at the end of 2.1 (sig. D3) and enters with her in the next scene, and he and the King and Queen leave her onstage to hear Hamlet's "To be or not to be" soliloquy and to be confronted by him in the "nunnery scene." Both Quarto 1 and Folio correct another Quarto 2 duplication: Hamlet instructs the players in 2.2 (sig. F4ᵛ) to insert a "speech of some dosen lines, or sixteene lines," while in Quarto 1 and Folio (sig. E4ᵛ; TLN 1581) he asks for a "speech of some dosen or sixteene lines." The textual inconsistencies which do not appear in Quarto 1 may have been unconsciously omitted by a reporter with an imperfect memory or consciously cut by Shakespeare or a bookkeeper in the abridged version in which the reporter performed.

Another inconsistency which certainly derives from a change in intention during Shakespeare's composition of the play appears in 3.4, during Hamlet's angry confrontation with his mother. In Quarto 2 (sig. I4ᵛ), Hamlet reveals to Gertrude that he knows what function Rosencrantz and Guildenstern have been asked to perform:

> Ther's letters seald, and my two Schoolefellowes,
> Whom I will trust as I will Adders fang'd,
> They beare the mandat, they must sweep my way
> And marshall me to knauery: let it worke,
> For tis the sport to haue the enginer
> Hoist with his owne petar, an't shall goe hard
> But I will delue one yard belowe their mines,
> And blowe them at the Moone: ô 'tis most sweete
> When in one line two crafts directly meete.

However, later in 5.2 (sigs. N1-N1ᵛ), Hamlet tells Horatio that one night on board ship to England he felt uneasy, so he stole Rosencrantz and Guildenstern's packet of letters, and discovered when he read them "a royall knauery": Claudius's order for his death. At that moment he decided to forge the letters to ensure the deaths of Rosencrantz and Guildenstern, and afterward he returned the letters to their hiding place.

Hamlet's remark to Gertrude in 3.4 in Quarto 2 suggests that he knew about the existence and contents of the "letters seald," marshalling him to "knauery," before he left Denmark, but his narration of events to Horatio in 5.2 implies that he first learned about the letters while aboard ship. Shakespeare may not then have planned on the events of 5.2 when writing 3.4 or may have been uncertain about how to proceed with this subplot on the treachery of Rosencrantz and Guildenstern. The Folio text eliminates the contradiction by not reprinting the "Ther's letters seald" passage in 3.4. As John Kerrigan points out, the omission of these lines could not have been accidental since in Quarto 2 Rosencrantz and Guildenstern next enter in 4.1, the scene following 3.4, in the company of Claudius, while in the Folio they enter only after Claudius, who is already onstage, sends for them.[13] Quarto 1 avoids the duplication, as Hamlet does not mention sealed letters in the closet scene, and Horatio briefly tells Gertrude in the scene substituted for that of the sailors and Horatio in Quarto 2/Folio that Hamlet had found the "Packet" (sig. H2ᵛ).

The most striking duplication in Quarto 2 indicates not *currente calamo* revisions but later marginal additions in the foul papers to accommodate the larger addition of the rebellion of Laertes against Claudius. In 4.5 (sig. K4ᵛ) after the exit of the mad Ophelia, the King begins his speech:

> Follow her close, giue her good watch I pray you.
> O this is the poyson of deepe griefe, it springs all from her Fathers
> death, and now behold, ô *Gertrard. Gertrard,*
> When sorrowes come, they come not single spyes,
> But in battalians: first her Father slaine,
> Next your sonne gone, and he most violent Author
> Of his owne iust remoue . . .
> > poore *Ophelia*
> Deuided from herselfe . . .
> . . . . .
> Last, and as much contayning as all these,
> Her brother is in secret come from Fraunce,
> Feeds on this wonder, keepes himself in clowdes,
> And wants not buzzers to infect his eare
> With pestilent speeches of his fathers death.

The Folio (TLN 2811–2314) prints the beginning of the passage as:

> Follow her close,
> Giue her good watch I pray you:
> Oh this is the poyson of deepe greefe, it springs
> All from her Fathers death. Oh *Gertrude, Gertrude.*

"Now behold" may have been a false start in the foul papers which was meant to be canceled, as Philip Edwards argues;[14] however, it seems more likely from the position of the printed lines that "It springs all from her Fathers death" was a marginal addition. A few lines after Claudius has stated that Ophelia's deep grief springs "all" from her father's death, he notes the four sorrows that have come to the kingdom: Polonius's death, Hamlet's absence, Ophelia's madness, and Laertes's confusion. Shakespeare may have begun with the intention of naming four "sorrows" but then decided to expand the speech to explain how the death of Ophelia's father engendered the current dissension in the kingdom, causing the exile of Hamlet, the madness of Ophelia, and the secret return of Laertes, giving a single, powerful source for the dangerous events which are to come.

Immediately after Claudius's speech in Quarto 2 and Folio, a Messenger enters with news that the "rabble" is crying for Laertes to be made King (sig. L1; TLN 2838–2848). Shortly afterward, Laertes, in open "rebellion," breaks open the doors and enters with others to confront Claudius. However, in Quarto 1, Laertes enters alone immediately after Claudius's short speech on the swiftness of time, which is prefaced by only one remark on Ophelia's condition, "A pretty wretch! this is a change indeede" (sig. H1). The passages in which the messenger brings news of the rabble's rebellion and in which Laertes forcibly enters are omitted. Instead, Quarto 1 begins the confrontation with passages reprinted in the other texts in which Laertes demands vengeance for his father's death.

These variants appear to indicate that the rebellion of Laertes was cut for the abridged version which later served as copy for Quarto 1. Yet the two conflicting versions about the source of dissension in Quarto 2, the first version noting the four sorrows, including Laertes's infection by others with "pestilent" speeches, and the second version intensifying and justifying his rebellion as resulting from a single cause of crisis, his father's death, suggest instead that Laertes's rebellion was a later addition in the foul papers. If so, Quarto 1 records the scene before it received additions. The other plot discrepancies between Quarto 1 and Quarto 2/Folio do not appear to have arisen from this type of revision in foul papers.

That Shakespeare revised *Hamlet* once again after this period, perhaps in the process of transcribing it, is apparent given the substantial evidence of careful and deliberate large-scale cutting, additions, and minor tinkering, especially in small substitutions, in the Folio text. The Folio omits two hundred thirty lines which appear in Quarto 2, most of them in the speeches of Hamlet in the last acts of the play, including his last soliloquy, in 4.4 (sigs. K3-K3$^v$), "How all occasions doe informe against me," a powerful speech in which Hamlet is spurred on to vengeance after he watches Fortinbras and his men march past and realizes that "god-like reason" separates man from beasts and arms him for battle. Greg is willing to see Shakespeare's hand in the cuts, even those which substantially change the audience's perception of Hamlet's character, such as the loss of the "How all occasions" speech, but not in the minor tinkering, claiming that "it is absurd to suppose that Shakespeare, when dissatisfied with a word in his text, commonly replaced it by another of generally similar appearance."[15] Harold Jenkins, who discounts the possibility of *any* authorial revision in the play, also argues that "we cannot suppose that all these little repetitions, interjections, and similar small elaborations show the way in which Shakespeare would have gone about revision."[16] But duplications in *Romeo and Juliet, Love's Labor's Lost,* and several other plays indicate that Shakespeare frequently made substitutions of words of similar appearance as well as additions which slightly elaborated the sense of a passage; these revisions demonstrate Shakespeare's extraordinarily meticulous attention to the state of the text.

As discussed earlier, Shakespeare apparently made some of the Folio cuts in order to eliminate the inconsistencies which appear in Quarto 2. Critics have argued that other cuts in Acts 3, 4, and 5 may have been made to speed up the final actions of the play.[17] Three Quarto 2 passages in the long exchange among Hamlet, Horatio, and Osric in 5.2 (sigs. N2-N3$^v$) do not appear in the Folio; however, rather than simply extending Hamlet and Horatio's opportunity to comically taunt the foppish Osric, the first and the third passages offer information which sets up specific dramatic expectations for the play's conclusion (which immediately follows this scene). In the first passage, Osric twice commends Laertes as a "Gentleman," prompting Hamlet's satiric comparison of Laertes and Osric. This praise of Laertes from the comic character is both ironic and comical, as the audience has already been told by Laertes that he will poison his sword for his match with Hamlet in a most ungentlemanly fashion.

The third passage (sig. N3ᵛ) also stresses the abilities of Laertes: a Lord enters to summon Hamlet to the fencing match, prompting this exchange:

> *Lord.*  The Queene desires you to vse some gentle entertainment to *Laertes,*
> before you fall to play.
> *Ham.*  Shee well instructs me.
> *Hora.*  You will loose my Lord.
> *Ham.*  I doe not thinke so, since he went to France, I haue bene in continuall
> practise, I shall winne at the ods; thou would'st not thinke how ill all's
> heere about my hart, but it is no matter.

In these lines, the audience learns that Gertrude has asked Hamlet to reconcile with Laertes before the duel, and in his first speech after the entrance of the King, the Queen, Laertes, and members of the court, Hamlet offers Laertes a seventeen-line apology (sig. K3ᵛ; TLN 3678–3696; all but one line of this speech appears in the Folio). Also, Horatio expresses doubt about Hamlet's ability to defeat Laertes, but Hamlet assures him that he has been in "continuall practise," and the duel takes on more intensity as an evenly matched competition. The subject of Laertes's fencing ability is also discussed at length in 4.7; however, Quarto 2 presents more of this dialogue between Laertes and Claudius than the Folio does.

The loss of these two passages in 5.2 in the Folio assigns Hamlet's attempt at reconciliation with Laertes to his own motives rather than to Gertrude's entreaty, and it also avoids the sense of uncertainty about the outcome of the duel in the minds of Horatio and Hamlet, and consequently of the audience. If Shakespeare intentionally cut these lines, and speeches such as "How all occasions doe informe against me," it was not merely to move other episodes on at a faster pace but to subtly alter character motives and audience expectations in the final scene, presenting a revised final act, and thus, a revised vision of the final state of the play John Kerrigan agrees that Shakespeare carefully and consciously made these cuts to reshape the entire play, particularly in hastening the arrival of the Ghost in the first act, softening the sensuality of the closet scene, and blunting the audience's skepticism about Fortinbras as the Danes' new king, rather than simply advancing the action in the last acts.[18]

In addition to cutting passages in the Folio, Shakespeare added five passages, totalling seventy lines, which are not found in the Quarto 2. One passage was inserted into the play to comment on the War of the Theatres, a pseudo or genuine running battle between the boys' and men's company dramatists, including Ben Jonson, John Marston, and Thomas Dekker, who satirized each other in various plays from 1598 to 1602. In Quarto 2/Folio 2.2, as Rosencrantz and Hamlet discuss the newly arrived Players, Hamlet asks, "Doe they hold the same estimation they did when I was in the City? Are they so follow'd?" Rosencrantz answers, "No indeed, they are not." In the Folio only (TLN 1384–1408) this long passage next appears:

> *Ham.*   How comes it? doe they grow rusty?
>
> *Rosin.*  Nay, their indeauour keepes in the wonted pace; But there is Sir an
>          ayrie of Children, little Yases, that crye out on the top of question;
>          and are most tyrannically clap't for't: these are now the fashion, and
>          so be-ratled the common Stages (so they call them) that many
>          wearing Rapiers, are affraide of Goose-quils, and dare scarse come
>          thither.
>
> *Ham.*   What are they Children? Who maintains 'em? How are they escoted?
>          Will they pursue the Quality no longer then they can sing? Will they
>          not say afterwards if they should grow themselues to common Players
>          (as it is like most if their meanes are not better) their Writers do
>          them wrong, to make them exclaim against their owne Succession.
>
> *Rosin.*  Faith there ha's bene much to do on both sides: and the Nation holds
>          it no sinne, to tarre them to Controuersie. There was for a while, no
>          mony bid for argument, vnlesse the Poet and the Player went to
>          Cuffes in the Question.
>
> *Ham.*   Is't possible?
>
> *Rosin.*  Oh there ha's beene much throwing about of Braines.
>
> *Ham.*   Do the Boyes carry it away?
>
> *Rosin.*  I that they do my Lord. *Hercules* & his load too.

The comment on Hercules and his load alluded to the emblem of the Globe theatre,[19] a playhouse that evidently suffered financially during the boys' companies' successes in the popular *Poetomachia* plays. *Hamlet* was entered in the Stationers' Register in July 1602, and this passage could have been added to the manuscript which served as printer's copy for the Folio at any time before the interest in the War of the Theatres had waned, but probably by the end of 1602. A slight allusion to this

War of the Theatres appears in Quarto 1 (sig. E3) when Hamlet asks how it comes that the tragedians travel, and Gilderstone replies: "The principall publicke audience that / Came to them, are turned to priuate playes, / And to the humour of children"; this reported version may imperfectly represent Shakespeare's first attempt, after the play had originally been composed, to mock his private-theatre competition, which later found fuller and more satiric expression in the Folio text.

Another passage of thirty-two lines in 2.2 (TLN 1285–1316), which includes Hamlet's remark, "Denmark's a Prison," was probably also added at the same time as the boys' company passage to the Folio, rather than cut in the Quarto. Many critics have argued that the "Denmark's a Prison" passage was cut from foul papers (but later restored to the Folio manuscript) to avoid offending King James's Danish-born wife, Anne; however, only half of the passage concerns Denmark, as the other half comments on ambition and kingship. Marcellus's comment at the end of 1.4 that "something is rotten in the State of Denmarke" appears in Quarto 1, Quarto 2, and the Folio (sigs. C3$^v$; D2; TLN 678), and it and the numerous other references to corruption in the Danish court throughout the three texts of the play seem as offensive as Hamlet's comparison of Denmark to a prison, supposedly censored in Quarto 2. Shakespeare may have deliberately cut this passage in the foul papers to make room for the additional lines on the boys' companies, and the cut but not the addition appeared in Quarto 2. But both Folio-only passages in this scene were more probably added in the revisions which cut so many other Quarto passages.

If Shakespeare revised *Hamlet* to increase its commercial appeal during the War of the Theatres by adding one passage on the success of the boys' companies in performing satiric plays in private theatres, it seems likely that he made the other revisions to the play during the same period, probably between the completion of the foul papers and his later transcription of them. The foul papers, used to print Quarto 2, and the transcript, used to print the Folio, probably each contained cuts, additions (possibly on inserted sheets), and minor alterations, resulting in separate, substantive versions of the play. The reporter of Quarto 1 may have imperfectly transcribed an abridged version of the promptbook, which was at least one remove from the foul papers in which some subplots, such as Laertes's rebellion against Claudius, did not appear. The three texts of *Hamlet,* a play which has served for centuries as the literary, cultural, and historical archetype for the ultimate achievement of the creative process, preserve not only a remarkable record of the act of dramatic creation but of the ever-transformative and ever-transmutable act of authorial re-creation.

## Troilus and Cressida

As W. W. Greg has stated, *Troilus and Cressida* has long been considered "a play of puzzles, in respect of its textual history no less than its interpretation, and any attempt to solve them cannot be other than speculative";[20] however, there are probable solutions to at least some of its interpretive and textual problems. Between the Quarto and Folio texts are more than five hundred substantive differences.[21] The play as acted by the Chamberlain's Men was entered in the Stationers' Register in 1603, but it did not appear in print until six years later. The two states of the 1609 Quarto 1 of *Troilus and Cressida* offer some evidence that the play was involved in controversy before or during its printing. The title page of the first state advertises the play "as it was acted by the Kings Maiesties seruants at the Globe," and the text does not contain the prologue, which was later printed in the Folio. The title page of the second state cancels the King's Men/Globe Theatre notice, substituting the description, "Excellently expressing the beginning of their loues, with the conceited wooing of Pandarus Prince of Licia," without noting the company or the place of performance.

The second state of Quarto 1 of *Troilus and Cressida* also adds an epistle (¶2-¶2ᵛ) entitled, "A neuer writer, to an euer reader. Newes," advising the "eternall" reader:

> You haue heere a new play, neuer stal'd with the Stage, neuer clapper-clawd with the palmes of the vulger, and yet passing full of the palme comicall; for it is a birth of your braine, that neuer vnder-tooke any thing commicall, vainely: And were but the vaine names of commedies changde for the titles of Commodities, or of Playes for Pleas; you should see all those grand censors, that now stile them such vanities, flock to them for the maine grace of their grauities: especially this authors Commedies, that are so fram'd to the life, that they serue for the most common Commentaries, of all the actions of our liues.

The "neuer writer" continues in this Epistle to proclaim the great power of this play and its author to instill "witte" into the audience, finally intoning,

And beleeue this, that when hee is gon, and his Commedies out of sale, you will scramble for them, and set vp a new English Inquisition. Take this for a warning, and at the perrill of your pleasures losse, and Iudgements, refuse not, nor like this the less, for not being sullied, with the smoaky breath of the multitude; but thanke fortune for the scape it hath made amongst you. Since by the grand possessors wills I beleeue you should haue prayd for them rather then beene prayd. And so I leaue all such to bee prayd for (for the states of their wits healths) that will not praise it. *Vale.*

The fact that the writer calls himself a "neuer writer" and calls the play, performed since 1602/1603, "new," suggests, as R. A. Foakes argues, that the epistle could have been "a publisher's blurb, written by someone with a legal turn of mind to present a play not seen for some years, and newly published."[22] The strongest argument for not assigning the epistle to Shakespeare is its omission from the Folio. Yet, the printing of the play in the Folio collection was suspended for a period of time, apparently because the printers had not received permission from the owners of the play, and then abandoned; when permission was finally granted, the play was hastily worked into a different place in the collection, creating spacing and continuity problems.[23]

Greg and several critics who have followed him speculate that the Quarto was surreptitiously printed with an unknowingly false title page and that the printers attempted to placate the angry King's Men by altering the title page and adding the epistle in the second issue.[24] However, Quarto 1 appears to have been printed directly from foul papers,[25] so the play's printing in 1609 was probably not unauthorized or surreptitious. The 1603 Stationers' Register entry may not have been a "blocking entry," suggesting authorization, but an unauthorized one, which would explain why the play was not printed in this year, and the 1609 entry by a different printer was thus the authorized entry rather than the unauthorized one. It is doubtful that the Quarto printers would have bothered to stop press and correct an edition if it was a piracy; evidence in other Shakespearian "bad" Quartos suggests that printers of such texts paid little attention to the condition of the text and apparently did not heed complaints from the rightful owners.

The epistle does not acknowledge or apologize for piracy, and there is no evidence that the printing of the Quarto was interrupted for anything other than to make some type of correction or addition, as in the case of the 1600 Quarto 1 of *2 Henry IV,* whose second issue inserted the politically controversial scene of 3.1, presumably written out by

Shakespeare on a separate sheet (this Quarto and the *Troilus and Cressida* Quarto were not published by the same printers). The epistle may even have been inserted into the Quarto of *Troilus and Cressida* when printing was interrupted to make several corrections other than in the title page. Kenneth Palmer argues that disturbances in setting Quarto 1 suggest that some material may have been added to 3.2, the "wooing" scene, which becomes the focus of the substituted second state title page, and perhaps to 3.1 during printing.[26]

Because the epistle writer attacks those "grand censors" who consider the author's plays "vanities" and asserts that the play, which has made a "scape," serves as commentary for "actions of all our liues," E. A. J. Honigmann concludes that the play had been censored because it indirectly referred to Essex's rebellion and could not be publicly presented, except at Cambridge, until after the deaths of Robert Cecil and others who would have taken offense.[27] Yet the epistle may not refer to censorship but to the play's theatrical failure during the War of the Theatres. The writer's use of "clapper-clawd," a term Thersites repeats in 5.4 (sig. L2ᵛ), the self-mocking tone of his praise of the play's author, and his stubborn refusal to accept the unenthusiastic response of an audience of "such dull and heauy-witted wordlings" to the comedy suggest that Shakespeare, chafing at the audience's reaction to the play, wrote or participated in the writing of the epistle. The writer's command of legal terms may not have been beyond the reach of Shakespeare, who had displayed his familiarity with the law in *The Merchant of Venice* and other plays.[28] The printer of the 1622 Quarto 1 of *Othello* states that "to set forth a booke without an Epistle, were like to the old English prouerbe, *A belew coat without a badge,* & the Author being dead, I thought good to take that piece of worke vpon mee," implying that a dramatist often provided his own epistle.

If the epistle was written by Shakespeare or someone familiar with the play's performances, its complaints should be taken more seriously to represent the displeasure of the audience with the play itself rather than the displeasure of the King's Men with the piracy of their text. Critics such as Greg and Gary Taylor, who dates the epistle 1603 and assigns it to someone associated with the Inns of Court, whom he conjectures surreptitiously acquired the foul papers,[29] have been more concerned with the epistle's remarks about the play being new and never clapper-clawed than with the bulk of its comments which castigate a specific type of unappreciative audience. The epistle writer's continued defense of the theatrical value of the author and this particular play, "So much and such fauored salt of witte is in his Commedies, that they seeme (for their height of pleasure) to be borne in that sea that brought forth *Venus*. Amongst all there is none more witty than this," and his continued and sardonic attack of those who do not appreciate the commercial value of such wit, like the grand censors, and perhaps the grand possessors who refused to release it, imply that the play had fared badly with an audience which did not appreciate it. The author's title of "a neuer writer" may have been Shakespeare's ironic comment on his stinging failure as dramatist in this play.

Judging from the legal allusions in the epistle and epilogue, the play was originally performed at the Inns of Court, and the play's salty wit apparently irritated this audience, so recently offended by Jonson's *Poetaster*, more than it entertained them. As Kenneth Muir argues, the insertion of the epistle and the cancellation of the title page seem to suggest that "the play was not successful enough to remain for long in the Globe repertory."[30] The King's Men/Globe theatre advertisement in the first state of the Quarto may have been incorrect as the play may only have been performed by the Chamberlain's Men privately, and the advertisement was subsequently replaced with a title page and epistle intended to attract a literary audience after the play failed to attract a theatrical one.

A few allusions within the play suggest it was, like *Hamlet*, involved in the War of the Theatres begun by John Marston's portrayals of Ben Jonson in *Histriomastix* (1598/1599), *Jack Drum's Entertainment* (1600), and *What You Will* (1601), continued by Thomas Dekker in *Satiromastix* (1602), and answered by Jonson in *Every Man Out of His Humor* (1599), *Cynthia's Revels* (1600) and *Poetaster* (1601). The epistle of *Troilus and Cressida* particularly marks the play as Shakespeare's contribution to this *Poetomachia*. Shakespeare (who, according to a speech given by Will Kemp in *The Second Part of the Return from Parnassus*, gave Jonson, as author of *Poetaster*, a "purge that made him beray his credit"[31]) mocks *Poetaster* by borrowing its "armed" prologue. In addition, Shakepeare's use of "masticke" to describe Thersites in 1.3 alludes to *Histriomastix*, which presents the story of Troilus and Cressida in a play within the play,[32] and *Satiromastix*.[33]

There are also verbal echoes between the Quarto epistle in *Troilus and Cressida* and Jonson's "apologeticall Dialogue," which was "only once spoken vpon the Stage" as an Epilogue to *Poetaster*, and between the

Quarto epistle and Dekker's preface to *Satiromastix*. The Dialogue defends the genre of comedy by comparing Jonson's satirical comedy to those by Aristophanes, Persius, and Juvenal, while the epistle defends the genre of comedy by comparing Shakespeare's satirical comedy to those of Terence and Plautus. The Dialogue's author also mocks the players among the audience who took offense to his play (Folio, sig. Gg2):

> It is true, I tax'd 'hem,
> And yet, but some; and those so sparingly,
> And all the rest might haue sate still, vnquestion'd,
> Had they but had the wit, or conscience,
> To thinke well of themselues.

And the Epistle writer similarly mocks the witless members of the audience:

> And all such dull and heauy-witted worldlings, as were neuer capable of the witte of a Commedie, comming by report of them to his [Shakespeare's] representations, haue found that witte there, that they neuer found in themselues, and haue parted better wittied then they came: feeling an edge of witte set vpon them, more than euer they dreamd they had braine to grinde it on.[34]

The original performance of Jonson's *Poetaster* had provoked angry reactions from the audience, particularly the lawyers, players, and soldiers whom the play had satirized, and Jonson may have barely escaped legal prosecution for libel; it seems probable that this audience constitutes the "grand censors" to which the writer of the epistle of *Troilius and Cressida* refers.

Or does the epistle single out the dramatists involved in the War of the Theatres as the "grand censors" who are not able to produce witty plays? Dekker's comment on Jonson in his preface (Quarto, sigs. A3-A3ᵛ) to *Satiromastix*, a play performed by Shakespeare's company,

> If before *Apollo* himselfe (who is *Coronator Poetarum*) an *Inquisition* should be taken touching this lamentable merry murdering of Innocent Poetry: all mount *Helicon* to *Bun-hill*, it would be found on the *Poetasters* side *se defendendo,*

echoes in the *Troilus and Cressida* epistle writer's comment that when Shakespeare is gone and his plays out of sale, "You will scramble for them, and set vp a new English Inquisition." George E. Rowe agrees that *Troilus and Cressida* is the Shakespearian "purge" described by Will

Kemp and "presents a powerful, if indirect, analysis of the causes, characteristics, and ultimate futility of the theatrical quarrel itself."[35] Shakespeare had first commented on this "throwing about of Braines" some months earlier in an addition to the text of *Hamlet* and had acknowledged that "there was for a while, no mony bid for argument, vnlesse the Poet and the Player went to Cuffes in the Question"; he may have decided to go to cuffs himself with an entire play. The futile War of the Trojans in *Troilus and Cressida,* set in ancient times as was *Poetaster,* in its revised form satirizes the futile War of the Theatres.

Whether the "grand censors" referred generally to the lawyers in attendance at an Inns of Court performance, or referred specifically to an audience, including lawyers and dramatists, which had been angered by *Poetaster,* Shakespeare's play appears to have received the same unappreciative response as Jonson's satiric play. Jonson's stinging apologetical Dialogue was prohibited after a single performance, and he states in the 1602 Quarto edition of the play (sig. N1$^v$) that he was restrained by "Authoritie" from printing it (it first appeared in print in the 1616 Folio of his works). The printer of the first issue of *Troilus and Cressida* may have feared the same censure and thus at first withheld the epistle, finally printing it in the second state of Quarto 1 without the author's name but with the pseudonym of "a neuer writer."

Numerous loose ends and duplications within the Quarto text suggest that it was printed from Shakespeare's foul papers, which were reworked during the course of composition. For example, the description of Ajax before he appears on stage bears little resemblance to the character as he is portrayed, so Shakespeare changed his conception of the character as he wrote. It is also possible that, as Kenneth Palmer argues, Shakespeare added the long exchange in 3.2 (sigs. F2-F2$^v$) between Troilus and Cressida beginning with Cressida's comment, "Will you walke in my Lord," and concluding forty lines later with her repetition of the same line[36] so that Troilus's seduction of Cressida in Act 3 was originally as abrupt as Diomede's seduction of her in Act 5.

The prologue and the description of Thersites's "masticke" jaws, which allude to *Poetaster, Histriomastix,* and *Satiromastix,* appear only in the Folio text. Shakespeare apparently revised *Troilus and Cressida* after composition in order to comment satirically on the War of the Theatres by adding the prologue and reworking characters' speeches, and at a later point, altering the play's ending in the theatrical manuscript which served as copy for the Folio.[37] The thirty-one-line prologue, which "leapes ore the vaunt and firstlings of those broyles, / Beginning in the middle" (TLN 28–29) of the Trojan war by narrating the arrival of the Greeks in Troy, served at least two purposes: it set the historical perspective of the Trojan War and it set the historical perspective of the Poets' "broyles."[38] The prologue's comment after summarizing the causes of the Trojan war, "And that's the Quarrell" (TLN 11), could allude to the "quarrell," the contemporary term for the Jonson-Marston feud.[39]

Other probable alterations between the Quarto and Folio texts also serve the two purposes of establishing the old Trojan War and the new Trojan War. At least one speech prepares the audience for a character who has not yet been seen: in the Folio only, Agamemnon interrupts Ulysses's long conciliatory speech to the Trojans in 1.3 (TLN 529–533) with the comment:

> Speak Prince of *Ithaca,* and be't of lesse expect:
> That matter needlesse of importlesse burthen
> Diuide thy lips; then we are confident
> When ranke *Thersites* opes his Masticke jawes,
> We shall heare Musicke, Wit, and Oracle.

Shakespeare apparently added the passage, which prefigures Thersites's role in the rest of the play, at some point after he decided to establish him as a satiric commentator on the Trojan War and the Poets' War.[40] Another passage more directly refers to past and future events. Agamemnon's greeting of his army in Quarto 4.5 (sig. I3), "Worthy all armes as welcome as to one / That would be rid of such an enemy. / From heart of very heart, great *Hector* welcome," has a six-line insertion between lines two and three in the Folio (TLN 2732–2737):

> But that's no welcome: vnderstand more cleere
> What's past, and what's to come, is strew'd with huskes
> And formelesse ruine of obliuion:
> But in this extant moment, faith and troth,
> Strain'd purely from all hollow bias drawing
> Bids thee with most diuine integritie.

Agamemnon offers this triple perspective of time, which becomes the central theme throughout the play, to both his army and the audience.

Although some of the numerous single-word or short speech variants between the Quarto and Folio texts do not appear to follow a pattern, other Folio additions subtly enhance a character's speech. For example, in the Quarto at the end of a speech in 4.5 (sigs. I2-I2ᵛ) Agamemnon asks:

> *Aga.*  *Vlisses:* what Troyan is that same that lookes so heauy?
> *Vlis.*  The yongest sonne of *Priam,*  a true knight,
>          Not yet mature, yet matchlesse firme of word,
>          . . . . .
>          They call him *Troylus.*

However, the passage varies in the Folio, with the insertion of an extra line by Ulysses and a duplication, possibly from a marginal addition, in his description of Troilus (TLN 2655–2670):

> *Vlis.*  They are oppos'd already.
> *Aga.*  What Trojan is that same that lookes so heauy?
> *Vlis.*  The yongest Sonne of *Priam;*
>          A true Knight; they call him *Troylus;*
>          Not yet mature, yet matchlesse firme of word,
>          . . . . .
>          They call him *Troylus.*

The addition of Ulysses's line, "They are oppos'd already," coincides with other later insertions in the Folio speeches of Ulysses, perhaps as Shakespeare's attempt to strengthen his role; the Folio thus seems to present a revised version rather than the original version of the passage.

Shakespeare also reworked the play's conclusion after he had reworked these other passages. Troilus's comment to Pandarus, "Hence broker, lacky, ignomyny, shame, / Pursue thy life, and liue aye with thy name," appears at the end of play in the Quarto (sig. M1ᵛ), immediately preceding the epilogue; the passage appears in this place and also earlier in 5.3 in the Folio text (TLN 3571–3572, 3329–3330). Nevill Coghill and Gary Taylor have each argued that Shakespeare moved the passage to 5.3 after dispensing with the epilogue, intended only for a private audience, when reworking the play for a public audience, but that the canceled passage was printed inadvertently in 5.10.[41] Pandarus's bawdy pun in the Quarto and Folio epilogue (sig. M1ᵛ; TLN 3577–3581),

> Let me see,
> Full merrily the humble Bee doth sing,
> Till he hath lost his hony and his sting.
> And being once subdude in armed taile,
> Sweet hony, and sweet notes together faile,

seem to attack that "B" with the "armed" tale, Ben Jonson (whose name frequently appeared on Quarto title pages as "B.I."), accused by John Marston of "venerie" as well as personal satire.[42] If Shakespeare decided to cancel the epilogue, it may have been at some point after the audience's interest in the War of the Theatres had passed and he planned to rework the play, particularly in the concluding act, for later public theatre audiences.

Evidence from the variant texts of *Troilus and Cressida* suggests that the first and second states of the Quarto represent the play as originally composed in the foul papers for a private theatre audience, and that the Folio represents the play as immediately reworked in a theatrical manuscript to capitalize on that audience's interest in the newly intensified War of the Theatres. In anticipation of the printing of an edition in 1603, the foul papers apparently acquired an epistle by Shakespeare or someone familiar with the 1601 performed text of *Poetaster,* including the once-performed "apologeticall Dialogue," and the 1602 printed text of *Satiromastix.* When the play was finally issued in 1609 from foul papers, its printing was interrupted to correct an inadvertently false title page and to insert the epistle, and perhaps the additions in the wooing scene, 3.2, which had been written out on separate leaves. Shakespeare revised the theatrical manuscript which served as Folio copy at least once between 1602 and 1603, in "the middle" of the Jonson-Marston-Dekker "broyles," and may have tinkered with it again before 1609 for a planned revival of the play for the King's Men at the Globe. Thus, as R. A. Foakes argues, the Folio "seems to represent the latest Shakespearian version we have of the play";[43] yet this text derives not simply from the "latest" version but from the composite version, offering an endlessly revisable vision of the play.


## Othello

Modern editors and critics have been nearly unanimous in arguing that *Othello,* which exists in two substantively variant texts, the 1622 Quarto and 1623 Folio, can serve as a textbook example of, although not an archetype for, authorial revision in Shakespeare's plays after performance. David Bevington, skeptical of authorial revision in other Shakespearian plays, argues of *Othello* that "indeed we may see here a genuine Shake-spearean revision showing the author at work when evidently he was not under constraint to eliminate material for practical considerations."[44] M. R. Ridley had earlier suggested that the Quarto and Folio texts contain Shakespeare's first and second thoughts as well as nonauthorial variants.[45] Nevill Coghill followed in seeing Shakespeare's *"strategy of revision"* in his alteration of passages with which he did not seem wholly satisfied in performance while he was purging oaths for a revival of the play in or after 1606, and these alterations included revising the role of Emilia in the last two acts to "endear" her to the audience.[46] E. A. J. Honigmann supported Coghill's conclusions, deciding that Shakespeare revised the play to sharpen the play's sexual imagery.[47] Thus Norman Sanders's recent assertion that the Quarto and Folio represent "two Shakespearian versions" of the play[48] raises little objection from critics who dismiss revision in such plays as *King Lear*. None of these critics sees revision within the Quarto text itself; yet there is evidence of revision during composition within the Quarto as well as evidence of revision after performance between the Quarto and Folio, suggesting that Shakespeare reworked at least the ending of his play in his foul papers and reworked it again at some later period in a theatrical manuscript.

The Quarto and Folio texts of *Othello* were printed within the same year (the majority of typesetting for the First Folio occurred during 1622), so it is unlikely that the one hundred sixty lines which appear only in the Folio were added during that year. The fact that the two texts were printed nearly simultaneously rather than decades apart may explain why editors have been so willing to recognize authorial revision in this play and to dismiss it in all of the other plays; ironically, these editors support authorial revision in texts which were *not* printed in the author's lifetime. As the play had been performed since 1604, behind the texts of the play were manuscript copies which had existed for some years. The Quarto text was printed from foul papers or a scribal transcript of them, and the Folio text derived from a reworked theatrical manuscript, probably authorial, which acquired editorial corrections, including the purging of oaths and the alteration of difficult passages, before being printed.[49] Hundreds of the variants between the two texts are classed by Stanley Wells, among others, as "literary sophistications."[50]

More significant variants include the numerous passages absent from the Quarto but printed in the Folio. Two notable absences in the Quarto are the Willow Song, sung by Desdemona in 4.3, and a reference to it in 5.2. Greg, arguing that the Folio-only passages were cut from the Quarto rather than added to the Folio, conjectures that the song was cut for a revival in which a non-singing boy played Desdemona.[51] However, Greg ignores the Quarto title-page evidence that the play had been "diuerse times acted at the Globe and at the Black-Friers," so it is possible that the play was subjected to revisions when it moved from a public to a private theatre.[52] The King's Men acted the play at Whitehall in 1604, at the Globe and in Oxford in 1610, again at court in 1612/13 for the marriage festivities of Princess Elizabeth,[53] and apparently at Blackfriars after 1608.

The Quarto is the earlier text, and most of the editors and critics who argue for later revision see the Folio-only passages as later additions, for artistic reasons, to the Folio rather than earlier cuts, for theatrical reasons, from the Quarto which were restored in the Folio.[54] Norman Sanders notes that the Folio-only passages enhance clear exposition, character portrayal, psychological verisimilitude, dramatic effect, unnatural images of Desdemona's choice of a husband, and the supernatural quality of Othello's love.[55] The additions range from one line to whole speeches, and most are self-contained insertions into the middle of a character's speech or an exchange between characters which elaborate on the current situation. One example is Roderigo's seventeen-line expansion in 1.1 in his speech warning Brabantio that his daughter is in bed with Othello: Roderigo further emphasizes in the addition that Desdemona has "made a grosse reuolt" and also relates how she managed to steal from her father's house, escorted by a "Gundelier" (TLN 134–150); he provides the audience with information it does not receive elsewhere in the play.

The scene with the inserted song, 4.3, also has a number of other insertions, including a five-line exchange between Desdemona and Emilia on women who "abuse" their husbands with cuckoldry, and an eighteen-line addition to Emilia's final speech in the scene on husbands' treatment of wives which concludes, "Then let them vse vs well: else let them know, / The illes we do, their illes instruct vs so" (TLN 3030–3034, 3059–3076). The entire passage serves as an ironic prefigurement of the events of the last act. Honigmann argues that Shakespeare also made "sexually specific" additions, including the Willow Song, after performance to sharpen the play's moral commentary on sexual abnormality.[56]

Other additions to the speeches of Emilia in the last two acts serve, as Coghill has demonstrated, to soften her character and absolve her of complicity in Iago's plotting with the stolen handkerchief, as well as to offer dramatic perspective to the preceding events. In two additional passages in 5.2 (TLN 3425–3429, 3468–3478) she laments Desdemona's murder, reaching a peak in the last passage:

> Villany, villany, villany:
> I thinke vpon't, I thinke: I smel't: O Villainy:
> I thought so then: Ile kill my selfe for greefe.
> O villany, villany!

These additions also inform the newly entered Montano, Gratiano, and Iago that Desdemona has been murdered, as Coghill points out.[57] Yet Ridley has argued that some variants in the Folio text of *Othello* may have been made at actors' requests or reflect actors' contributions which were entered into the manuscript from which the Folio was printed,[58] and the repetitive nature of this addition to Emilia's speech suggests an actor, if not the author, attempting to emphasize the dramatic intensity of her grief.

At least one of the Folio "additions" in Othello's speech in 5.2 after his murder of Desdemona and Iago's murder of Emilia reveals Shakespeare's reworking of the play's ending in the foul papers and again in the theatrical manuscript. In both texts, Montano announces that he has taken a weapon from Othello; in the Quarto (sig. M4$^v$) he tells Gratiano, "Take your weapon, / Which I haue here recouered from the Moore," while in the Folio (TLN 3536–3537) he tells him, "Take you this weapon / Which I haue recouer'd from the Moore." In the Quarto, Othello seizes a weapon from Gratiano, and in the Folio Othello is already armed with his own weapon (Emilia had told Othello earlier in the scene, "I care not for thy sword" [sig. M3$^v$; TLN 3442], so he may have been armed from the beginning of the scene).[59] After disarming Othello, Montano tells Gratiano to "guard the dore without" and warns him not to let Othello escape. Apparently both Montano and Gratiano exit the stage at this point: in the Quarto, the stage direction reads "Exit Montano and Gratiano," while in the Folio, the stage direction "Exit" follows at the end of Montano's speech. Othello then laments in both the Quarto and Folio texts, "I am not valiant neither, / But every puny whipster gets my sword" (sig. M4$^v$; 3541–3542).

Yet Othello twice announces that he has again armed himself. He first admits (sig. M4$^v$; TLN 3551–3558):

> I haue another weapon in this chamber,
> It is a sword of Spaine, the Ise brookes temper;
> Oh heere it is: Vnkle I must come forth.

The Quarto stage direction here, "Gra. *within*.," which does not appear in the Folio, suggests that Gratiano has remained onstage but hears only part of Othello's speech. Gratiano advises him not to attempt escape and adds, "Thou hast no weapon." Othello tells him, "Looke in vpon me then, and speake to [with *F*] me, / Or naked as I am I will assault thee." Gratiano inquires, "What is the matter?" and Othello responds (sigs. M4ᵛ-N1; TLN 3559–3565):

> Behold, I haue a weapon:
> A better neuer did it selfe sustaine
> Vpon a Souldiers thigh. I haue seene the day,
> That with this little arme, and this good sword,
> I haue made my way through more impediments,
> Then twenty times you [your *F*] stop. But O vaine boast
> Who can controule his Fate? tis not so now.

At this point in the Quarto text, Othello concludes his speech with a seeming non sequitur, "Pale as thy smocke: when we shall meete at count, / This looke of thine, will hurle my soule from heauen"; apparently he is looking at the dead Desdemona and considering the sin he has committed by murdering her. However, in the Folio, seven additional lines appear between "Who can control . . . Tis not so now," and "Pale as thy smocke . . . at compt." In an apparent addition, Othello once more tells Gratiano that he is armed (TLN 3566–3572):

> Be not affraid, though you do see me weapon'd:
> Heere is my iournies end, heere is my butt
> And verie Sea-marke of my vtmost Saile.
> Do you go backe dismaid? 'Tis a lost feare:
> Man but a Rush against *Othello*'s brest,
> And he retires. Where should Othello go?
> Now: how dost thou looke now? Oh ill-Starr'd wench.

Because the last line of the passage, "Now: how dost thou look" helps to introduce the original line which follows it, "Pale as thy Smocke," this Folio passage appears to be a restored cut from the original play rather than an addition to the later play. If the passage were a later addition it would have been Shakespeare's attempt to fill in a rather abrupt return to the subject of the dead Desdemona marked by "Pale as thy smocke."

This restored cut (or later addition) also marks the third declaration by Othello within fifteen lines that he has another weapon, and although it may have been a second-thought addition in the original text, it more plausibly signals that the other two passages and Montano's mention of having stripped Othello of another weapon were reworkings of the end of the play during or after composition in the foul papers. Shakespeare may have originally written one of the three passages in which Othello admits that he is armed, then canceled it and started over with a second version, and finally ended with three versions. The variant stage directions in Quarto and Folio, and Gratiano's oddly placed question, "What's the matter?" after Othello's first announcement that he will come forth make it clear that the first version is the one in which Othello warns, "Behold, I haue a weapon."

Perhaps most of the final actions of Othello, beginning with Montano's remark that he has taken a weapon from him and concluding with Othello's suicide with another weapon (sigs. M4$^V$-N2; TLN 3536–3671) and Cassio's remark, "This did I feare, but thought he had no weapon," were heavily revised in the foul papers, and at least the passage beginning, "Be not affraid, though you do see me weapon'd," was cut to omit one of the duplications. Furthermore, the alteration in Montano's mention to Gratiano of "your weapon" in the Quarto to "this weapon" in the Folio suggests that Shakespeare later tried to clear up the duplications in his fair copy. The reworkings may have been the result of Shakespeare's observation of the scene in rehearsal or performance, so that the textual irregularities in the Quarto derive from these reworked foul papers if not a transcript of them.[60] The few passages which appear in the Quarto but not in the Folio were not accidentally omitted in the Folio, as most critics have asserted, but deliberately cut by Shakespeare. As the revising dramatist, Shakespeare controlled the shaping vision of *Othello*.

The Quarto and Folio texts of *Hamlet, Troilus and Cressida,* and *Othello* thus offer substantiating canonical evidence of consciously planned and deliberately made authorial revision. Even when the revision was minor, it served a function; as Kerrigan argues, "the subtlest attention is paid in revision to that which holds between characters, and between characters and their senses of self."[61] In these three plays, it is the sense of self of Hamlet, Thersites, Ulysses, Othello, and other major and minor characters which undergoes stunning dramatic revision; these revisions re-determined the interlocking shapes of the plot, the themes, the structure, and the settings of these plays as well as what holds between characters. Furthermore, in each case Shakespeare offered the texts of his plays as representations of the composition and revision *process,* insisting on their very transmutability and infiniteness. He understood each play as not simply finally resulting from but as continuously representing this process. Arguments that dismiss the possibility of revision or approve the canonical sanctity of the tragedies ignore this process; therefore they cannot illuminate but rather they obscure, circumscribing a false, external, and dangerously limiting interpretation of the plays and their playwright which does not enlighten or elucidate but darkens and subjugates.

# ❧ 6 ❧

# Revising *King Lear* and
# Revising "Theory"

T. H. Howard-Hill noted in 1985 that "more has been written about the text of *King Lear* in the last six years than in any similar span of years before," with the result that "in a short time the theory that Shakespeare substantially revised his early version of the play has become almost commonplace in journal articles on *Lear*."[1] This "commonplace" and now routine reconsideration of textual theories about *King Lear* and consequently Shakespeare's other plays inevitably affects the critical interpretations and theoretical discourses which are derived from them. When new historicist, deconstructive, semiotic, psychoanalytic, or feminist and gender critics discuss and analyze the "text" of a Shakespearian play, they are, in great measure, creating the "text" as they interpret it; for them, the word "text" is synonymous with "literary work" and is concerned with that work's inherent meaning and possible interpretations. For a textual scholar the "text" is primarily the physical object that descends from the author in all its various forms and permutations, and is also in some measure created by the editor and other agents who reproduce it in print.

Yet that abstract textuality sought by literary critics is still based on the physical property or materiality of the text; since the advent of the "New Bibliography," the word text has connoted an edited text—not the original single or multiple versions of the text, but one created and synthesized through the editorial reconstruction process. Both textual and literary critics must now reevaluate and redefine the idea of "the text"; it is no longer editorially or theoretically composite or finite, but multiple and ever-revising. The literary interpretations of the interlocking elements of plot, structure, setting, theme, and characterization, and the critical ideologies and methodologies used to understand them, *all* depend on their establishment in a physical text. If, as has become apparent, the conflated physical text is fraudulent because it synthesizes and reduces the multiple versions produced by the author in the process of revision, methods of textual and literary analysis for dealing with such texts are also fraudulent (as Jerome McGann, Hans Walter Gabler, Bernard Brun, Michael Warren, Gary Taylor, Steven Urkowitz, Stanley Wells, and others have so recently argued).

The specific revisions in *King Lear* provide ample material for a discussion of the possible reasons for and implications of the author's changing treatment of the text. More important, by using *King Lear,* especially the character of Cordelia, as an example, I will show how a "theory" of textual revision *establishes* and *determines* a "theory" of literary criticism.

## The Texts of *King Lear*

The Folio text of *King Lear* varies substantively from the Quarto: the Quarto contains about three hundred lines which are not in the Folio, the Folio has about one hundred lines not in the Quarto, and there are more than eight hundred fifty verbal variants between them.[2] The textual irregularities of Quarto 1, which are characteristic of Shakespeare's first drafts, suggest that it was printed from foul papers. The 1619 Quarto 2 was an unauthorized reprint, like several others printed by Thomas Pavier, of Quarto 1, with the false date of 1608. The Folio was printed from Quarto 2.[3] Because the 1608 Quarto 1 of *King Lear* was for many years considered a memorial reconstruction which was corrupted by errors, it was not held to be a reliable base upon which to judge variants as representing revisions in the Folio text.

Madeleine Doran first challenged this conception of Quarto 1 as unreliable by arguing in 1931 that the variants between it and the Folio stemmed primarily from authorial revision within each copy; she asserted that the first Quarto represented Shakespeare's original and extensively revised manuscript, with a heightening of Edmund's role, and the Folio represented the prompt-copy transcript of the original, which had been censored, abridged, and somewhat revised.[4] Doran's theories provoked this skeptical response from W. W. Greg:

Besides a certain improbability in such extensive literary revision, especially after the foul papers had been handed over, the theory had to meet the difficulty of believing that Shakespeare, and that at the height of his powers, could ever have written the clumsy and fumbling lines we find in Q, or that these could in general represent a stage in the development of F.

Greg dismissed arguments of "literary revision once a play has taken final form in the prompt-book," citing E. K. Chambers's essay on "The Disintegration of Shakespeare" for support. Greg saw the omissions in the Quarto as accidental and the omissions in the Folio as due to externally imposed censorship and theatrical cutting.[5]

By 1960, G. I. Duthie, who had agreed with Alice Walker's conclusion that Quarto 1 was a reported text, concluded that there was "no basis for any theory of a Shakespearian revision separating Q1 and F (apart from whatever share Shakespeare may have had in the work of abridgement)."[6] Editions such as Kenneth Muir's, published in 1952 and revised in 1972, did not even note the possibility of authorial revision in analyses of the texts of the play. Greg's and Duthie's rejections of revision theories remained unchallenged, despite Kristian Smidt's 1964 assertion that each text represented equally authentic variant editions deriving from authorial papers,[7] and despite E. A. J. Honigmann's 1965 argument for unstable second-thought variants in the play, until Michael Warren in 1976 provoked a reconsideration of revision between the Quarto and Folio texts. Warren's conclusion that the Quarto presents a weak Edgar and a strong Albany and the Folio a strong Edgar and a weak Albany allowed him to assert that there is no single "ideal play" of *King Lear,* that the Quarto is an authoritative version of the play, and that the Folio is "Shakespeare's considered modification of the earlier text."[8]

Because P. W. K. Stone saw Quarto 1 as a reported text, he argued in his 1980 study, *The Textual History of King Lear,* for editorial rather than authorial revision between it and the Folio text.[9] However, in the same year Gary Taylor traced the differing portrayals of the war that divides Lear's kingdom in each text, concluding that the Quarto had the same authority as the Folio and that "it is hard to believe that such a succession of interrelated changes happened by accident, and it would be churlish (let alone unnecessary) to attribute them to anyone but Shakespeare."[10] Also in 1980, Steven Urkowitz in *Shakespeare's Revision of King Lear* examined textual variants in dramatic contexts in several scenes, such as those in 4.2 which alter the relationship between Goneril and Albany, those in players' entrances and exits, those in the entrance of Cordelia in 4.4, those in the speeches of Kent and the Gentleman, particularly in 3.1, and those throughout the role of Albany. Urkowitz concluded that

> the Quarto was printed from Shakespeare's foul papers, and the Folio was printed from the Quarto version that was carefully brought into agreement with the official prompt book. The prompt book itself embodied all of Shakespeare's own revisions, including additions, cuts, substitutions, and rear-rangements. The Quarto and Folio do not represent two partial copies of a single original, but instead they are different stages of a composition, an early and a final draft.

Urkowitz assigned the revisions to the period immediately after the completion of the foul papers and before the preparation of the prompt book.[11] His arguments that each text of the play has its own authority and that revisions were added to a post–foul paper manuscript, in this case the prompt-copy, were also raised in Peter Blayney's study of Quarto 1; he concluded in 1982 that as the Folio derives partly from the Quarto and partly from another source which altered many Quarto readings, "if the alterations can be shown to be of high authority, they may be either authoritative corrections of a corrupt Q text or Shakespearean revisions of an earlier authoritative draft."[12]

The earlier conclusions of Warren, Taylor, and Urkowitz about revisions in characters and themes were restated and expanded in 1983 in *The Division of the Kingdoms,* along with new conclusions by other scholars who had begun studying the relationship of the Quarto and Folio texts. Roger Warren examined the Folio omission of Lear's mock trial of Goneril and Regan in 3.6 and concluded that Shakespeare cut the passage to give the same type of material more effective and devel-oped treatment later in the play, particularly in 4.6.[13] Several contributors discussed revisions in the roles of particular characters: Michael Warren argued that the Folio diminishes the Quarto role of Kent; Thomas Clayton found a more intense and dramatic Lear in the last acts of the Folio than in the Quarto; Beth Goldring saw a slightly stronger Cordelia in 1.1 in the Folio than in the Quarto; Randall McLeod argued for the greater moral ambiguity in the Folio portrayals of Goneril, Regan, and Edmund but defended the integrity of each text; and John Kerrigan asserted that the Folio Fool is dramatically superior to his Quarto counterpart.[14] Gary Taylor dismissed external censorship as the cause of the revisions between the Quarto, printed from foul papers, and the Folio, printed from a marked-up copy of Quarto 2 (itself deriving from an authorially revised prompt book), and proposed that the play was revised during the winter of 1609–10, most probably for the opening of Blackfriars.[15] Only one of the contributors to *The Division of the Kingdoms,* Paul Werstine,[16] did not assert that the Folio variants resulted from Shakespeare's deliberate rewriting of his original text as printed in the Quarto to suit his own artistic demands.

Sidney Thomas, John L. Murphy, Marion Trousdale, and a few other reviewers of *Shakespeare's Revision of King Lear* and *The Division of the Kingdoms* have questioned the individual theories and bibliographic methods of these revisionists and have rejected revision as the primary cause of variants between the texts. They have especially objected to the contributors' rejection of traditional editions of *King Lear,* which conflate Quarto and Folio readings.[17] Kenneth Muir particularly attacked the "new and proselytizing orthodoxy" of printing the two texts as separate and equally authoritative plays.[18] Other reviewers, such as Honigmann and Howard-Hill, have offered more cautious support of some of the revision theories, agreeing that the possibility of authorial revision should be taken into account in further editions and studies of the play.[19] Yet, Howard-Hill pointed out that in the study of variants due to revision in *The Division of the Kingdoms,*

> the trivial or indifferent character of many of the variations which are brought forward to illustrate revision can allow readers reasonably to suspect that (although textual variations do affect the character of the play in which they appear, and variations as numerous as those in Q and F must have considerable effects) the distinctive literary consequences of the variation are more a measure of the critical sensitivity of the scholars who interpret them than an indication of a purposed, consistent revision of an existing play into another distinct form.[20]

However, Michael Warren had argued in his 1976 essay that Shakespeare's audience showed the same sensitivity as the modern critics. Warren contended that "play texts are scripts for performance; when they are realized on the stage, presence, absence, action, inaction, speech, and silence have far more impact than when they are noted on the printed page."[21]

Discussion of revision in *King Lear* has continued; for example, in 1985 R. A. Foakes argued that the Folio's alterations in the speeches of the Fool present him as more sardonically mocking than in the Quarto and concluded that "there seems little doubt that the changes were made as conscious revision, and that Shakespeare was responsible for most if not all of them."[22] The editors of the 1986 Oxford *Complete Works* (Stanley Wells, Gary Taylor, John Jowett, and William Montgomery) print the Quarto and Folio texts as two separate plays, *The History of King Lear* and *The Tragedy of King Lear,* in their edition. Taylor argues that printer's copy consisted of a copy of Quarto 2 annotated with a manuscript, either theatrical or nontheatrical, derived from Quarto 1, so that Shakespeare's initial revisions were made on a copy of Quarto 1.[23]

The textual variants in the Quarto and Folio have thus recently been catalogued and related to extensive revision in the play's major themes, such as war and family relationships, and figures, such as Lear, Kent, Albany, Edgar, and the Fool. Yet very little attention, with the exception of brief discussions by Steven Urkowitz and Beth Goldring, has been paid to the textual variants and deliberate revisions in the dialogue of and about Cordelia which establish and define her character and which in great measure *create* the presentation of other major characters and themes in each text. Cordelia is not a supporting, peripheral, or dispensable character, as previous critics have argued, but an essential, central, and foundationally necessary character, and *all* of the lines which frame and contain her character have an intrinsic though unrecognized worth. Warren, Taylor, and Urkowitz, for example, have not recognized their value; each has examined the omission of eighty lines in the 1623 Folio text which appear in the 1608 Quarto text and refer to the French army's impending invasion of Lear's kingdom. These critics claim that the substantial omission of these Quarto lines in the Folio may shift the audience's view of war from an "unprovoked" foreign invasion to a "provoked" civil rebellion. In discussing the Folio's omission of these lines and seventy-four others in Acts 3 and 4 of Quarto 1, Taylor decides that

> the structural value of these omissions can be simply stated: they clearly and strongly establish the narrative expectation of war, and they reduce the amount of time that Lear himself is offstage . . . And what the Folio sacrifices is for the most part eminently dispensable. The narrative prelude to Cordelia's return (IV,iii) is hardly necessary; it is much more immediately satisfying to hear and see Cordelia than to be told about her.[24]

Yet fifty-six lines of 4.3 as well as a total of twenty-four other lines in Acts 3, 4, and 5 in the Quarto referring to the French army do more than delay the expectation of war, and are not "eminently dispensable" to the characterization of Cordelia in the text. These lines substantively alter the audience's view of the character and of the dramatic power of Cordelia as well as her integral relationship to other characters and to the play's major themes.

The additional eighty lines in the Quarto establish Cordelia as an active, foreign queen who exercises strength even when not present on stage, and although Howard-Hill argues that "the only textual evidence for the revision of *King Lear* is printed in the Folio,"[25] the Quarto shows signs of Shakespeare's revisions during or after composition, particularly in marginal additions in passages involving Cordelia. The omission in the Folio of the lines found in the Quarto recasts her as a submissive, nonpolitical, and nonmonarchical daughter who embodies strength only when present on stage. A conflation of the two texts, the usual strategy of the play's modern editors, produces a fraudulent and inconsistent characterization of Cordelia which minimizes her form and function in the play; thus it minimizes her interpretation and her ultimate meaning. If the audience is to accept, as the Quarto and Folio texts each imply, the reintroduction of Cordelia in Act 4 as a "moral force,"[26] it is essential to examine the differing evolutions of her character, and thus the differing degrees of moral force which Shakespeare gave her in the Quarto and the Folio texts.

## Revising Cordelia

Geoffrey Bullough cites as the primary sources of the *King Lear* story the anonymous play, *The True Chronicle History of King Leir,* and Holinshed's account of Leir, both of which mention how Leir's daughter, the Gallian Queen, accompanied by her exiled father, invades Leir's kingdom, now ruled by her sisters. According to Holinshed, Cordeilla's husband, Aganippus, readied his army

> to passe over into Britaine with Leir his father in law, to see him againe restored to his kingdome. It was accorded, that Cordeilla should also go with him to take possession of the land, the which he promised to leaue unto hir, as the rightfull inheritour after his decesse, notwithstanding any former grant made to hir sisters or to their husbands in anie maner of wise.[27]

In both sources, the King and Queen of Gaul succeed in returning possession of the English throne to Leir. Although in *King Lear* Cordelia acts militarily before reconciling with her father, the explicit use of this episode in the Quarto in the form of numerous references to the French army, and its omission, or at least thematic muddiness, in the Folio has produced various explanations from critics. Harley Granville-Barker had questioned the dramatic success of this subplot in the Quarto:

> The King of France comes armed with Cordelia to Lear's rescue, as is natural. Then, by virtue of the clumsiest few lines in the play, he is sent back again. Did Shakespeare originally mean Cordelia to restore her father to his throne as in the old play; but would a French victory in England not have done? It may be; though I cannot think he ever intended Lear to survive.[28]

Rather than stating that Shakespeare had begun at this point in the Quarto to rework his plot and then eliminated the clumsiness altogether in the Folio (as Granville-Barker does), Madeleine Doran argues that the omission of lines referring to France was due to the censorship of the Master of the Revels, "who was on guard to catch any matter in plays which might be offensive to the court or to the foreign ambassadors."[29] Most modern critics such as Taylor dismiss any theory of censorship in the Folio's redaction of the passages on France and argue instead that the Folio excises extraneous dialogue which interferes with the swift flow of action.[30]

The omitted lines are from the following scenes:

Q:   3.1   12 lines [revised in Folio as 9 lines discussing Albany and Cornwall]
    4.2   6 lines
    4.3   56 lines [entire scene]
    5.1   6 lines
    5.2   stage-directions

As Cordelia is seen only briefly in 1.1 and does not appear on stage again until 4.4 Quarto (4.3 Folio), it is striking that most of these lines come in the long gap between her introduction in Act 1 and her reintroduction in Act 4. Of all these passages, the omission of 4.3 in the Folio has produced the most critical speculation. 4.4, 4.5, and 4.6 in the Quarto become 4.3, 4.4, and 4.5 in the Folio, but 4.7 Quarto remains 4.7 in the Folio, as the scene numbering in the Folio skips from 4.5 to 4.7 with no scene marked as 4.6. Taylor reviews the previous textual studies of this compositorial error and explains that "according to Madeleine Doran, W. W. Greg, G. I. Duthie, G. K. Hunter and others, this error establishes—or at least 'suggests'—that the omission of 4.3 must have post-dated the preparation of the manuscript, and must therefore be without

Shakespearian authority." He concludes that the misnumbering of this scene in the Folio is characteristic of the Folio printers' treatment of the other plays and it

> thus, demonstrably proves nothing about the circumstances under which 4.3 was removed. If the Folio had correctly numbered the first two scenes and then misnumbered the remaining four (4.4–4.7), that would indeed suggest that 4.3 once stood in the prompt-book, though even then one could hardly prove that Shakespeare himself did not make the change after the book was prepared.[31]

Textual study of this scene has often become embroiled in discussions of the error in the numbering of the scenes of Act 4 in the Folio, and to what degree it reflects Shakespeare's authorial interference, so that the scene's thematic offering to the rest of the play has been neglected and its effect on the characterization of Cordelia has been dismissed.

These omissions appear in the last three acts of the play, but minor textual variants between the two texts in the early scenes, particularly 1.1, begin to consciously and strikingly shape the audience's differing views of Cordelia. She comes to acquire a moral strength in the later scenes, yet she behaves badly in 1.1, even though Beth Goldring sees her as demonstrating "courage" in this scene.[32] In the Quarto, Cordelia acts badly, and in the Folio, she speaks badly. Puzzling over how to respond to her father's demand for the measure of her love, she decides (sig. B1ᵛ; TLN 67):

> Q: What shall *Cordelia* doe, loue and be silent.
> F: What shall *Cordelia* speake? Loue, and be silent.

Where does the difference lie in *doing* love and *speaking* love and why do these texts diverge here in the evolution of Cordelia's character? It appears that in each text, Cordelia makes a deliberate choice that will govern her dramatic portrayal, form, and meaning: in the Quarto she decides to do nothing and in the Folio she decides to say nothing. A few lines later (sig. B2; TLN 79), Regan compares her own speech to Goneril's, resolving to "professe" that she is enemy to all other joys,

> Q: Which the most precious square of sence possesses.
> F: Which the most precious square of sense professes.

It is possible that the Folio compositor slipped and repeated the "professe" of two lines earlier here in this line; however, this variant would logically follow from the direction that each text has already taken: in the Quarto, filial love is tied to action and possession, and in the Folio, it is tied to verbal declarations. In the Quarto, Cordelia decides after Regan's speech that her love's "more richer" (in terms of possession?) than her tongue, while in the Folio Cordelia decides that her love's "more ponderous" (in terms of speaking?).

A more curious but still significant variant (sig. B2; TLN 88–91) occurs when Lear then addresses Cordelia as

> Q:                                    Our ioy,
> Although the last, not least in our deere loue.
> F:                                    Our Ioy,
> Although our last and least: to whose yong loue
> The Vines of France, and Milke of Burgundie,
> Strive to be interest.

In the Quarto, "least" appears to mean "not least in Lear's love," while in the Folio, "least" is used to mean "youngest," so that Lear offers her his affection in the Quarto and offers her affection to France and Burgundy in the Folio. He asks her in the Quarto what she can "win" (in action?), rather than "draw" (in speech?) in the Folio, more opulent than her sisters. Her response, "Nothing my Lord," provokes two additional lines of dialogue in the Folio, Lear's "Nothing?" and Cordelia's "Nothing," presenting a stronger confrontation in speech between them (sig. B2; TLN 91, 93–95). Again, the focus on action in the Quarto and speech in the Folio causes Lear to advise her (sig. B2; TLN 100–101):

> Q:                          Mend your speech a little,
> Least it may mar your fortunes.
> F:                          Mend your speech a little,
> Least you may marre your Fortunes.

In the Quarto, she and her speech are separated, and "it" will be responsible for marring her fortunes, and in the Folio, she alone is the cause of her marred fortunes.

Although Beth Goldring and Steven Urkowitz argue that the additional line in the Folio, "*Alb. Cor.* Deare Sir forbeare" in defense of Kent, and Gloucester's line in the Quarto assigned to "*Cor.*" (possibly either Cornwall or Cordelia) in the Folio, "Heer's *France* and *Burgundie* my noble Lord" (sig. B3ᵛ; TLN 176, 204), could be spoken by Cordelia and would thus present her as a much more forceful character in this scene,[33] it is highly unlikely that Cordelia would speak either line. Albany and

Cornwall are spoken of together in the scene's first lines, "I Thought the King had more affected the Duke of *Albany,* then *Cornwell,*" and in fact Albany and Cornwall enter together immediately after Lear a few lines later, so it would not be unusual for them to speak together. Cordelia has evidently been stunned by Lear's stinging rejection of her and would probably not caution her father to have patience with Kent when she has failed to caution him to do so in her own case. Also, she probably would not formally announce her own suitors; either the courtier Cornwall or the courtier Gloucester, who speaks the line in the Quarto, is a more appropriate speaker of that line.

This methodical and strict pattern of variants in the acting Cordelia and the speaking Cordelia continues in her next speech in which she asks that Lear "may know" in the Quarto and "make knowne" in the Folio (sig. B4; TLN 248) the true causes of her sudden loss of his grace and favor. In the Quarto, she appears to appeal to him to understand the reasons for her actions, while in the Folio, she demands that he state publicly the reasons for her words. The audience's last view of Cordelia for three acts is as she leaves with the man who has accepted her, the King of France. The audience is told of her in 1.4 and reminded of her connection with France when Lear asks why his Fool is absent and is informed, "Since my yong Ladies going into *France* sir, the foole hath much pined away." Later in the scene, she is again recalled when Lear, angry with Goneril, says, "O most small fault, how vgly did'st thou in *Cordelia* shewe" (sigs. C4, D2; TLN 602–603, 777–778). These minor references do not create any strong sense of her presence on stage, but Michael Warren feels that Kent and the Fool stand in for her: "With the Fool, whose attachment to Cordelia is established even before his first entrance, Kent-as-Caius maintains the link with Cordelia in the abstract—they are both honest and faithful individuals."[34]

In 2.2 (sig. E3; TLN 1244–1249), she is no longer abstract, for the stocked and disguised Kent peruses a letter which he has just received from Cordelia, who, he says,

> hath most fortunately bin informed
> Of my obscured course, and shall find time
> From this enormious state, seeking to giue
> Losses their remedies, all wearie and ouerwatch
> Take vantage heauie eyes not to behold
> This shamefull lodging.

This valuable piece of information, often overlooked by critics who treat both the question of war and Cordelia's role in it, may be related to the first omission in the Folio of references to France in 3.1. W. W. Greg ingeniously charted the time-space sequences of the two texts and concluded from Kent's lines on the French army found only in 3.1 in the Quarto that there can be no doubt that "the French army had actually landed before Lear had any quarrel with his daughters."[35] Yet Kent had already appealed to Cordelia for aid prior to receiving her letter in 2.2.

In 3.1, the Folio has a speech of nine lines substituted for the twelve lines in the Quarto, in which the news of Albany's and Cornwall's servants who are spying for the French replaces the news of foreign invasion. After Kent tells the Gentleman of the division between Cornwall and Albany, he continues in the Quarto (sig. F3ᵛ):

> But true it is, from *France,* there comes a power
> Into this scattered kindgome, who alreadie wise in our negligence
> Haue secret feet in some of our best Ports,
> And are at point to shew their open banner,
> Now to you, if on my credit you dare build so farre,
> To make your speed to Douer, you shall find
> Some that will thanke you, making iust report
> Of how vnnaturall and bemadding sorrow
> The King hath cause to plaine.
> I am a Gentleman of blood and breeding,
> And from some knowledge and assurance,
> Offer this office to you.

The mislining in the second line signals that "wise in our negligence" was marginally added, perhaps when Shakespeare remembered that Kent had been sending and receiving letters to and from Cordelia in France. The word "negligence" is ambiguous in Kent's speech; it could represent the mistreatment of Lear, supported by Kent's comments in 2.2, rather than the misgoverning of the kingdom, which brings France to Britain's shores.

Yet, in the Folio (TLN 1631–1638), Kent speaks not of the French army but of Albany and Cornwall,

> Who haue, as who haue not, that their great Starres
> Thron'd and set high; Seruants, who seeme no lesse,
> Which are to France the Spies and Speculations
> Intelligent of our State. What hath bin seene,

> Either in snuffes, and packings of the Dukes
> Or the hard Reine which both of them hath borne
> Against the old kinde King; or something deeper,
> Whereof (perchance) these are but furnishings.

The Quarto and Folio speeches proceed from the same line: "With mutuall cunning, twixt *Albany* and *Cornwall*," and the syntactical awkwardness of the first few lines of the Folio variant suggests that it was deliberately inserted as a revision. Greg, Taylor, and other critics argue convincingly that the Quarto speech describes an unprovoked, and perhaps opportunistic, foreign invasion, while the Folio speech begins to set up the need for civil rebellion. Urkowitz also stresses that "the expedition of the French in the Quarto text is unrelated to Lear's plight, of which they have no knowledge prior to their landing," and in the Folio, "rebellion is suggested instead."[36]

Yet, the striking point about this variant in 3.1 is not whether war takes on a different definition in the view of the audience or whether Cordelia acquires guilt through association, but how Cordelia exerts a powerful and active presence in the Quarto and is revised to become incidental and subordinate in the Folio. The lines immediately following these variants again connect Kent to Cordelia through a letter in both the Quarto and Folio. Kent tells the Gentleman (sig. F3ᵛ; TLN 1642–1646):

> Open this purse, and take
> What it containes, if you shall see *Cordelia*
> As feare not but you shall, shew her this ring,
> And she will tell you who your [that *F*] fellow is
> That yet you doe not know.

In the Quarto, Kent sends the Gentleman to Dover, the site of the French army's camp, so it is logical that he will encounter Cordelia soon. However, in the Folio, the Gentleman is not sent to any particular place but is told confidently by Kent that he will see Cordelia, without being told where he is to see her.

The lines in 2.2, printed in both the Quarto and the Folio, do not mark Cordelia as ambitious in returning to her father's defense; yet the Quarto links her with the French army while the Folio does not. In the Quarto, she remains a character who has evidently been taking action since quitting her father's land, and she begins to fulfill her promise as a physical and moral force for reconciliation and remedy. In the Folio, she remains the more submissive character who is only incidentally involved in remedying her father's situation and becoming reconciled to him. Perhaps Shakespeare was attempting here and elsewhere in the Folio text to weaken the external forces supporting Lear, such as Cordelia in the Quarto, so that Lear could be more intensely and centrally portrayed as struggling alone throughout the play; through this meticulous and interwoven pattern of revision, Shakespeare succeeded in restructuring and reconstructing the very meaning of tragedy itself.

The discussion of whether Cordelia directly (in the Quarto) or indirectly (in the Folio) hopes to restore her father's moral and political power can be extended in the interlocking treatment of Gloucester's direct or indirect involvement with the French/rebel forces in the Quarto and Folio. In 3.3 (sig. G1; TLN 1762–1764), he confides to Edmund that he has received a letter and,

> these injuries
> The King now beares, will be reuenged home
> Ther's part of a power already landed [footed *F*],
> We must incline to the King.

Again, in 3.6, Gloucester informs Kent of the plot against Lear's life and advises, "Ther is a Litter ready lay him in't, & driue towards Douer frend, / Where thou shalt meet both welcome & protection, take vp thy master" (sig. G4ᵛ; TLN 2049–2051). However, because this passage is badly mislined in the Quarto, as are the following three lines (the Folio attempts to correct the mislineation), it appears to have been marginally reworked. The Quarto text has repeatedly connected Cordelia with Dover, so Gloucester first appears to send Lear simply to "welcome and protection," but after Shakespeare's revision, Gloucester sends him specifically to Dover. However, the Folio text does not explicitly connect Cordelia with Dover, and Gloucester sends Lear to the protection and welcome of someone whom he does not name. In the Folio, Gloucester appears to be taking matters into his own hands, unless he, like Kent, received his letter from Cordelia. Thus, only the Quarto suggests that Gloucester's cruelty to his sons is tempered here by his kindness to Lear in entrusting him to the care of his loving daughter.

Immediately following this scene, the audience watches Gloucester being punished for his alliance with the Dover group. Betrayed by Edmund to Cornwall, Regan, and Goneril, Gloucester is called to account for the letter he has received and for sending Lear to Dover. In the opening of 3.7, Cornwall tells Goneril in the Quarto and Folio, "Post speedily to my Lord your husband shew him this letter, / The army of France is landed," knowledge which the Quarto audience had six scenes earlier. Cornwall's next line varies (sig. G4^v; TLN 2061–2062):

> Q: Seeke out the vilaine *Gloster*.
> F: Seeke out the Traitor *Glouster*.

In the Quarto, in which Cordelia is perhaps associated with a "traitorous" army, the man who has knowledge of her actions (and has been aiding her?) is called a "vilaine." In the Folio, in the eyes of the Cornwall-Regan-Goneril group, with the absence of a building-up of Cordelia as "traitress" or leader, Gloucester becomes the focus for treachery. Other similarly patterned variants appear in 3.7 in the texts: in the Quarto, Gloucester is called "traitor" four times (five times, *F*), "traitorous" one time (one time, *F*), and "villain" four times (twice, *F*, "treacherous villain" once, *F*). In the Folio, Gloucester is more intensely termed a traitor rather than a villain in this scene, but only by a group that the audience recognizes as vicious and corrupt, and, ultimately, more dangerously traitorous.

Cornwall also demands to know what letters Gloucester has received "from France" and asks him, "What confederacy haue you with the tratours late footed in the kingdome?" (sig. H1^v; TLN 2111–2112). In the Quarto, Kent says that the French army has "secret feet" in the kingdom, and the Folio borrows this term in 3.3 when Gloucester tells Edmund of the "part of a power" that is "already footed" in the kingdom (rather than "landed" in the Quarto). Perhaps these "tratours" refer to Cordelia in the Quarto, and to the unidentified leader of the French troops in the Folio. Gloucester does not name the author of the letter he has received, but describes it as "gessingly set downe / Which came from one, that's of a neutrall heart, / And not from one oppos'd" (sig. H1^v; TLN 2115–2116). As "neutrall" could mean "not inclining toward either party, view, etc., assisting neither of two contending parties" or "occupying a middle position with regard to two extremes" (*OED*), in the Quarto text the audience could assume that the letter advising Gloucester to send Lear to Dover came from Cordelia. In the Folio, which lacks the clear connection of Cordelia to the French army, the author of the letter remains ambiguous and unimportant; Gloucester is the central focus here, not Cordelia. Asked three times in this scene why he has sent Lear to Dover, Gloucester finally replies that he wanted to save Lear from the cruelty of Goneril and Regan. In the Quarto, Gloucester sends Lear to his kindest daughter while in the Folio he sends Lear to his kindest ally.

Goneril again takes up the impending crisis of France's invasion of the kingdom only in the Quarto while berating her husband, Albany, in 4.2 (sig. H4):

> France spreds his banners in our noyseles land,
> With plumed helme, thy state begins thereat
> Whil'st thou a morall foole sits still and cries
> Alack why does he so.

Although critics have debated whether 4.3 in the Quarto "emblematizes" Cordelia, this scene should be seen in juxtaposition with 4.2, for in a Quarto-only passage, 4.2 de-emblematizes Goneril when Albany responds to his wife's attack:

> Thou changed, and selfe-couerd thing for shame
> Be-monster not thy feature, wer't my fitnes
> To let these hands obay my bloud,
> They are apt enough to dislecate and teare
> Thy flesh and bones, how ere thou art a fiend,
> A woman's shape doth shield thee.

Cordelia's "woman's shape" is immediately described in 4.3 in the Quarto as her sister's opposite: she is not the bemonstered fiend when the true "morall" fools are distinguished from the false ones.

In the Quarto in 4.3, a scene not printed in the Folio, the audience hears that the King of France has returned to his own country, leaving behind him "the Marshall of *France* Monsier *la Far*" (sig. H4ᵛ). Although Granville-Barker saw this sudden departure of France in the Quarto as Shakespeare's turning away from his original intentions for this character, the absence of the King of France removes any last stigma of "traitor" from Cordelia's character. It may also signal the merging of the foreign queen with the loving daughter. Beth Goldring argues that this presence of Monsieur la Far in the Quarto and his absence in the Folio establish him as the leader of the invading army in the Quarto and Cordelia as its leader in the Folio.[37] Yet Cordelia is portrayed as a suffering daughter as well as a Queen and commander-in-chief in 4.3 in the Quarto. Maynard Mack writes that Kent and the Gentleman "wrap Cordelia in a mantle of emblematic speech,"[38] and Michael Warren agrees that in Kent's speech "she develops almost emblematic status in her joyful suffering."[39] Yet before becoming the suffering child, she is strongly represented as a monarch (sig. H4$^v$):

> Now and then an ample teare trild downe
> Her delicate cheeke, it seemed she was a queen ouer her passion,
> Who most rebell-like, fought to be King ore her.

She is further softened as an emblem of pity (sigs. H4$^v$-I1):

> Not to a rage, patience and sorow streme,
> Who should expresse her goodliest you haue seene,
> Sun shine and raine at once, her smiles and teares,
> Were like a better way those happie smilets,
> That playd on her ripe lip seeme not to know,
> What guests were in her eyes which parted thence,
> As pearles from diamonds dropt in briefe,
> Sorow would be a raritie most beloued,
> If all could so become it.

Here she seems to fulfill the expectations of Kent in 2.2 (Quarto and Folio) and in 3.1 (Quarto only) that the news of Lear's "vnnaturall and bemadding sorrow" would move Cordelia to action. "Holy water" flows from her eyes as she cries, "Sisters, sisters, shame of Ladies sisters," and the words of Albany in the previous scene sharpen the contrast between the "fiend" Goneril and the "holy" Cordelia.

4.3 does not merely serve to "emblematize" Cordelia but deliberately and majestically extends the direction of her character which the Quarto has been building for four acts. She is represented as the strong queen and the loving daughter, and her roles merge as she acquires the power to act as one of the play's moral spokespersons. Although Goneril calls Albany a "morall foole," it is she who becomes the fool while Cordelia becomes the moral sage. Because the Folio text lacks these lines in 4.3 and 4.2, it weakens the establishment of moral strength in Cordelia by reducing her at this point in the play to a supporting character rather than a fundamental one.

Warren sees 4.3 as "representative of Kent's function in the Quarto as spokesman for deep human feeling and profound moral concern. The absence of this scene from the Folio diminishes our awareness of Kent and removes this function."[40] Yet the absence of 4.3 also diminishes the audience's awareness of Cordelia and her power over Lear and those opposed to him. Granville-Barker and Urkowitz have each argued that the scene is a dramatic failure. Granville-Barker complains, "I could better believe that Shakespeare cut it than wrote it. There is, certainly, a little life in the description of Cordelia, and a case can be made for so heralding her return to the play. The rest is explanation of what is better left unexplained." Urkowitz also decides that "Cordelia's immediate appearance onstage, the alternative found in the Folio, may be a *better* continuation of Cordelia's story than the report of her behavior in 4.3, however beautiful the report may be."[41] Yet it is not the continuation of Cordelia's story that is significant here but the consistent continuation of her character; it is this careful consistency which plays a necessary role in establishing and interweaving the major themes of each text. Cordelia is the measure by which other characters, themes, and a large portion of the plot seek their reflection and meaning.

Cordelia enters in Quarto 4.4 with "*Docter and others,*" but the stage directions in the Folio for 4.3 (Quarto 4.4) read "*Enter with Drum and Colours, Cordelia, Gentlemen, and Souldiours.*" Urkowitz asserts that "according to the Folio text only Cordelia acts like the leader,"[42] but as Edmund, Regan, Albany, and Goneril will also enter with "*Drumme and Colours*" in 5.1 in the Folio, Cordelia's entrance in the Folio is made parallel to that of her sisters. Cordelia explains in this scene that she does not act from ambition but from love (sig. I1ᵛ; TLN 2376–2380):

> O deere father
> It is thy business that I go about therfore great *France*
> My mourning and important [importun'd *F*] teares hath pitied
> No blowne ambition doth our armes in sight [incite *F*]
> But loue, deere loue, and our ag'd fathers right.

The mislining in "It is thy business . . . France," may indicate that the lines "therfore great France. . . hath pitied" were marginally added in the foul papers; if so, Shakespeare began Cordelia's speech by focusing on her lack of ambition and her Christ-like attention to her father's business but added a reference to the King of France's lack of political interest in supporting her invasion. She cannot be seen by the audience as anything less than sympathetic and sacred here, and it is significant that Shakespeare in both the Quarto and Folio chooses to reintroduce her as a moral force after she has been first introduced in 1.1 as a brutally honest child. This reportrayal of the reentering Cordelia causes critics to reexamine her character, although they have not noticed how that character is strengthened in the Quarto by constant and consistent focus on her successive actions and weakened in the Folio by sporadic and inconsistent focus on her previous words. For example, Kenneth Muir decides that "Cordelia's honesty is not the best policy; and her virtue is literally its own reward";[43] this scene, set against 1.1, of course suggests that honest expression from emotion is better than action or speech from expectation. Yet the change in Cordelia's character from her first entrance in 1.1 and her next entrance in 4.4, ironically, does not exist solely within one, eclectically edited text of the play, but is constituted outside of it. The genuine change in her character is not from one entrance to another but from one text to another. She serves as a constantly self-revising moral force and moral center which constantly revises the audience's sense of what is essential in the tragedy it is witnessing.

Cordelia's lines in the Quarto and Folio 4.7 show fewer variants than those in the earlier scenes in the play, except for four additional lines in the Quarto in which she extends her metaphor on natural elements ("dread bolted thunder," sig. K2) that have hurt her father. This reconciliation of Lear and his daughter appears to reach its emotional peak in their exchange (sig. K2ᵛ; TLN 2830–2833):

*Lear.* I know you doe not loue me, for your sisters
　　　Haue as I doe remember, done me wrong,
　　　You haue some cause, they haue not.
*Cord.* No cause, no cause.

Whether the active Cordelia of the Quarto or the more submissive Cordelia of the Folio speaks in this scene, she gains strength in her morally compassionate and generous response to Lear's just remark. The audience cannot question her strength but can see it derive from a different transformation in the Quarto and the Folio.

Only the Quarto again brings up the problem of France's invading troops in 5.1 (sig. K3). Albany informs the others of the business of Lear's reunion with his daughter: "It touches vs, as *France* inuades our land / Not bolds the King, with others whome I feare, / Most iust and heauy causes make oppose." There is overwhelming dramatic tension in the Quarto between the external conflict with France and the internal conflict between the forces of Albany and Edmund, and this tension creates an insupportable sense of crisis. In the Folio, both conflicts are replaced by a single internal struggle that seems tolerable in comparison, but is actually more perilous in its consequences. Taylor argues that

> by making Cordelia's resistance an armed uprising rather than a foreign invasion the Folio removes the last vestige of an 'explanation' for her eventual unexpected defeat. In short, the Folio deliberately raises our hopes higher in order, apparently, to dash them lower.[44]

This revision makes Lear and those aiding him more pathetic and tragic in the Folio. Ultimately Shakespeare revises his very concept of tragedy for both his characters and his audience: tragedy becomes a self-reflexive process practiced both within and without the play itself.

Shakespeare further redefines public and private tragedy in the concluding act of *King Lear*. The stage directions for 5.2 (sig. K3$^v$; TLN 2917–2918) have Cordelia enter regally and emblematically:

> Q: *Alarum. Enter the powers of France ouer the stage,*
>     *Cordelia, with her father in her hand.*
> F: *Alarum within. Enter with Drumme and Colours,*
>     *Lear, Cordelia, and Souldiers, ouer the Stage, and*
>     *Exeunt.*

Neither Cordelia nor Lear speaks in this scene; they act as emblems and icons. Cordelia, accompanied by her father, enters as the head of the French powers in the Quarto (certainly not subordinate to Monsieur la Far, as Goldring argues, who is not singled out), while Lear, accompanied by Cordelia, enters as the head of a group of soldiers in the Folio. Again, the active Cordelia in the Quarto becomes the passive companion in the Folio, led by her father rather than leading him by the hand. In 5.3 (sig. K4$^v$), Edmund remarks only in the Quarto that "the question of *Cordelia* and her father / Requires a fitter place," as the focus of Cordelia *and her father* in the Quarto shifts to Lear *and his daughter* in the Folio.

The variants in the last lines of Lear's final speech in the play canonize the context of the two differing treatments of Cordelia. Granville-Barker, the critic so carefully theatrical in his analyses, finds the entrance of the dead Cordelia in Lear's arms at the end of 5.3 more poignant and dramatic than any other type of entrance, for "dumb and dead, she that was never apt of speech—what fitter finish for her could there be?"[45] Such a literary reading or a theatrical rendering of Cordelia mistakes even a single text's appropriation of her form and meaning. In the Quarto (sig. L4), Lear apparently believes that the daughter who was most "deere" in his love is dead before he dies, and he suffers the most pain at the tragic recognition of his part in her death. In the Folio (TLN 3282–3283), he murmurs, "Do you see this? Looke on her? Looke her lips, / Looke there, looke there," and he dies, perhaps triumphantly, believing that Cordelia is still alive. In the shift from Cordelia and her father in the Quarto to Lear and his daughter in the Folio, it is Lear's tragedy, rather than his shared with Cordelia, that becomes the final focus in this later version of the play. Cordelia pleads in 1.1 (sig. B4; TLN 246–247) that she lacks "the glib and oyly Art, / To speake and purpose not"; ironically, in the Quarto she learns primarily how to "purpose" with power while in the Folio she learns primarily how to "speak" with power. The play's final lines (sig. L4; TLN 3298–3299), whether spoken by Albany, as in the Quarto, or Edgar, as in the Folio,

> The waight of this sad time we must obey,
> Speake what we feele, not what we ought to say,

recommend in each text that ultimately the true power to interpret and transform derives from heartfelt speech, and it is to this moral lesson which the rewritten and re-presented Folio Cordelia finally conforms.

Any edition of *King Lear* which conflates the Quarto and Folio texts, as Kenneth Muir's does, produces an inconsistent treatment of themes such as war and familial conflict, a confused presentation of the play's structure and form, and, most important, a falsely conflated version of Cordelia and so many other characters, creating a counterfeit and non-Shakespearian foundation upon which only the most limited literary interpretation and meaning can be built. For example, Muir generally follows the Folio for Cordelia's lines and much of the text, yet places references to France side by side with the Folio variants: in 3.1 he presents first the variants in the Folio on the French spies, immediately followed by the lines on France in the Quarto. How can the spies bring word of the "negligence" to the French forces in France if the forces are now at Dover? Similarly, Muir's Cordelia, who decides, "What shall Cordelia speak? Love, and be silent" (1.1.61), becomes the active queen coexisting with the tragically submissive one, ultimately negating any sense of her character and her essential contributions to the larger world of the play. And a critic such as William Elton, who does not examine the textual variants of the Quarto and Folio but works with a modern conflated edition, bases his entire treatment of Cordelia and her significant contribution to the play on her "resolution to 'Love and be silent'" (but preceded by which verb, "do" or "speak"?), leading to the "inception of a capability whose nature speaks louder than words."[46] Even in the Folio, Cordelia's nature must be expressed before it can speak louder than words; in the Quarto, this expression takes the form and the meaning of action.

Even the recent feminist readings of Cordelia's contribution to the play by such scholars as Juliet Dusinberre and Marianne Novy, which do not discuss or even acknowledge the differences between the portrayals of Cordelia in the two texts,[47] present nothing more than a general argument about an editorially revised and recreated Cordelia rather than a specific argument about the textually extant Cordelias. In essence, modern literary and textual critics interpret and analyze a Shakespearian female character who does not exist, because she is not the character that Shakespeare created and recreated in revision; her varying essentiality has been stripped away and replaced with a new, synthesized, non-Shakespearian form and meaning. Such modern criticism endows editors with the power to revise while denying that power to Shakespeare himself.

The title page of the Quarto *King Lear* advertises that it was performed "*at Whitehall vpon S.* Stephans *night in Christmas Hollidayes*" by the King's Men, "playing vsually at the Gloabe"; since the play was entered in the Stationers' Register in 1607 with the same description, the play was evidently performed privately at court in 1606. Shakespeare's extensive and intricately consistent revisions in characterizations, themes, and plots were almost certainly made during the same period in the course of preparing the original play for later performances. Thus, the Quarto represents the play as first composed, perceived, and performed, and the Folio offers revisions, written out in an authorial manuscript or recorded in a transcript which served as a promptbook, which re-present the ever-transformative power of the dramatist and the poet to represent tragedy.

The careful and consistent revision of so many of the other characters in the play, particularly Lear, the Fool, Kent, Albany, and Edgar, as discussed by Roger Warren, John Kerrigan, R. A. Foakes, Steven Urkowitz, and Michael Warren, and the themes of war and kingship, as discussed by Steven Urkowitz and Gary Taylor, were made by Shakespeare apparently to suit his altered vision of the play as a theatrical piece. The leaner and more intense portrayal of these characters and of Cordelia in the Folio were evidently made in the course of tightening the play for greater dramatic effect. As E. A. J. Honigmann argues, "a *major* revision by someone other than Shakespeare seems unlikely, when one considers the converging evidence: strategies of revision that imply an awareness of the minutiae of characterization."[48] These strategies of revision, so demonstrable here, both draw on and are drawn from the strategies of revision Shakespeare used throughout his career in so many of his plays.

This study of the original texts of plays by Shakespeare and his contemporaries demonstrates with clarity and certainty that dramatists during the Elizabethan and Jacobean ages produced foul papers full of loose ends, false starts, duplications, and major and minor alterations, including deletions and additions. These same dramatists also reworked their foul papers or the later transcripts of them after composition in a process which revised their plays and their very power as creative artists. In his elegy to Shakespeare printed in the First Folio, Ben Jonson remarked,

> And that he,
> Who casts to write a liuing line, must sweat,
>    (such as thine are) and strike the second heat
> Vpon the *Muses* anuile. turne the same,
>    (And himselfe with it) that he thinkes to frame,
> Or for the lawrell, he may gaine a scorne,
>    For a good *Poet's* made, as well as borne.
> And such wert thou.

As John Kerrigan notes, Jonson's praise "reads like a conscious correction of Heminge and Condell,"[49] who had remarked of Shakespeare that "what he thought, he vttered with that easinesse, that wee haue scarse receiued from him a blot in his papers." Shakespeare extensively "struck the second heat" in many of his early plays, expanding and cutting dialogue in an effort to clarify characters, plots, and themes, making slight changes that would have major consequences for the plays' larger structures. His revising hand is especially apparent in plays written later in his career, including *Hamlet, Troilus and Cressida, Othello,* and *King Lear,* in which he continuously altered numerous passages to isolate and intensify the presentation and the focus of the interlocking elements of character, structure, setting, plot, and theme, re-presenting and re-creating the worlds of the plays. Through revision, Shakespeare made his plays private or public, endowing them with a personal and a cultural identity, multiplying rather than reducing their possibilities for interpretation. Whether these minor and major revisions were made during or immediately after composition, during rehearsals, some months or years after performance, or after publication cannot always be determined from the variant texts of the plays, but it is certain that they were made by the author himself.

In *William Shakespeare: A Textual Companion,* Gary Taylor states that the Oxford *Complete Works* presents the Quarto and Folio *King Lear* as two separate plays because the texts differ "in ways not paralleled by other collateral texts (like the good quartos of *Hamlet, Troilus,* and *Othello*)," and because the revisions were made "several years after the original composition."[50] However, the types of revisions in *King Lear,* which were both "massive in scale and intricate in detail,"[51] are not substantially different from those in these three plays written a few years earlier. In all four plays mentioned by Taylor, major and minor painstaking revisions coexist with theatrical, editorial, and compositorial changes, and thus the Quarto and Folio texts of *Hamlet, Troilus and Cressida, Othello,* and other plays should also be printed in separate versions if scholars are ever to come to terms with all that they offer.[52]

At the beginning of the *King Lear* controversy in the early 1980s, a critic warned that "a deep crack is opening in Shakespeare studies, and the paying public needs to know where it stands and which side to take."[53] Because of this "deep crack" scholars can no longer debate what constitutes, as well as how to establish, a copy-text that stands as the "best" or "most authoritative" or "definitive" version of a Shakespearian play without reconsidering the implications of revision on traditional textual theories and literary interpretations. The *possibility* and indeed the *probability* of revision can no longer be ignored by scholars producing an edition of a text, even if it exists in only *one* substantive version; revisions during or shortly after composition in a single text are as significant as revisions made years later in a subsequent text. Scholars demanding such critical investigations of revision can no longer, like Ben Jonson, be accused of making "a malevolent speech," but should be recognized as advocating the multiple and not the reduced vision of Shakespeare as a creative artist. Nor can the real constitution and canonicity of Shakespeare be displaced; the revising Shakespeare and the variant texts of his plays constitute his canon.

Many modern editors, who insist on reconstructing a copy-text, have ignored critical bibliography, which can point toward revision as a cause of variants, and instead have focused on their own taste and judgment in dismissing variants which they consider inferior or un-Shakespearian. And many eclectic editions present a text as the product of the printing process, utterly discounting it as the product of the author and as a work which underwent different authorial stages of composition and paths of transmission. This type of editorial treatment must be recognized as fraudulent and presumptuous; editors cannot claim that Shakespeare did not revise and at the same time revise for him. Textual critics can preserve Shakespeare's individual sanctity and his canonical importance only by presenting the integrity of *each* of his texts.[54]

For Shakespeare's plays, the institutionalization of the theory of unblotted lines has ended, and the "rationale of copy-text" must yield to that of genetic or parallel texts. And when the editing of Shakespeare's texts changes, so must the interpretation of them; scholars are beginning to recognize "that editing and interpreting, that bibliography and hermeneutics, are only heuristically separable."[55] Basing criticism on a fraudulent text has serious consequences for both the literary and the textual scholar; no significant theoretical mode of discourse, ideology, method, or approach can effectively proceed from a fabricated textual foundation or a falsified literary base. All Shakespearian scholars, textual editors, literary critics, and students of Shakespeare must attempt to deal with the multiplicity of the variant texts, the implications of this textual revolution, and the interrelationship of textual and literary studies. Scholars need to study Shakespeare's plays, as Michael Warren has proposed, in the photographic reproductions of the earliest texts with their "primal confusions and corruptions unsullied by the cleansing corruption of later sophistication" and not solely in modern eclectic editions, so that

> the scholar and perhaps the student would meet the existential text or texts of the play and see each for what it is—an individual manifestation called by a specific name, produced under certain economic and historical circumstances for a particular purpose that it fulfills to a greater or lesser degree, not the author's 'original' perhaps, but what he hath left us.[56]

Thus Warren's proposal brings all of us as scholars closer to Shakespeare because an eclectic text of a Shakespearian play is by its very nature *two or more removes* from Shakespeare's text. The farther the original text from the reader the farther we are from Shakespeare, and this distance has created and contributed to the current crisis in reading, writing, watching, and understanding Shakespeare.

Yet, textual scholars calling for a return to the original texts can impose another kind of distance; although Stanley Wells notes that he would like to see editions of *Hamlet, Troilus and Cressida,* and *Othello* which are limited "to one or the other text," he also implies that different values can be assigned to texts when he asserts that editors present Shakespeare's plays "in the form in which he finally preferred them if we choose the theatrically influenced texts."[57] However, there is no evidence that any of the texts presents Shakespeare's "final" form, only a *later* form. As Warren's proposal makes clear, scholars must simply examine the texts as they exist, as they were left us. And in hermeneutical study, whether from the vantage point of deconstruction or new historicism or any other prevailing methodology, the text, as the product of the author and not of the critic, must be allowed to take shape in all its varying physical and abstract forms.

Rather than worrying about the increased burden on an editor when adding in the integer of revision in the textual transmission process (as David Bevington does in asking, "What is an editor to do with indeterminacy? What compromises will we accept in the imprecise business of setting down in print what we think an author meant to say?"[58]), the editor and the critic must assume that revision is already an existing and an integral factor in, rather than a tangential by-product of, the textual transmission process of a theatrical or a literary work. Nor can the editor argue, as E. A. J. Honigmann recently has, that the Quarto and Folio *King Lear* texts require "firm editorial 'interference'" to conform them into editions of the play.[59] Editorial interference and determinacy are forces which exist *outside* of the text and which immediately assume that the original text is corrupt, and nothing outside of the texts matters as much as the various and varying incorruptible texts themselves.

Textual study serves as the only solid foundation on which to build literary criticism, precisely because it examines a text as an authorially derived social product: from author to literary audience, through the medium of the printing house, and through the medium of the playhouse and the theatrical process in the case of a play. D. F. McKenzie has recently described bibliography as "the sociology of texts" because it reveals the physical forms, textual versions, technical transmission, institutional control, perceived meanings, and social effects of books and non-books. For books which exist in more than one version because of revision, it follows that, "since any single version will have its own historical identity, not only for its author but for the particular market of readers who bought and read it, we cannot invoke the idea of one unified intention which the editor must serve."[60] It is this very relationship between the author and the reader and the very identity of the text itself that are jeopardized by a limited and limiting theory of textual and critical interpretation.

Scholars, students, and the general theatrical and reading public have already been forced to accept unacceptable compromises when they are confronted with traditional, eclectic editions which limit the vision, the range, the creative artistry, and the shaping fantasy of an author occasionally or continually shaping and reshaping his text. The final result of the new debate about authorial revision in the plays of Shakespeare is that, as John Kerrigan has noted, "the *details* of revision change our idea of Shakespeare. He becomes a self-considering artist": a "poet willing to engage with his own work critically, as reader and rethinker."[61]

What appears to have disturbed literary and textual scholars from the seventeenth to the twentieth century who have resisted theories of authorial revision in Shakespeare's plays is that they must rethink their conception of his image, his methods, and his meanings, as well as his texts. But in denying revision these scholars deny Shakespeare the power he *wanted* to exert as a poet: he must be able, as he proclaims in *A Midsummer Night's Dream,* to use the poet's pen to turn the forms of things unknown bodied forth by imagination into shapes and to give to them a local habitation and a name. Shakespeare must be allowed the ability to shape fantasies which apprehend *more* than the cool reason of scholars, textual or literary, ever comprehends. Indeterminacy is not an unfortunate product of the process of constructing or reconstructing the physical text alone but a fortunate and necessary product of interpreting both the physical and the abstract text. Those textual and literary ideologies and theoretical discourses, which scholars so scrupulously create and apply in order to capture the determined elusiveness of a literary work, can only thrive on a text's own indeterminacy and its own lack of finality for both the author and his audience.

# APPENDIX

# Early Printing History of the Plays

A brief outline of the printing history of Shakespeare's plays from the later sixteenth century to the middle of the seventeenth century appears below. Plays are listed in the same order as in the First Folio. Quartos with a bracketed date or an actual date of 1619 are part of a spurious collection of plays attempted by Thomas Pavier.

## Comedies

*The Tempest*
>       First printed in the Folio

*The Two Gentlemen of Verona*
>       First printed in the Folio

*The Merry Wives of Windsor*

| (bad) | Quarto | 1 | 1602 by T. C. for Arthur Johnson |
|-------|--------|---|----------------------------------|
| (bad) |        | 2 | 1619 for Arthur Johnson          |
|       |        | 3 | 1630 by T. H. for R. Meighen     |

*Measure for Measure*
>       First printed in the Folio

*The Comedy of Errors*
> First printed in the Folio

*Much Ado About Nothing*
> Quarto   1   1600 by V. S. for Andrew Wise and William Aspley

*Love's Labor's Lost*
> Quarto   1   1598 by W. W. for Cuthbert Burby
>               2   1631 by W. S. for John Smethwicke

*A Midsummer Night's Dream*
> Quarto   1   1600 by Thomas Fisher
>               2   [1619] by James Roberts

*The Merchant of Venice*
> Quarto   1   1600 by I. R. for Thomas Heyes
>               2   [1619] by J. Roberts
>               3   1637 by M. P. for Laurence Hayes

*As You Like It*
> First printed in the Folio

*The Taming of the Shrew*
> First printed in the Folio

*All's Well That Ends Well*
> First printed in the Folio

*Twelfth Night*
> First printed in the Folio

*The Winter's Tale*
> First printed in the Folio

# Histories

## *King John*

First printed in the Folio

## *Richard II*

| | | | |
|---|---|---|---|
| Quarto | 1 | 1597 by Valentine Simmes for Andrew Wise |
| | 2 | 1598 by Valentine Simmes for Andrew Wise |
| | 3 | 1608 by W. W. for Mathew Lawe |
| | 4 | 1608 by W. W. for Mathew Lawe |
| | 5 | 1615 for Mathew Lawe |
| | 6 | 1634 by John Norton |

## *1 Henry IV*

| | | | |
|---|---|---|---|
| Quarto | 0 | 1598 for Andrew Wise (one sheet only extant) |
| | 1 | 1598 by P. S. for Andrew Wise |
| | 2 | 1599 by S. S. for Andrew Wise |
| | 3 | 1604 by Valentine Simmes for Mathew Lawe |
| | 4 | 1608 for Mathew Lawe |
| | 5 | 1613 by W. W. for Mathew Lawe |
| | 6 | 1622 by T. P. for Mathew Lawe |
| | 7 | 1632 by John Norton for William Sheares |
| | 8 | 1639 by John Norton for Hugh Perry |

## *2 Henry IV*

Quarto 1 1600 by V. S. for Andrew Wise and William Aspley (reissued in the same year)

## *Henry V*

(bad) Quarto 1 1600 by Thomas Creede for T. Millington and John Busby
(bad) 2 1602 by Thomas Creede for Thomas Pauier
(bad) 3 [1619] for T. P.

*1 Henry VI*

    First printed in the Folio

*2 Henry VI*

(bad)   Quarto  1   1594 by Thomas Creede for Thomas Millington
(bad)            2   1600 by Valentine Simmes for Thomas Millington
(Quartos titled *The First part of the Contention betwixt the two famous Houses of Yorke and Lancaster*)
(bad)   Quarto  3   1619 for T. P.
(Printed together with Quarto 3 of *The true Tragedie of Richard Duke of Yorke* as *The Whole Contention betweene the two Famous Houses, Lancaster and Yorke*)

*3 Henry VI*

(bad)   Octavo  1   1595 by P. S. for Thomas Millington
(bad)   Quarto  2   1600 by W. W. for Thomas Millington
(Octavo and Quarto titled *The true Tragedie of Richard Duke of Yorke*)
(bad)   Quarto  3   1619 for T. P.
(Printed together with Quarto 3 of *The First part of the Contention* as *The Whole Contention betweene the two Famous Houses, Lancaster and Yorke*)

*Richard III*

(bad)   Quarto  1   1597 by Valentine Simmes for Andrew Wise
(bad)            2   1598 by Thomas Creede for Andrew Wise
(bad)            3   1602 by Thomas Creede for Andrew Wise
(bad)            4   1605 by Thomas Creede for Mathew Lawe
(bad)            5   1612 by Thomas Creede for Mathew Lawe
(bad)            6   1622 by Thomas Purfoot for Mathew Lawe
(bad)            7   1629 by John Norton for Mathew Lawe
(bad)            8   1634 by John Norton

*Henry VIII*

    First printed in the Folio

# Tragedies

### Troilus and Cressida

> Quarto  1  1609 by G. Eld for R. Bonian and H. Walley (exists in two states)

### Coriolanus

> First printed in the Folio

### Titus Andronicus

> Quarto  1  1594 by John Danter
> 2  1600 by I. R. for Edward White
> 3  1611 for Edward White

### Romeo and Juliet

> (bad)  Quarto  1  1597 by John Danter
> 2  1599 by Thomas Creede for Cuthbert Burby
> 3  1609 for John Smethwicke
> 4  (undated) for John Smethwicke
> 5  1637 by R. Young for John Smethwicke

### Timon of Athens

> First printed in the Folio

### Julius Caesar

> First printed in the Folio

### Macbeth

> First printed in the Folio

### Hamlet

> (bad)  Quarto  1  1603 for N. L. and John Trundell
> 2  1604/5 by I. R. for N. L.
> 3  1611 for John Smethwicke
> 4  (undated) by W. S. for John Smethwicke.
> 5  1637 by R. Young for John Smethwicke

194

Printing History

*King Lear*

Quarto 1 1608 for Nathaniel Butter
2 [1619] for Nathaniel Butter

*Othello*

Quarto 1 1622 by N. O. for Thomas Walkley
Quarto 2 1630 by A. M. for Richard Hawkins

*Antony and Cleopatra*

First printed in the Folio

*Cymbeline*

First printed in the Folio

*Pericles*

Not printed in the Folio
(bad) Quarto 1 1609 for Henry Gosson
(bad) 2 1609 for Henry Gosson
(bad) 3 1611 by S. S.
(bad) 4 1619 for T. P.
(bad) 5 1630 by I. N. for R. B.
(bad) 6 1635 by Thomas Cotes

*The Two Noble Kinsmen*

Not printed in the Folio
Quarto 1 1634 by Thomas Cotes for John Waterson

# SELECTED BIBLIOGRAPHY

Bald, R. C. "'Assembled' Texts." *The Library*, 4th ser., 12 (1931–32), 243–248.

——— "The Foul Papers of a Revision." *The Library*, 4th ser., 26 (1946), 37–50.

Bentley, Gerald Eades. *The Profession of Dramatist in Shakespeare's Time, 1590–1642.* Princeton: Princeton University Press, 1971.

Bevington, David. "Determining the Indeterminate: The Oxford Shakespeare." *Shakespeare Quarterly*, 38 (1987), 501–519.

Blayney, Peter. *The Texts of King Lear and their Origins: Volume 1, Nicholas Okes and the First Quarto.* Cambridge: Cambridge University Press, 1982.

Bowers, Fredson. "Notes on Standing Type in Elizabethan Printing." *The Papers of the Bibliographic Society of America*, 40 (1946), 205–224.

——— *On Editing Shakespeare.* Charlottesville: University Press of Virginia, 1966.

——— *Essays in Bibliography, Text, and Editing.* Charlottesville: University Press of Virginia, 1975.

——— "Foul Papers, Compositor B, and the Speech-Prefixes Of *All's Well that Ends Well*." *Studies in Bibliography*, 32 (1979), 60–81.

——— "Shakespeare At Work: The Foul Papers of *All's Well That Ends Well*." In *English Renaissance Studies: Presented to Dame Helen Gardner*. Ed. John Carey. Oxford: Clarendon Press, 1980, pp. 56–73.

——— "Establishing Shakespeare's Text: Poins and Peto in *1 Henry IV*." *Studies in Bibliography*, 34 (1981), 189–198.

——— "Authority, Copy, and Transmission in Shakespeare's Texts." In *Shakespeare Study Today*. Ed. Georgianna Ziegler. New York: AMS Press, 1986, pp. 7–36.

Brun, Bernard. "Problèmes d'une édition génétique: L'atelier de Marcel Proust." In *Avant-texte, texte, après-texte*. Ed. Louis Hay and Peter Nagy. Paris: Editions du CNRS, 1982, pp. 77–82.

Chambers, E. K. *The Disintegration of Shakespeare.* London: Oxford University Press, 1924.

——— *William Shakespeare: A Study of Facts and Problems.* 2 vols. Oxford: Clarendon Press, 1930.

Coghill, Nevill. *Shakespeare's Professional Skills.* Cambridge: Cambridge University Press, 1965.

Craig, Hardin. "Revised Elizabethan Quartos: An Attempt to Form a Class." In *Studies in the English Renaissance Drama.* Ed. J. Bennett, O. Cargill, and V. Hall, Jr. New York: New York University Press, 1959, pp. 43–57.

de Grazia, Margreta. "The Essential Shakespeare and the Material Book." *Textual Practice,* 2 (1988), 69–86.

——— *Shakespeare Verbatim: The Reproduction of Authenticity and the 1790 Apparatus* (Oxford: Oxford University Press, 1991).

Doran, Madeleine. *The Text of King Lear.* 1931; rpt. New York: AMS Press, Inc., 1967.

Duthie, G. I. *The 'Bad' Quarto of Hamlet.* Cambridge: Cambridge University Press, 1941.

Fabian, Bernhard, and Kurt Tetzeli von Rosador, eds. *Shakespeare: Text, Language, Criticism: Essays in Honour of Marvin Spevack.* Hildesheim: Olms-Weidmann, 1987.

Feuillerat, Albert. *The Composition of Shakespeare's Plays: Authorship, Chronology.* New Haven: Yale University Press, 1953.

Foakes, R. A., "Textual Revision and the Fool in *King Lear.*" In *Essays in Honour of Peter Davison, Trivium,* 20 (1985), pp. 33–47.

——— Review, *William Shakespeare: The Complete Works* (ed. Wells and Taylor). *Modern Language Review,* 84 (1989), 436–439.

Foakes, R. A., and R. T. Rickert, eds. *Henslowe's Diary.* Cambridge: Cambridge University Press, 1961.

Greg, W. W. *Dramatic Documents From the Elizabethan Playhouses: Commentary.* Oxford: Clarendon Press, 1931.

——— "The Rationale of Copy-Text." *Studies in Bibliography,* 3 (1950), 19–36.

——— *The Editorial Problem in Shakespeare.* 3rd ed. Oxford: Clarendon Press, 1954.

——— *The Shakespeare First Folio: Its Bibliographical and Textual History.* Oxford: Clarendon Press, 1955.

——— *Collected Papers.* Ed. J. C. Maxwell. Oxford: Clarendon Press, 1966.

Hinman, Charlton. *The Printing and Proof-Reading of the First Folio of Shakespeare.* 2 vols. Oxford: Clarendon Press, 1963.

Honigmann, E. A. J. *The Stability of Shakespeare's Text.* London: E. Arnold Ltd, 1965.

——— "Shakespeare's Revised Plays: *King Lear* and *Othello.*" *The Library,* 6th ser., 4 (1982), 142–173.

——— "Shakespeare as a Reviser." In *Textual Criticism and Literary Interpretation.* Ed. Jerome J. McGann. Chicago: University of Chicago Press, 1985, pp. 1–22.

——— "The Date and Revision of *Troilus and Cressida.*" In *Textual Criticism and Literary Interpretation.* Ed. Jerome J. McGann. Chicago: University of Chicago Press, 1985, pp. 38–54.

——— "Do-It-Yourself Lear." Review, *The Complete King Lear, 1608–1623* (ed. Michael Warren). *The New York Review of Books,* 25 October 1990, 58–60.

Howard-Hill, T. H. "The Bridgewater-Huntington MS of Middleton's *Game at Chess.*" *Manuscripta,* 28 (1984), 145–156.

——— "The Challenge of *King Lear.*" *The Library,* 6th ser., 7 (1985), 161–179.

——— "The Author as Scribe or Reviser?" Middleton's Intentions in *A Game at Chess.* *TEXT,* 3 (1987), 305–318.

Jonson, Ben. *Conversations with William Drummond of Hawthornden, 1619.* Ed. G. B. Harrison. New York: E. P. Dutton & Company, 1923. Published with *Discoveries* (below).

———— *Discoveries, 1641.* Ed. G. B. Harrison. New York: E. P. Dutton & Company, 1923. Published with *Conversations* (above).

Jowett, John. "Ligature Shortage and Speech-Prefix Variation in *Julius Caesar.*" *The Library,* 6th ser., 6 (1984), 244–253.

Jowett, John and Gary Taylor, "Sprinklings of Authority: The Folio Text of *Richard II.*" *Studies in Bibliography,* 38 (1985), 151–200.

———— "The Three Texts of *2 Henry IV.*" *Studies in Bibliography,* 40 (1987), 31–50.

Kerrigan, John. "*Love's Labor's Lost* and Shakespearean Revision." *Shakespeare Quarterly,* 33 (1982), 337–339.

———— "Shakespeare at Work: The Katharine-Rosaline Tangle in *Love's Labour's Lost.*" *Review of English Studies,* n.s. 33 (1982), 129–147.

———— "Shakespeare as Reviser." In *English Drama to 1710.* Ed. Christopher Ricks. New York: Peter Bedrick Books, 1987, pp. 255–275.

Limon, Jerzy. *Dangerous Matter: English Drama and Politics in 1623–24.* Cambridge: Cambridge University Press, 1986.

Long, William B. "'A bed / for woodstock': A Warning for the Unwary." *Medieval and Renaissance Drama in England,* 2 (1985), 91–118.

———— "Stage-Directions: A Misinterpreted Factor in Determining Textual Provenance." *TEXT,* 2 (1985), 121–137.

McGann, Jerome J. *A Critique of Modern Textual Criticism* University of Chicago Press, 1983.

———— ed. *Textual Criticism and Literary Interpretation.* Chicago: University of Chicago Press, 1985.

McKenzie, D. F. *Bibliography and the Sociology of Texts.* London: British Library, 1986.

McKerrow, R. B. *An Introduction to Bibliography for Literary Students.* Oxford: Oxford University Press, 1928.

———— "The Elizabethan Printer and Dramatic Manuscripts." *The Library,* 4th ser., 12 (1931), 251–275.

———— *Prolegomena for the Oxford Shakespeare: A Study in Editorial Method.* Oxford: Clarendon Press, 1939.

McLeod, Randall (Random Cloud). "The Marriage of Good and Bad Quartos." *Shakespeare Quarterly,* 33 (1982), 421–431.

McMillin, Scott. "Casting for Pembroke's Men: The *Henry VI* Quartos and *The Taming of A Shrew.*" *Shakespeare Quarterly,* 23 (1972), 141–159.

———— *The Elizabethan Theatre and "The Book of Sir Thomas More."* Ithaca: Cornell University Press, 1987.

Muir, Kenneth. *Shakespeare: Contrasts and Controversies.* Norman: University of Oklahoma Press, 1985.

Nosworthy, J. M. *Shakespeare's Occasional Plays: Their Origin and Transmission.* New York: Barnes & Noble, Inc., 1965.

Orgel, Stephen. "What is a Text?" *Research Opportunities in Renaissance Drama,* 24 (1981), 3–6.

————— "The Authentic Shakespeare." *Representations,* 21 (1988), 1–25.

Patterson, Annabel. *Censorship and Interpretation.* Madison: University of Wisconsin Press, 1984.

Pollard, Alfred. *Shakespeare's Fight With the Pirates and the Problems of the Transmission of His Text.* London: A. Moring, 1917.

————— *The Foundations of Shakespeare's Text.* London: Oxford University Press, 1923.

Taylor, Gary. "The War in *King Lear.*" *Shakespeare Survey,* 33 (1980), 27–34.

————— "*Troilus and Cressida:* Bibliography, Performance, and Interpretation." *Shakespeare Studies,* 15 (1982), 99–136.

————— "The Fortunes of Oldcastle." *Shakespeare Survey,* 38 (1985), 85–100.

————— "William Shakespeare, Richard James and the House of Cobham." *Review of English Studies,* 38 (1987), 334–354.

————— "Revising Shakespeare." *TEXT,* 3 (1987), 285–304.

Taylor, Gary and Michael Warren, eds. *The Division of the Kingdoms: Shakespeare's Two Versions of King Lear.* 1983; rpt. Oxford: Clarendon Press, 1986.

Thomas, Sidney. "Shakespeare's Supposed Revision of *King Lear.*" *Shakespeare Quarterly,* 35 (1984), 506–511.

Thorpe, James and Claude M. Simpson. *The Task of the Editor.* Los Angeles: William Andrews Clark Memorial Library, 1969.

Trousdale, Marion. "Diachronic and Synchronic: Critical Bibliography and the Acting of Plays." In *Shakespeare: Text, Language, Criticism: Essays in Honour of Marvin Spevack.* Ed. B. Fabian and K. Tetzeli von Rosador. Hildesheim: Olms-Weidmann, 1987, pp. 304–314.

Turner, Robert K. "Act-End Notations in Some Elizabethan Plays." *Modern Philology,* 72 (1975), 238–247.

————— "Revisions and Repetition-Brackets in Fletcher's *A Wife for a Month.*" *Studies in Bibliography,* 36 (1983), 178–190.

Urkowitz, Steven. *Shakespeare's Revision of "King Lear."* Princeton: Princeton University Press, 1980.

————— "'Well-sayd olde Mole': Burying Three *Hamlets* in Modern Editions." In *Shakespeare Study Today.* Ed. Georgianna Ziegler. New York: AMS Press, 1986, pp. 37–70.

————— "Five Women Eleven Ways: Changing Images of Shakespearean Characters in the Earliest Texts." In *Images of Shakespeare.* Ed. W. Habicht, D. J. Palmer, and R. Pringle. Newark: University of Delaware Press, 1988, pp. 292–304.

Warren, Michael. "Quarto and Folio *King Lear* and the Interpretation of Albany and Edgar." In *Shakespeare: Pattern of Excelling Nature.* Ed. David Bevington and Jay L. Halio. Newark: University of Delaware Press, 1978, pp. 95–107.

————— "Textual Problems, Editorial Assertions in Editions of Shakespeare." In *Textual Criticism and Literary Interpretation.* Ed. Jerome J. McGann. Chicago: University of Chicago Press, 1985, pp. 23–37.

————— *The Complete "King Lear," 1608–1623.* Berkeley: University of California Press, 1989.

————— "The Theatricalization of Text: Beckett, Jonson, Shakespeare." *The Library Chronicle of the University of Texas at Austin,* 20 (1990), 39–59.

Wells, Stanley and Gary Taylor. *Modernizing Shakespeare's Spelling, with Three Studies in the Text of "Henry V."* Oxford: Clarendon Press, 1979.

—————— "The Oxford Shakespeare Re-viewed." *Analytical and Enumerative Bibliography,* n.s. 4 (1991, forthcoming).

Wells, Stanley and Gary Taylor, with John Jowett and William Montgomery, eds. *William Shakespeare: The Complete Works* (Old Spelling Edition). Oxford: Clarendon Press, 1986.

Wells, Stanley, and Gary Taylor, with John Jowett and William Montgomery. *William Shakespeare: A Textual Companion.* Oxford: Clarendon Press, 1987.

Wells, Stanley. *Re-Editing Shakespeare for the Modern Reader.* Oxford: Clarendon Press, 1984.

—————— "Revision in Shakespeare's Plays." In *Editing and Editors: A Retrospect.* Ed. Richard Landon. New York: AMS Press, 1988, pp. 67–97.

Werstine, Paul. "The Textual Mystery of *Hamlet.*" *Shakespeare Quarterly,* 39 (1988), 1–26.

Wilson, John Dover. "The Task of Heminge and Condell." In *Studies in the First Folio.* London: Oxford University Press, 1924, pp. 53–77.

—————— *The Elizabethan Shakespeare.* London: Oxford University Press, 1929.

# NOTES

Introduction

1. Werstine, "The Textual Mystery of *Hamlet,*" *Shakespeare Quarterly,* 39 (1988), 1.

2. Chambers, *The Disintegration of Shakespeare* (London: Oxford University Press, 1924).

3. Although E. A. J. Honigmann in *The Stability of Shakespeare's Text* (London: E. Arnold Ltd, 1965) and J. M. Nosworthy in *Shakespeare's Occasional Plays: Their Origin and Transmission* (New York: Barnes & Noble, Inc., 1965) each suggested that Shakespeare's "second thoughts" may have produced some of the variants in his plays, Michael Warren was the first to argue that Shakespeare revised *King Lear* with a specific plan and purpose in mind. See Warren, "Quarto and Folio *King Lear* and the Interpretation of Albany and Edgar," in *Shakespeare: Pattern of Excelling Nature,* ed. David Bevington and Jay L. Halio (Newark: University of Delaware Press, 1978), pp. 95–107. His essay is an enlarged version of the paper he delivered at the International Shakespeare Association Congress in 1976.

4. Taylor, "The War in *King Lear,*" *Shakespeare Survey,* 33 (1980), 27–34.

5. Urkowitz, *Shakespeare's Revision of "King Lear"* (Princeton: Princeton University Press, 1980), p. 3.

6. Stanley Wells, "The Once and Future *King Lear,*" in *The Division of the Kingdoms: Shakespeare's Two Versions of "King Lear,"* ed. Gary Taylor and Michael Warren (1983; rpt. Oxford: Clarendon Press, 1986), pp. 8–9.

7. For a discussion of these issues, see *The Division of the Kingdoms,* especially Stanley Wells, "The Once and Future *King Lear,*" pp. 1–22; Michael Warren, "The Diminution of Kent," pp. 59–73; and Gary Taylor, "*King Lear:* The Date and Authorship of the Folio Version," pp. 351–451.

8. Orgel, "What is a Text?" *Research Opportunities in Renaissance Drama,* 24 (1981), 3, 6; also see his essay "The Authentic Shakespeare," *Representations,* 21 (1988), 1–25, in which he contrasts five eighteenth-century performances of the same Shakespearian scene in order to argue that "what we want is not the authentic play, with its unstable, infinitely

revisable script, but an authentic Shakespeare, to whom every generation's version of a classic drama may be ascribed." The substantively variant Quarto and Folio texts demonstrate that the "authentic" Shakespeare precedes and produces the authentically revisable text.

9. Goldberg, "Textual Properties," *Shakespeare Quarterly,* 37 (1986), 213–214. Also see Michael D. Bristol's discussion of these issues in *Shakespeare's America, America's Shakespeare* (London: Routledge, 1990), pp. 91–119.

10. On the "death" of the author, see Michel Foucault, "What is an Author," in *Language, Counter-Memory, Practice: Selected Essays and Interviews,* ed. Donald F. Bouchard (Ithaca: Cornell University Press, 1977), pp. 113–138.

11. Margreta de Grazia, "The Essential Shakespeare and the Material Book," *Textual Practice,* 2 (1988), 71.

12. Gary Taylor, in "The Canon and Chronology of Shakespeare's Plays" (in Stanley Wells and Gary Taylor with John Jowett and William Montgomery, *William Shakespeare: A Textual Companion* [Oxford: Clarendon Press, 1987], p. 70; hereafter cited as *Textual Companion*), states that nineteen of the Folio plays had been printed in separate editions before 1623. However, I believe that he includes either *The Taming of a Shrew* or the nonextant play *Love's Labour's Won* in this list, which I do not.

13. A brief outline of the printing history of all of the plays appears in the Appendix.

14. My study of printed Quartos of plays by Renaissance dramatists other than Shakespeare shows that Quartos advertising "enlargement" or some other type of revision were not always preceded by "bad" or "pirated" editions, but were in fact often preceded by a "good" Quarto overseen by the author (see chapter 7).

15. W. W. Greg, *The Shakespeare First Folio: Its Bibliographical and Textual History* (Oxford: Clarendon Press, 1955), pp. 447–448; Charlton Hinman, *The Printing and Proof-Reading of the First Folio of Shakespeare,* vol. 1 (Oxford: Clarendon Press, 1963), pp. 361–362.

16. Jonson, *Discoveries, 1641,* ed. G. B. Harrison (New York: E. P. Dutton & Company., 1923), p. 28. Published with *Conversations with William Drummond of Hawthornden, 1619.*

17. Both Nosworthy and Bevington trust the "testimony" of Heminge, Condell, and Jonson that Shakespeare's drafts were unblotted (see Nosworthy, *Shakespeare's Occasional Plays,* p. 62, and Bevington, Introduction, *Henry IV, Part I* [Oxford: Clarendon Press, 1987], p. 90).

18. Bentley, *The Profession of Dramatist in Shakespeare's Time, 1590–1642* (Princeton: Princeton University Press, 1971), p. 262.

19. William Long, in his essay "'A bed / for woodstock': A Warning for the Unwary," *Medieval and Renaissance Drama in England,* 2 (1985), p. 93, argues that the term "prompt-book" should be replaced with "playbook," as the former term implies a neat, orderly, and regularized manuscript, which to judge from extant evidence was not often the case; however, while I recognize Long's objection, I use "promptbook" throughout this study as synonymous with "the book," the term used in several manuscripts as the title of the theatrical copy.

20. See chapter 1 for a discussion of W. W. Greg's and E. K. Chambers's skeptical attitudes about the type of revision performed by Shakespeare.

21. Honigmann, *The Stability of Shakespeare's Text,* pp. 11, 2. Honigmann has more recently argued for more large-scale revisions than those deriving from "instability"; see

for example his essay "Shakespeare as a Reviser," in *Textual Criticism and Literary Interpretation,* ed. Jerome J. McGann (Chicago: University of Chicago Press, 1985), pp. 1–22.

22. Thomas, "Shakespeare's Supposed Revision of *King Lear,*" *Shakespeare Quarterly,* 35 (1984), 509.

23. Werstine, "Folio Editors, Folio Compositors, and the Folio Text of *King Lear,*" *The Division of the Kingdoms,* p. 252.

24. Bowers, "Establishing Shakespeare's Text: Poins and Peto in *1 Henry IV,*" *Studies in Bibliography,* 34 (1981), 194–195. Hereafter "Establishing Shakespeare's Text."

25. Kerrigan, "Shakespeare as Reviser," in *English Drama to 1710,* ed. Christopher Ricks (New York: Peter Bedrick Books, 1987), p. 258. Gary Taylor also takes up this issue in "Revising Shakespeare," *TEXT,* 3 (1987), 285–304.

26. Wells, *Re-Editing Shakespeare for the Modern Reader* (Oxford: Clarendon Press, 1984), p. 112.

27. Chambers, *William Shakespeare: A Study of Facts and Problems,* vol. 1 (Oxford: Clarendon Press, 1930), pp. 509, 231–232 (also discussed by Urkowitz in *Shakespeare's Revision of King Lear,* p. 141).

28. Bentley, *The Profession of Dramatist,* p. 263.

29. *Henslowe's Diary,* ed. R. A. Foakes and R. T. Rickert (Cambridge: Cambridge University Press, 1961), p. 182.

30. Greene, *Groats-Worth of Witte,* ed. G. B. Harrison (New York: E. P. Dutton & Company, 1923), p. 45.

31. For discussions of this point, see, for example, J. Dover Wilson, "Malone and the Upstart Crow," *Shakespeare Survey,* 4 (1951), 56–68; and Samuel Schoenbaum, who in *William Shakespeare: A Compact Documentary Life* (New York: Oxford University Press, 1987), pp. 152–153, argues that this passage may refer either to Shakespeare's plagiarism or to his "audacity" in setting himself up as a rival to established dramatists (or possibly to both offenses). Russell Fraser, in *Young Shakespeare* (New York: Columbia University Press, 1988), p. 144, suggests that Shakespeare took revenge on Greene in *Hamlet* with Polonius's remark in 2.2 that "beautified" is a "vile phrase." E. A. J. Honigmann has recently argued that the use of "tygers hart" implied that Shakespeare had previously been a usurer ("'There is a World Elsewhere': William Shakespeare, Businessman," in *Images of Shakespeare,* ed. W. Habicht, D. J. Palmer, R. Pringle [Newark: University of Delaware Press, 1988], p. 42).

32. *The Works of Thomas Nashe,* ed. R. B. McKerrow, 5 vols. (Oxford: Basil Blackwell, 1904–1910), vol. 3, pp. 153–154.

33. Quarto 2: G4; Folio: TLN 1886–1891. Signatures (sigs.) from the original Quartos and Through Line Numbers (TLN) from the *First Folio Facsimile* prepared by Charlton Hinman (New York: W. W. Norton & Company, Inc., 1968) are given throughout for each citation from a Shakespeare play.

34. Honigmann, *The Stability of Shakespeare's Text,* p. 1.

35. Greg, "The Rationale of Copy-Text," *Studies in Bibliography,* 3 (1950), 21, 34. Marion Trousdale has recently argued that the "present crisis in Shakespeare studies," which she sees as a "crisis about the nature of our texts," is "a direct result of contradictions implicit in the methods so carefully developed by McKerrow and Greg. In brief, all editors from Pope to the present have sought a text that does not exist" ("Diachronic

and Synchronic: Critical Bibliography and the Acting of Plays," in *Shakespeare: Text, Language, Criticism: Essays in Honour of Marvin Spevack,* ed. B. Fabian and K. Tetzeli von Rosador [Hildesheim: Olms-Weidmann, 1987], p. 304; collection referred to hereafter by title only).

36. See Jerome J. McGann's discussion of this point in *A Critique of Modern Textual Criticism* (Chicago: University of Chicago Press, 1983), p. 28.

37. Bowers, "Scholarly Editions of Nineteenth-Century American Authors," in *Bibliography and Textual Criticism: English and American Literature, 1700 to the Present,* ed. O. M. Brack, Jr., and Warner Barnes (Chicago: University of Chicago Press, 1969), p. 197.

38. Bowers, *Essays in Bibliography, Text, and Editing* (Charlottesville: University Press of Virginia, 1975), p. 464.

39. James Thorpe and Claude M. Simpson, Jr., *The Task of the Editor* (Los Angeles: William Andrews Clark Memorial Library, 1969), p. 3.

40. McKerrow, *Prolegomena for the Oxford Shakespeare: A Study in Editorial Method* (Oxford: Clarendon Press, 1939), p. 1.

41. Steven Urkowitz, "'Well-sayd olde Mole': Burying Three *Hamlets* in Modern Editions," in *Shakespeare Study Today,* ed. Georgianna Ziegler (New York: AMS Press, 1986), p. 39.

42. See Nicholas Hytner, "A Stage for Second Thoughts," *The Times* (London), 30 June 1990, p. 25, and Peter Holland, "A Note on the Text," *King Lear,* souvenir program, Royal Shakespeare Company, 1990.

43. McGann, *A Critique of Modern Textual Criticism,* pp. 4–5.

44. Brun, "*Problèmes d'une édition génétique: L'atelier de Marcel Proust,*" *Avant-texte, texte, après-texte,* ed. Louis Hay and Peter Nagy (Paris: Editions du CNRS, 1982), p. 78.

45. Gabler, *Ulysses: A Critical and Synoptic Edition,* 3 vols. (New York: Garland Publishing, 1984). Gabler created more controversy by renaming this edition *Ulysses: The Corrected Text* when it was published by Random House, Penguin Books, and the Bodley Head Press in 1986 in a single, nonsynoptic, "reading" edition without the critical apparatus. In his afterword to this later edition, Gabler notes that "since it was the act of making fair copies that gave the impulse to revise which carried forward into the last revision of the final working manuscripts, the whole process of revision was in truth continuous. Hence, all recoverable changes it occasioned belong to the stage of the text's development that the documents comprise, and thus ultimately to a validly revised text of *Ulysses*" (p. 648). This argument, which can be applied to the "development" of Shakespeare's text, has signficant implications for revision theories.

46. Gabler, afterword, *Ulysses: A Critical and Synoptic Edition,* p. 1901. However, Gabler does impose some "stringent rules and restrictions" in recording revisions: "Unique fair-copy revisions are not admitted to the edition text if the context established for them by fair-copy/typescript agreement underwent revision in the subsequent textual development" (pp. 1902–1903). For a review of Gabler's editorial distinctions, see Jerome J. McGann, "*Ulysses* as a Postmodern Text: The Gabler Edition," *Criticism,* 27 (1985), 283–305.

47. This distinction, made by Gabler in a circulated but unpublished essay, is quoted by Charles Rossman in "The New *Ulysses*: The Hidden Controversy," *The New York Review of Books,* 8 December 1988, pp. 53–58. In the afterword to his 1984 edition, Gabler

argues that "Joyce's proofreading was characteristically corrective. Although one may be virtually certain that he never read proof against copy, his excellent memory and precise sense of his text largely served him in fully reversing the textual corruptions he spotted. Authorial interventions of such kind in the documents of transmission are unambiguously corrections and thus equally clearly distinct from the revisions on the same documents. Yet cases remain where correction and revision interpenetrate and the individual instances call for critical interpretation" (p. 1893).

48. Ted-Larry Pebworth and Ernest W. Sullivan II, "Rational Presentation of Multiple Textual Traditions," *The Papers of the Bibliographical Society of America,* 83 (1989), 44.

49. Bevington, "Determining the Indeterminate: The Oxford Shakespeare," *Shakespeare Quarterly,* 38 (1987), 502.

50. See Wells and Taylor et al., *Textual Companion,* especially "The Canon and Chronology of Shakespeare's Plays," pp. 69–109.

51. Warren, general introduction, *The Complete "King Lear," 1608–1623: Texts and Parallel Texts in Photographic Facsimile* (Berkeley: University of California Press, 1989), pp. xx–xxi.

52. Honigmann, "Do-It-Yourself Lear" (review of *The Complete "King Lear," 1608–1623,* ed. Michael Warren), *The New York Review of Books,* 25 October 1990, p. 60.

53. Because the loose ends, inconsistencies and variants within or between the Quarto and/or Folio texts of *The Comedy of Errors, The Taming of the Shrew, The Two Gentlemen of Verona, King John, The Merchant of Venice, Much Ado About Nothing, As You Like It, Twelfth Night, All's Well That Ends Well, Measure for Measure, Timon of Athens, Antony and Cleopatra, Pericles, Coriolanus, Cymbeline, The Winter's Tale, The Tempest, Henry VIII,* and *The Two Noble Kinsmen* appear to be due to collaboration or to scribal, censorial, editorial, and/or compositorial interference rather than to demonstrable authorial revision, these plays are not individually discussed in this study of authorial revision. For discussions of the variants in these plays see for example R. A. Foakes, introduction, *The Comedy of Errors* (London: Methuen & Co. Ltd, 1962), p. xvi; Ann Thompson, textual analysis, *The Taming of the Shrew* (Cambridge: Cambridge University Press, 1984), pp. 160–164; Clifford Leech, introduction, *The Two Gentlemen of Verona* (London: Methuen and Co. Ltd, 1969), pp. xxx–xxxv; W. W. Greg, *The Shakespeare First Folio,* pp. 248–249, 258, 279; Agnes Latham, introduction, *As You Like It* (London: Methuen and Co. Ltd, 1975), p. xxxiv; T. W. Craik, introduction, *Twelfth Night,* ed. J. M. Lothian and T. W. Craik (London: Methuen and Co. Ltd, 1975) pp. xxi–xxv; Greg, *The Shakespeare First Folio,* pp. 351–353; John Jowett, introduction, *Measure for Measure,* in *Textual Companion,* pp. 468–469; H. J. Oliver, introduction, *Timon of Athens* (London: Methuen and Co. Ltd, 1959), pp. xiv, xix, xxii–xxiii; Greg, *The Shakespeare First Folio,* p. 103; Philip Edwards, "An Approach to the Problem of *Pericles,*" *Shakespeare Survey,* 5 (1952), 26, 37, 45; Philip Brockbank, introduction, *Coriolanus* (London: Methuen and Co. Ltd, 1976), p. 5; Gary Taylor, introduction, *Cymbeline,* in *Textual Companion,* p. 604; J. H. P. Pafford, introduction, *The Winter's Tale* (London: Methuen and Co. Ltd, 1966), pp. xxii–xxvii; Frank Kermode, introduction, *The Tempest* (London: Methuen and Co. Ltd, 1961), pp. xvi–xxiv; R. A. Foakes, introduction, *Henry VIII* (London: Methuen and Co. Ltd, 1968), p. xxv; and G. R. Proudfoot, introduction, *The Two Noble Kinsmen* (Lincoln: University of Nebraska Press, 1970), p. xxiv, respectively. For example, the loose ends

and inconsistencies in the Folio texts of such plays as *The Winter's Tale* and *The Tempest* probably represent different layers of composition or a change of intention on the author's part rather than later revision. Shakespeare may have made marginal additions in the speeches of Caliban throughout *The Tempest* to rework his character, as Frank Kermode argues (introduction, *The Tempest,* p. xiv), but the only evidence for such a conclusion comes from an assumption that Caliban speaks more nobly than a monster should. Similarly, minor revision during composition may account for a few false starts, inconsistencies, repetitions, and confusions in characters, as with Salarino, Solanio, and Salerio in the 1600 Quarto of *The Merchant of Venice* and the Folio text printed from it, further annotated with playhouse alterations (Greg, *Shakespeare First Folio,* p. 260); however, all of these textual tangles may have arisen from the author's uncertainty about how to proceed while composing a work and not necessarily from concurrent or later revisions.

## 1. Theories of Revision, 1623–1990

1. Thomas, "Shakespeare's Supposed Revision of *King Lear,*" p. 507.

2. Both Kenneth Muir (*Shakespeare: Contrasts and Controversies* [Norman: University of Oklahoma Press, 1985], p. 52) and Sidney Thomas ("Shakespeare's Supposed Revision of *King Lear,*" p. 506) use the term "orthodoxy" to describe these new "revisionist" theories. Annabel Patterson calls *The Division of the Kingdoms* "the volume in which this revisionary movement has itself become institutionalized" (*Censorship and Interpretation* [Madison: University of Wisconsin Press, 1984], p. 61).

3. McGann, *A Critique of Modern Textual Criticism,* pp. 11, 4.

4. Steven Urkowitz, "The Base Shall to th'Legitimate: The Growth of an Editorial Tradition," in *The Division of the Kingdoms,* p. 37. Hereafter "Growth of an Editorial Tradition."

5. G. B. Evans, "Shakespeare's Text: Approaches and Problems," in *A New Companion to Shakespeare Studies,* ed. Kenneth Muir and S. Schoenbaum (Cambridge: Cambridge University Press, 1971), p. 237.

6. For a discussion of the "reforming" of the plays, see F. E. Halliday, *The Cult of Shakespeare* (London: Gerald Duckworth & Co. Ltd, 1957), pp. 14–43. Also see George R. Guffey's essay, "Politics, Weather, and the Contemporary Reception of the Dryden-Davenant *Tempest,*" *Restoration,* 8 (1984), 1–9, in which he argues that the revised *Tempest* "reflected the realities of recent domestic and foreign history."

7. *The Works of Mr. William Shakespear,* 7 vols., ed. Nicholas Rowe, vol. 1, (London: Printed for Jacob Tonson, 1709), sigs. A2-A2$^v$, pp. vii, xii. All editions of Shakespeare's complete works will be cited in full at the first instance, and referred to thereafter by the last name of the editor only.

8. The eighteenth-century debate about whether the extant Quartos of *The Troublesome raigne of John King of England* (1591 and later) and *The Taming of a Shrew* (1594 and later) served as sources for or first editions of the two Shakespearian plays has continued into the twentieth century.

9. Maynard Mack states that Pope had access to only six first Quartos (*Alexander Pope: A Life* [New York: W. W. Norton & Co., 1985], p. 425), but Pope lists at least nine

that he has seen in "A Table of the Several Editions," *The Works of Mr William Shakespear*, 7 vols. (London: Printed for Jacob Tonson, 1725), vol. 6.

10. Pope, vol. 1, pp. viii, xvii, 233, xvi, xxii.

11. Thomas R. Lounsbury, *The First Editors of Shakespeare* (London: David Nutt, 1906), p. 101.

12. Pope, vol. 1, p. xx, xxii.

13. *The Works of Shakespeare*, ed. Lewis Theobald, 7 vols. (London: Printed for A. Bettesworth et al., 1733), vol. 1., pp. xvi, xxxvii–xxxviii. Alfred Pollard's "bad" Quarto theory, based on similar conclusions, helped in the twentieth century to displace arguments of revision, as modern critics agreed that a reported text could not also be accepted as an author's first draft. However, many (including some "new" revisionists) now question whether any Quarto can be considered "bad" when it may indeed be the author's first draft, and they reject Pollard's theories.

14. Theobald, vol. 1, pp. xxxviii, 223; vol. 2, p. 179. For a recent discussion of Theobald's achievements, see Peter Seary, *Lewis Theobald and the Editing of Shakespeare* (Oxford: Clarendon Press, 1990).

15. *The Works of Shakespear*, ed. Thomas Hanmer, 9 vols. (London: Printed for J. and P. Knapton et al., 1744–1747).

16. *The Works of Shakespear*, ed. Alexander Pope and William Warburton, 8 vols. (London: Printed for J. and P. Knapton et al., 1747), vol. 1, pp. viii, ix.

17. Grey, *An Answer to Certain Passages in Mr. W——'s Preface to His Edition of Shakespear* (London: Printed for H. Carpenter, 1748).

18. Edwards, *A supplement to Mr. Warburton's edition of Shakespear. Being the Canons of Criticism* (London: M. Cooper, 1748).

19. *The Plays of William Shakespeare*, ed. Samuel Johnson, 8 vols. (London: Printed for J. and R. Tonson et al., 1765), vol. 1, sig. C1$^V$.

20. Johnson's comment in the preface, "I collated such copies as I could procure, and wished for more, but have not found the collectors of these rarities very communicative" (vol. 1, sig. D7$^V$), appears to allude to his reluctance to "court" David Garrick for access to his collection (see J. W. Krutch, *Samuel Johnson* [New York: H. Holt, 1944], p. 288).

21. In his 1765 edition, Johnson discusses in the footnotes at the beginning of each play which Quarto and Folio texts he has seen, and offers his own revision theories and admits his indebtedness to other editors in footnotes throughout the text. He is often incorrect, as most eighteenth-century editors were, in listing which Quartos are "first" Quartos.

22. Johnson, vol. 4, p. 105; vol. 1, sig. C7$^V$; vol. 8, p. 282.

23. Johnson, vol. 2, p. 295.

24. Kenrick, *A Review of Doctor Johnson's New Edition of Shakespeare* (London: Printed for J. Payne, 1765), pp. 85–86.

25. *Twenty of the Plays of Shakespeare*, ed. George Steevens, 4 vols. (London: Printed for J. and R. Tonson, et al., 1766), vol. 1, p. 10, vol. 2, sig. N7$^V$.

26. Urkowitz, *Shakespeare's Revision of King Lear*, p. 140.

27. Farmer, *An Essay on the Learning of Shakespeare: Addressed to Joseph Craddock Esq; The Second Edition, with Large Additions* (Cambridge: J. Archdeacon, 1767), p. 85.

28. Whiter, *A Specimen of a Commentary on Shakespeare. Being the text of the first (1794)*

*edition revised by the author and never previously published,* ed. Alan Over, completed by Mary Bell (London: Methuen & Co. Ltd, 1967), pp. 94, 62–63.

29. *Bell's Edition of Shakespeare's Plays,* ed. by the Authors of the Dramatic Censor, 9 vols. (London: Printed for John Bell, 1774), vol. 1, pp. 8–9; Vol. 9, pp. 14–15, 19, 9.

30. *Mr. William Shakespeare his Comedies, Histories, and Tragedies,* ed. Edward Capell, 10 vols. (London: Dryden Leach, 1767–8), vol. 1, pp. 9–11, 2.

31. Samuel Schoenbaum mentions a revised version found among Malone's posthumous papers (*Shakespeare's Lives* [Oxford: Clarendon Press, 1970], p. 171), but it is unclear whether this is the version that Boswell the younger added to the 1821 posthumous edition.

32. *The Plays of William Shakspeare,* ed. Samuel Johnson and George Steevens, 2nd ed., 10 vols. (London: Printed for C. Bathurst et al., 1778), vol. 1, p. 305.

33. Urkowitz, "Growth of an Editorial Tradition," in *The Division of the Kingdoms,* p. 39.

34. Johnson and Steevens, vol. 1, pp. 305–306.

35. *Prolegomena to the Dramatick Writings of Will. Shakspere,* vol. 2 (London: John Bell, 1788), p. 351.

36. *The Plays and Poems of William Shakspeare,* ed. Edmond Malone, 10 vols. (London: H. Baldwin, 1790), vol. 1, part 1, p. 325. Hereafter 1790 Malone.

37. On this point, see Margreta de Grazia, *Shakespeare Verbatim: The Reproduction of Authenticity and the 1790 Apparatus* (Oxford: Oxford University Press, 1991).

38. 1790 Malone, vol. 1, pt. 1, pp. x–xviii.

39. Albert Feuillerat, *The Composition of Shakespeare's Plays: Authorship, Chronology* (New Haven: Yale University Press, 1953), p. 32.

40. 1790 Malone, vol. 1, pt. 1, pp. lix–lx.

41. 1790 Malone, vol. 6, p. 399.

42. Kerrigan, "Revision, Adaptation, and the Fool in *King Lear,*" in *The Division of the Kingdoms,* p. 195.

43. For further discussions of Malone's achievements as an editor see Gary Taylor, *Reinventing Shakespeare: A Cultural History from the Restoration to the Present* (London: The Hogarth Press, 1989), and Margreta de Grazia, *Shakespeare Verbatim.*

44. Malone repeatedly uses this term in "A Dissertation on the Three Parts of *King Henry VI,*" 1790 Malone, vol. 6, pp. 381–429.

45. Urkowitz examines this point in "Growth of an Editorial Tradition," in *The Division of the Kingdoms,* pp. 37–40.

46. 1790 Malone, vol. 1, pt. 1, p. xviii. Malone may have, in fact, compared copies of the 1608 Q1 with copies of the 1619 (falsely dated 1608) Q2.

47. *The Plays and Poems of William Shakespeare,* ed. Edmond Malone, 21 vols. (London: F. C. and J. Rivington et al., 1821), vol. 1, p. xiii.

48. 1790 Malone, vol. 1, pt. 1, p. lxiii.

49. Coleridge, *Lectures 1808–1819: On Literature,* ed. R. A. Foakes, 2 vols. (London: Routledge & Kegan Paul, 1987), vol. 1, p. 313.

50. For a discussion of these manuscripts, see Collier, *Reasons for a New Edition of Shakespeare's Works,* 2nd ed. with additions (London: Whittaker & Co, 1842), p. 10.

51. *The Works of William Shakespeare,* ed. J. Payne Collier, 8 vols. (London: Whittaker

& Co, 1844), vol. 1, pp. cxiii–cxiv, 173; vol 2, p. 110; vol. 3, p. 204; vol. 4, pp. 461–462; vol. 5, pp. 4, 107, 227; vol. 6, p. 369; vol. 7, pp. 96, 192, 353.

52. For example, the stage direction for 4.1 of *As You Like It* reads, "Rosalind's Cottage." The title page of Collier's 1856 edition of Coleridge's *Seven Lectures on Shakespeare and Milton* (London: Chapman and Hall) announced that its appendix contained a complete list of the emendations but in fact provided only a partial list.

53. Andrew Brae, first in 1853 in a series of letters to *Notes and Queries* and later in 1855 in his anonymously published pamphlet, *Literary Cookery, with Reference to Matter Attributed to Coleridge and Shakespeare* (London: J. R. Smith, 1855), p. 7, opened the Perkins Folio debate by complaining virulently of "the presumption—the plagiarism—the vulgarity—the imbecility—of those wretched libels on the text of Shakespeare." Brae also implied that Collier had forged the dates of some Coleridge lectures so that he could reprint them as new lectures. Samuel Weller Singer and Rev. Alexander Dyce, who were soon to produce their own editions of the plays, and others also joined Brae in attacking Collier, noting that some of the "emendations" were reminiscent of textual work done by previous editors, including Edmond Malone.

54. Ingleby, *A Complete View of the Shakspere Controversy* (London: Nattali and Bond, 1861), p. 323.

55. Dewey Ganzel has defended Collier against all charges of forgery and has also argued that he was the "first" editor to have respected the integrity of Quarto and Folio texts in *Fortune and Men's Eyes: The Career of John Payne Collier* (Oxford: Oxford University Press, 1982), p. 86. However, Edmond Malone appears to have been the first editor to have respected the integrity of Quarto and Folio texts. Georgianna Ziegler, who examined some recently discovered manuscripts concerning Collier, reassesses his later reputation in "A Victorian Reputation: John Payne Collier and His Contemporaries," *Shakespeare Studies*, 17 (1985), 209–234.

56. After examining the Perkins Folio, I concluded that the "old corrector" had noticed these seventeenth-century annotations and decided to make similar marks throughout the volume. I have compared the hands in the Perkins Folio with Collier's hand as it appears in his several page transcription of scenes from John Bale's *King Johan* (also in the collections of the Huntington Library), and although Collier's hand does not exactly match any of those in the Perkins Folio, I see some slight resemblance between some of Collier's transcribed words and some Perkins Folio words.

57. *The Pictorial Edition of the Works of Shakspere*, ed. Charles Knight, 8 vols., *Histories*, vol. 2 (London: Charles Knight and Co 1839), p. xxxi.

58. Knight's strictures were supported by H. N. Hudson, probably the first American critic to venture into Shakespearian textual study. In 1848, Hudson asked of Shakespeare: "How many of those foul, misshapen, monstrous forms he drew forth from their dark prison-house, and moulded into the beauty, and animated with the breath of his genius, cannot be ascertained. Traces of his inimitable hand are perceptible in many plays published under the name of contemporary dramatists; several of those published in his own name, are known to have been regenerations of pre-existing stock-copies; and some which drew vitality from his embraces perished in the subsequent wreck of theatrical wealth" (*Lectures on Shakspeare*, 2 vols. [New York: Baker and Scribner, 1848], vol. 1, p. 21). Hudson's florid rhetoric represents the continuance of the school of criticism begun

by those like Theobald who over-praised Shakespeare in order to protect him from charges of being a "re-toucher" or "re-handler" of inferior plays.

59. *The Dramatic Works of William Shakespeare,* ed. Samuel Weller Singer, 10 vols. (London: Bell and Daldy, 1856), vol. 3, pp. 235–236, 371; vol. 4, p. 259.

60. *The Works of William Shakespeare,* ed. Rev. Alexander Dyce, 6 vols. (London: Edward Moxon, 1857), vol. 1, p. xxxv.

61. *The Works of William Shakespeare,* ed. W. G. Clark, J. Glover, and W. A. Wright, 9 vols. (Cambridge, Eng.: Macmillan and Co., 1863–1866) vol. 1, p. xxiii; vol. 2, p. 195; vol. 5, p. 639; vol. 6, p. ix; vol. 7, p. viii; vol. 8, p. xi.

62. Howard Staunton's edition of the *The Works of Shakespeare* (London: George Routledge & Sons, 1866), drew many of the same conclusions as the Cambridge Shakespeare.

63. Gary Taylor notes that a 1948 survey of English professors by Harcourt, Brace and Company showed that nearly all preferred a reprint of the Cambridge edition rather than the publication of a new text based on the latest scholarship (*Textual Companion,* p. 56). He also discusses this edition in *Reinventing Shakespeare,* pp. 184–189.

64. Fleay, *A Chronicle History of the Life and Work of William Shakespeare* (London: John C. Nimmo, 1886,) pp. 19, 59.

65. Robertson, *The Genuine in Shakespeare: A Conspectus* (London: George Routledge & Sons, Ltd, 1930), pp. 25, 9, 29.

66. Fleay, *Introduction to Shakespearian Study* (London: William Collins, Sons, and Co., 1877), p. 11.

67. Mackail, *Shakespeare After Three Hundred Years* (New York: Oxford University Press, 1916), p. 11.

68. Pollard, *Shakespeare Folios and Quartos: A Study in the Bibliography of Shakespeare's Plays 1594–1685* (London: Methuen & Co. Ltd, 1909).

69. Pollard, *Shakespeare's Fight With the Pirates and the Problems of the Transmission of His Text* (London: A. Moring, 1917), p. 62. This book, revised and reprinted in 1920 and 1967, continues to influence textual and literary scholars.

70. For a discussion of the methods of the New Bibliography, see R. B. McKerrow, *An Introduction to Bibliography for Literary Students* (Oxford: Clarendon Press, 1928); for a recent critique, see de Grazia, "The Essential Shakespeare and the Material Book."

71. Wilson, "The Task of Heminge and Condell," *Studies in the First Folio* (London: Oxford University Press, 1924), pp. 76–77.

72. Pollard, *The Foundations of Shakespeare's Text* (London: Oxford University Press, 1923), pp. 13–14.

73. Chambers, *The Disintegration of Shakespeare,* pp. 1, 3–4. He states that Malone "accepted Ravenscroft's account of *Titus Andronicus,* worked out the relation of 2 and 3 *Henry VI* to the *Contention* plays, took Shakespeare for their reviser, supposed *Henry VIII* to have undergone revision by a later hand, and beyond these only doubted 1 *Henry VI.*"

74. Chambers, *The Disintegration of Shakespeare,* p. 4, 18.

75. For example, in 1942, Alfred Hart rejected Robertsonian "double revision" theories, terming any revision by Shakespeare of predecessors' plays "fanciful" (*Stolne and Surreptitious Copies: A Comparative Study of Shakespeare's Bad Quartos* [Melbourne: Melbourne University Press, 1942], pp. 46, 62).

76. Wilson, *The Elizabethan Shakespeare* (London: Humphrey Milford, 1929), p. 4. In "The Task of Heminge and Condell" (pp. 57–58), he had attacked the editors of the *Cambridge Shakespeare* who had questioned the authority and truthfulness of Heminge and Condell's Folio address and defended the two actors without concluding whether their statements on "cur'd" copies and "unblotted lines" should be taken literally: "It is pleasant to think that in 1923, when we are feeling particularly grateful to Heminge and Condell, their veracity is no longer seriously open to question."

77. Lawrence, *Notes on the Authorship of the Shakespeare Plays and Poems* (London: Gay and Hancock Ltd, 1925), p. 183.

78. Greg, *The Shakespeare First Folio*, p. 102. For his earlier discussions of textual revision, see *The Editorial Problem in Shakespeare* (Oxford: Clarendon Press, 1942, reprinted in 1951 and 1954).

79. Bowers, *On Editing Shakespeare* (Charlottesville: University Press of Virginia, 1966), pp. 87, 80 (first published as *On Editing Shakespeare and the Elizabethan Dramatists* [Philadelphia: University of Pennsylvania Library, 1955]).

80. Mahood, *Unblotted Lines: Shakespeare at Work,* (London: Oxford University Press, 1972), pp. 3–4, 7. F. P. Wilson had earlier made the same point about Shakespeare's carelessness in *Shakespeare and the New Bibliography,* rev. and ed. Helen Gardiner (Oxford: Clarendon Press, 1970), p. 113.

81. See Wilson's response to Chambers, *The Elizabethan Shakespeare,* and his discussions of various plays in the introductions and textual commentaries to the Cambridge Shakespeare series; Doran, *The Text of King Lear* (Stanford: Stanford University Press, 1931); Feuillerat, *The Composition of Shakespeare's Plays;* Craig, "Revised Elizabethan Quartos: An Attempt to Form a Class," in *Studies in the English Renaissance Drama,* ed J. Bennett, O. Cargill, V. Hall, Jr. (New York: New York University Press, 1959); Honigmann, *The Stability of Shakespeare's Text;* Nosworthy, *Shakespeare's Occasional Plays;* Coghill, *Shakespeare's Professional Skills* (Cambridge: Cambridge University Press, 1965).

82. Honigmann, *The Stability of Shakespeare's Text,* pp. 2–3.

83. Stanley Wells, "The Once and Future *King Lear,*" in *The Division of the Kingdoms,* pp. 10–11.

84. Honigmann, "The New Lear" (review of *The Division of the Kingdoms*), *New York Review of Books,* 2 February 1984, p. 18; also see "Shakespeare's Revised Plays: *King Lear* and *Othello,*" *The Library,* 6th ser., 4 (1982), 142–173; Howard-Hill, "The Challenge of *King Lear*" (review of *The Division of the Kingdoms*), *The Library,* 6th ser., 7 (1985), 170–173.

85. Edwards, Review, *Modern Language Review,* 77 (1982), 698.

86. Muir, *Shakespeare: Contrasts and Controversies,* pp. 51–52.

87. McLeod, "UnEditing Shakespeare," *Sub-stance,* 33–34 (1982), 26–55; Warren, "Textual Problems, Editorial Assertions in Editions of Shakespeare," in *Textual Criticism and Literary Interpretation,* ed. Jerome J. McGann (Chicago: University of Chicago Press, 1985), pp. 23–37; Urkowitz, "Good News about 'Bad' Quartos," in *'Bad' Shakespeare: Revaluations of the Shakespeare Canon,* ed. Maurice Charney (Rutherford, N. J.: Fairleigh Dickinson University Press, 1988), pp. 189–206.

88. See Kerrigan, "Shakespeare as Reviser"; Taylor, "Revising Shakespeare"; and Wells, "Revision in Shakespeare's Plays," in *Editing and Editors: A Retrospect,* ed. Richard Landon (New York: AMS Press, 1988), pp. 67–97.

89. Wells, Letter, *Times Literary Supplement,* 18 January 1985, 63.

90. Sams, Letter, *TLS,* 1 February 1985, 119.

91. Thomas, "Shakespeare's Supposed Revision of *King Lear,*" p. 508.

92. Jenkins, introduction, *Hamlet* (London: Methuen, 1982), p. 5.

93. Taylor, "The Canon and Chronology of Shakespeare's Plays," in *Textual Companion,* p. 71.

94. Taylor, general introduction, in *Textual Companion,* p. 4.

95. Stanley Wells, general introduction, *William Shakespeare: The Complete Works* (Old Spelling Edition) (Oxford: Clarendon Press, 1986), p. xxxiv. Also see the introductions to the various plays in *Textual Companion.*

96. See Wells and Taylor, "The Oxford Shakespeare Re-viewed," *Analytical and Enumerative Bibliography,* n.s. 4 (1991, forthcoming).

97. See Wells's essay (first read in 1985), "Revision in Shakespeare's Plays," p. 93.

98. Bevington, "Determining the Indeterminate: The Oxford Shakespeare," pp. 502–503.

99. Samuel Schoenbaum includes among Malone's "enduringly admirable" characteristics "his refusal to push the interpretation of evidence beyond legitimate bounds" (*Shakespeare's Lives,* p. 170), while Brian Vickers credits him with being too "cautious and careful" to indulge in the "disintegration" of Shakespeare's plays (*Shakespeare: The Critical Heritage, Vol. 6: 1774–1801* [London: Routledge & Kegan Paul, London, 1981], p. 47). It was perhaps this concern with "legitimate bounds" and "careful" editing that encouraged both Malone's theory of limited authorial revision, which did not concern itself solely with enhancing or denigrating Shakespeare's reputation as a creative artist, and his rejection of simple or speculative conclusions to complex textual problems.

## 2. Revision in the Manuscripts of Shakespeare's Contemporaries

1. Anne Lancashire, for example, believes that the average manuscript passed through the hands of "at least three correctors in the course of initial production: the censor, a playhouse reviser (either directly, or indirectly via the scribe), and the author or scribe or another literary corrector or second playhouse reviser" (introduction, *The Second Maiden's Tragedy* [Manchester, Eng.: Manchester University Press, 1978], p. 67, note 62). Lancashire also points out that individual correctors did not make only one kind of change in a manuscript: "The censor, for example, might make a technical or a literary correction; the author might censor his own work; the scribe might do theatrical revision or literary alteration (though perhaps under direction)" (p. 11).

2. Howard-Hill, "The Challenge of *King Lear,*" p. 170.

3. Peter Ure's 1953 comments on revision in George Chapman's *Bussy D'Ambois* typify many editors' and critics' unnecessary concern with judging the "improved" quality of a reworked play. Ure finds both "blunders" and "improvements" in the 1641 Quarto text of the play, and thus decides that "about half the reviser's busy activity seems to have been totally wasted" ("Chapman's *Tragedy of Bussy D'Ambois:* Problems of the Revised Quarto," *Modern Language Review,* 48 [1953], 17).

4. Numerous manuscripts display these symbols; see for example those bound together as Egerton 1994 in the British Museum for crosses, stars, arrows, etc., and the

manuscripts of *The Wasp* (Alnwick Castle) and *The Welsh Embassador* (Cardiff Central Library) for drawings of a hand with a pointing index finger to mark additions to the texts.

5. The amount of scribal interference in a dramatic manuscript has continued to interest scholars. In 1931, R. B. McKerrow suggested that "one of the reasons for the badness of dramatic texts is that they were often set up from the author's manuscript." If the author's foul papers were readable, no scribal transcript was necessary, and the original manuscript was submitted to the Master of the Revels for licensing and afterwards used as prompt-copy. However, if "the author's copy contained revisions or corrections, or was not clearly written, we may suppose that a transcript would be made from it by a scrivener regularly employed by the company for the purpose and practised in dealing with dramatic copy. It would, no doubt, be his business to regularize and, when necessary, expand the speakers' names, see that the entries and exits were properly supplied, and, in short, to some extent edit the play . . . It is a point that must be insisted on that no copy but a good, orderly, and legible one could possibly serve as a prompt-copy" ("The Elizabethan Printer and Dramatic Manuscripts," *The Library*, 4th ser., 12 [1931], 264–266). McKerrow's strict distinctions between the conditions and uses of foul and fair copies are still influential, yet my study of manuscripts demonstrates that professional scribes, such as Ralph Crane, were not always employed to transcribe, and in fact, scribal practices do not prove consistent, so that McKerrow's theory that scribes *edited* cannot be applied to all or most manuscripts. Similarly, J. Q. Adams's stricture that "only in exceptional cases—as very extensive revision of the text, or the wretched handwriting of the author—was a scribe employed to make a more legible copy" ("Elizabethan Playhouse Manuscripts and Their Significance for the Text of Shakespeare," *Johns Hopkins Alumni Magazine*, 21 [1932–1933], p. 26), is also too severe. The reasons and occasions for employing a scribe varied.

6. The manuscript of John Fletcher's play, *Bonduca* (British Museum manuscript Add. 36758), has a similar scribal summary of lost scenes. At the beginning of Act 5 (F. 23) the scribe summarizes scenes 1 and 2, and remarks that the beginning of the next scene is "wanting" because "the booke where by it was first Acted from is lost: and this hath beene transcribed from the fowle papers of the Authors w^ch were found" (See *Bonduca*, ed. W. W. Greg [Oxford: Oxford University Press, 1951], p. 90).

7. W. W. Greg, in *Dramatic Documents From the Elizabethan Playhouses: Commentary* (Oxford: Clarendon Press, 1931), pp. 201–202, 229–233, 355, 362–363, and 366, discusses some of these plays, concluding that they were revised due to censorship by the Master of the Revels, and credits, in most cases, playhouse revisers rather than the authors with such revisions; yet in many manuscripts, revisions due to censorship coexist with revisions made for other reasons and often in a variety of hands.

8. British Museum manuscript Egerton 1994, F. 349^v. This command is part of the second, revised license of Herbert; the first license demanded a removal of oaths, the second demanded a cleaner copy as well as the removal of "Oathes, prophaness & publick Ribaldry," suggesting that Herbert made the first command when brought the original manuscript and made the second command when presented with the revised manuscript. (I am indebted to Susan P. Cerasano for calling attention to the fact that Herbert's license underwent revision for the revised manuscript.)

9. See William B. Long's discussions of this point in "'A bed / for woodstock': A Warning for the Unwary," and also in "Stage-Directions, A Misinterpreted Factor in Determining Textual Provenance," *TEXT,* 2 (1985), 121–137.

10. Turner, "Act-End Notations in Some Elizabethan Plays," *Modern Philology,* 72 (1975), 238–247, and "Revisions and Repetition-Brackets in Fletcher's *A Wife for a Month,*" *Studies in Bibliography,* 36 (1983), 178–190.

11. For a discussion of authorial revision between the foul and fair copies of *Bonduca,* see my essay "'The Final Revision of *Bonduca*': An Unpublished Essay by W. W. Greg," *Studies in Bibliography,* 43 (1990), 62–80.

12. Jonson's remark in the preface to the 1605 Quarto 1 of *Sejanus*—that the play "is not the same with that which was acted on the publike Stage, wherein a second Pen had good share: in place of which I haue rather chosen, to put weaker (and no doubt lesse pleasing) of mine own, then to defraud so happy a *Genius* of his right, by my lothed vsurpation"—appears to refer to his own revision of the original and controversial play written collaboratively, probably with Chapman, and not to any dissatisfaction with a later reviser (see W. F. Bolton, introduction, *Sejanus his Fall* [London: Ernest Benn Limited, 1966], pp. xi–xxi).

13. Craig, in "Revised Elizabethan Quartos: An Attempt to Form a Class," pp. 55–56, and Bentley, *The Profession of Dramatist,* pp. 242–245, discuss the veracity of the claims of the title pages of some of these plays.

14. Murray, "From Foul Sheets to Legitimate Model: Antitheater, Text, Ben Jonson," *New Literary History,* 14 (1983), 653.

15. Bowers, "Notes on Standing Type in Elizabethan Printing," *The Papers of the Bibliographic Society of America,* 40 (1946), 211, 219–223.

16. *Henslowe's Diary,* ed. Foakes and Rickert, pp. 137, 175, 182, 206–207, 216, 224.

17. Scott McMillin persuasively argues that revivals called for revisions because changes in the acting companies' personnel effected the casting of doubled roles (*The Elizabethan Theatre and "The Book of Sir Thomas More"* [Ithaca: Cornell University Press, 1987], p. 76). John Freehafer claims George Chapman revised *Bussy D'Ambois* in order to protect his rights to the play, which became a subject of contention between two rival acting companies during a War of the Theatres from 1622–1624 ("The Contention for *Bussy D'Ambois,*" *Theatre Notebook,* 23 [1968], 68–69).

18. Cited by Albert Feuillerat in *The Composition of Shakespeare's Plays,* p. 7.

19. Bentley, *The Profession of Dramatist,* p. 263.

20. Feuillerat, *The Composition of Shakespeare's Plays,* pp. 7–8.

21. Lancashire, introduction, *The Second Maiden's Tragedy,* p. 69, note 92.

22. Freehafer, "The Contention for *Bussy D'Ambois,*" p. 68. A. H. Tricomi also contends that Chapman was responsible for the revisions in the play, as the reworked version "reveals a pattern of revision consistent with Chapman's deepening Neo-Stoic thought in the later years of his dramatic career" ("The Problem of Authorship in the Revised *Bussy D'Ambois,*" *English Language Notes,* 17 [1979], 28). However, Nicholas Brooke argues that the play was revised twice, first by Chapman and later by Nathan Field, the actor-manager of Whitefriars Theatre (introduction, *Bussy D'Ambois* [London: Methuen & Co. Ltd, 1964], pp. lxv–lxxiv).

23. Loewenstein, "The Script in the Marketplace," *Representations,* 12 (1985), 109.

24. Kerrigan, "Revision, Adaptation, and the Fool in *King Lear*," in *The Division of the Kingdoms*, p. 206.

25. See Allan Holaday's introduction to his edition of *The Rape of Lucrece* (Urbana: University of Illinois Press, 1950), pp. 1–34, for a discussion of the extent of Heywood's revisions.

26. Madeleine Doran, introduction, *If You Know Not Me You Know Nobody, Part I* (Oxford: Clarendon Press, 1934), pp. v–xix.

27. Greg, *Collected Papers,* ed. J. C. Maxwell (Oxford: Clarendon Press, 1966), p. 169. H. D. Janzen also discusses Heywood's revisions to the play in his introduction to the Malone Society Reprints edition of *The Escapes of Jupiter* (Oxford: Clarendon Press, 1976), p. ix.

28. For a discussion of revision by Dekker in these plays, see Fredson Bowers's introductions and notes to *The Dramatic Works of Thomas Dekker* (Cambridge: Cambridge University Press, 1953–1961) and Cyrus Hoy's *Introductions, Notes, and Commentaries to texts in "The Dramatic Works of Thomas Dekker"* (Cambridge: Cambridge University Press, 1980).

29. For a discussion of revision by Beaumont and Fletcher in these plays, see the introductions and notes to *The Dramatic Works in the Beaumont and Fletcher Canon,* gen. ed. Fredson Bowers, 7 vols. (Cambridge: Cambridge University Press, 1966–1989), vols. 1–6; also see Robert K. Turner, Jr., introduction, *A King and No King* (Lincoln: University of Nebraska Press, 1963) and "Revisions and Repetition-Brackets in Fletcher's *A Wife for a Month*"; and Andrew Gurr's introductions to *Philaster* (London: Methuen & Co. Ltd, 1969) and *The Maid's Tragedy* (Edinburgh: Oliver & Boyd, 1969).

30. For a discussion of the political implication of Massinger's revision of *The Bondman* and other plays, see Jerzy Limon, *Dangerous Matter: English Drama and Politics in 1623/24* (Cambridge: Cambridge University Press, 1986), pp. 66–76.

31. For a discussion of Massinger's collaboration with Fletcher and later revisions of existing plays, see Cyrus Hoy's series of essays, "The Shares of Fletcher and His Collaborators in the Beaumont and Fletcher Canon," *Studies in Bibliography,* particularly volumes 8 (1956), 9 (1957), 11 (1958), and 14 (1961). Also see Robert K. Turner, Jr., "Collaborators at Work: *The Queen of Corinth* and *The Knight of Malta*," in *Shakespeare: Text, Language, Criticism: Essays in Honour of Marvin Spevack*, pp. 315–333.

32. Greg, *Collected Papers,* p. 176.

33. Chambers, *The Disintegration of Shakespeare*, pp. 15–17.

34. Bald, "The Foul Papers of a Revision," *The Library,* 4th ser., 26 (1946), 38.

35. Knutson, "*Henslowe's Diary* and the Economics of Play Revision for Revival, 1592–1603," *Theatre Research International,* 9 (1984), 1; she also takes up these issues in "Influence of the Repertory System on the Revival and Revision of *The Spanish Tragedy* and *Dr. Faustus*," *English Literary Renaissance,* 18 (1988), 257–274.

36. McMillin, *The Elizabethan Theatre and "The Book of Sir Thomas More,"* pp. 77, 95.

37. Philip Edwards, introduction, *The Spanish Tragedy* (Cambridge, Mass.: Harvard University Press, 1959), p. xxvii.

38. Scott McMillin provides a comprehensive study of revision in the play, which was originally written for Lord Strange's Men, suggesting that, among other reasons, it was revised to suit casting requirements of the Admiral's/Prince's Men for a revival (*The*

*Elizabethan Theatre and "The Book of Sir Thomas More,"* pp. 53–95). For the date of the
additions, see Giorgio Melchiori, "The Master of the Revels and the Date of the Additions
to *The Book of Sir Thomas More,"* in *Shakespeare: Text, Language, Criticism: Essays in
Honour of Marvin Spevack,* pp. 164–179; and Gary Taylor, "The Date and Auspices of
the Additions to *Sir Thomas More,"* in *Shakespeare and "Sir Thomas More": Essays on the
Play and its Shakespearian Interest,* ed. T. H. Howard-Hill (Cambridge: Cambridge
University Press, 1989), pp. 101–129.

39. W. W. Greg and D. N. Smith, introduction, *The Spanish Tragedy (1592)* (Oxford:
Oxford University Press, 1948), pp. vi–ix.

40. Edwards, introduction, *The Spanish Tragedy,* pp. xxxvi–xlii.

41. Edwards, introduction, *The Spanish Tragedy,* p. lxiii; he also questions the attri-
bution of the additions to Jonson and discusses other possible candidates for them.
However, Anne Barton assigns them to Jonson in *Ben Jonson, Dramatist* (Cambridge:
Cambridge University Press, 1984), pp. 13–28.

42. E. A. J. Honigmann, "Shakespeare as a Reviser," *Textual Criticism and Literary
Interpretation,* ed. Jerome J. McGann (Chicago: University of Chicago Press, 1985), p. 3.

43. Kerrigan, "Revision, Adaptation, and the Fool in *King Lear,"* in *The Division of
the Kingdoms,* p. 195. L. A. Beaurline also presents three distinct categories of variants:
simple deletions, theatrical adaptations, and literary revision ("The Director, the Script,
and Author's Revisions: A Critical Problem," in *Papers in Dramatic Theory and Criticism,*
ed. David M. Knauf [Iowa City: University of Iowa, 1969], p. 89).

44. Carter, introduction, *Every Man in His Humour* (New Haven: Yale University
Press, 1921), pp. xxxiv.

45. Lever, introduction, *Every Man in His Humour* (Lincoln: University of Nebraska
Press, 1971), p. xii, xx. Also see Michael Warren, who argues in "The Theatricalization
of Text: Beckett, Jonson, Shakespeare," in *The Library Chronicle of the University of Texas
at Austin,* 20 (1990), p. 41, that "Jonson suppressed a great deal in his revisions" and
"obscured the theatrical reality while giving details of the plays' theatrical histories."

46. Honigmann, *The Stability of Shakespeare's Text,* pp. 2–3.

47. Greg, *Collected Papers,* p. 173.

48. According to G. K. Hunter in the introduction to his edition of *The Malcontent*
(London: Methuen & Co. Ltd, 1975), p. xxxiv, only two extant copies of Quarto 2 contain
the prologue, printed at the end of the play on the leaf following the epilogue. Could
Quarto 2 then have been issued twice, first without the prologue, and again with the
prologue (titled "an imperfect Ode") newly added?

49. Hunter, introduction, *The Malcontent,* p. xxxviii.

50. The Huntington Library copies of Quarto 1, 2 and 3 suggest that at least Malevole's
remark early in 1.3, that he had just come "from the publick place of much dissimulation;
the Church," was censored: one copy of Q1 allows the line to stand as it is, while in
another, the words "the Church" have been rubbed out and the space closed up when
the sheet was still wet from printing; in Q2, "the Church" has been omitted by the
printer and replaced by "(     )"; Q3 restores "(the Church)," but it has been sliced out
of one copy and allowed to remain in another. G. K. Hunter argues in the introduction
to his edition (p. xxix) that Marston himself, in order to protect the "integrity" of his
authorial intentions, proposed these methods of censorship.

51. Hunter, introduction, *The Malcontent,* pp. xxvi–xxxi.

52. Hunter, introduction, *The Malcontent,* pp. xlvi–liii; Lake, "Webster's Additions to *The Malcontent:* Linguistic Evidence," *Notes and Queries,* 226 (1981), 153–158. Macdonald P. Jackson and Michael Neill endorse the conclusions of both Hunter and Lake in their introduction to the play in *The Selected Plays of John Marston* (Cambridge: Cambridge University Press, 1986), pp. 189–194.

53. Harris, introduction, *The Malcontent* (London: Ernest Benn Limited, 1967), p. xviii.

54. Barry B. Adams, introduction, *John Bale's "King Johan"* (San Marino: The Huntington Library, 1969), pp. 3–4, 11–12. J. H. Pyle Pafford and W. W. Greg offer similar conclusions in the introduction to their Malone Society Reprints edition of the play (Oxford: Oxford University Press, 1931), pp. v–xxix. Greg, in *Dramatic Documents From the Elizabethan Playhouses: Commentary,* p. 204, states that promptbooks were written on Folio sheets so that the prompter would have to turn pages less frequently. The Folio sheets of *King Johan* might suggest that the early version represented some type of theatrical copy, while Bale's additions on Quarto sheets would not.

55. I use Adams's dates (Introduction, pp. 20–24), based on topical allusions, for the composition and revision of the play. Pafford and Greg argue that the play was composed between 1538 and 1540 and revised between 1560 and 1563 (introduction, p. xvii).

56. In the manuscript of *The Second Maiden's Tragedy,* a scribe similarly used circles in the margin to mark the place to insert additions written out on slips.

57. For transcriptions of these lines from the manuscript, (F. 20, 22$^v$ and 27$^v$), see Pafford and Greg's edition of *King Johan,* pp. 84–85, 104–105.

58. Greg, *Collected Papers,* p. 176.

59. John Payne Collier, the first editor of this Bridgewater manuscript, assumed that these act notations and Bale's comments in his catalogue of his works about the play being in "two books" implied that the author had used a now lost added passage to divide *King Johan* into two separate plays (introduction, *Kynge Johan* [London: J. B. Nichols & Son, 1838], p. xi). Later editors Pafford and Greg argue that the play existed in two parts, was recast as one play by 1538, and that by 1561 Bale had reincorporated material into it from the original two-part play to produce the final version (introduction, pp. xxii–xxiii). Adams rejects this argument and accepts the final version of the play as two books, speculating that "book" may mean "as much of a play as could be presented conveniently without a break" (introduction, p. 22). However, "Book" was the common name for a theatrical promptbook.

60. Pafford and Greg, introduction, *King Johan,* p. xix.

61. Dale B. J. Randall, *Jonson's Gypsies Unmasked: Background and Theme of "The Gypsies Metamorphos'd"* (Durham, N. C.: Duke University Press, 1975), p. 69, 173 n 41.

62. W. W. Greg, introduction, *Jonson's "Masque of Gipsies" in the Burley, Belvoir, and Windsor Versions, An Attempt at Reconstruction* (London: Oxford University Press, 1952), pp. 1–5.

63. Orgel, introduction, *Ben Jonson: The Complete Masques* (New Haven: Yale University Press, 1969), p. 494.

64. The significance of the later revisions is dismissed by at least one scholar, who claims: "No matter how valuable the insights afforded by Jonson's later modifications of

the masque, a search for its essence should be concentrated on its first performance. The reason is simple: a masque was by definition conceived and designed for a particular audience in a particular place on a particular occasion" (Randall, *Jonson's Gypsies Unmasked*, p. 68). However, the very fact that Jonson produced three versions of the masque, each specific to a particular place and occasion, should imply that each version has its own "essence" and significance.

65. Greg, introduction, *Jonson's "Masque of Gipsies,"* p. 46, note 1.

66. Charles J. Sisson, introduction, *Believe as You List* (Oxford: Oxford University Press, 1927), pp. v–xx.

67. Greg, introduction, *Jonson's "Masque of Gipsies,"* p. 52.

68. See "Glossarial and Explanatory Notes" to *The Gypsies Metamorphosed,* ed. George Watson Cole (New York: The Century Co., 1931), pp. 217ff., for futher information on specific allusions in the masque to audience members.

69. For a transcription of these lines from the manuscript (F. 23), see Greg's edition, p. 131.

70. C. J. Sisson, introduction, *Believe as You List,* p. xix.

71. Bald, preface, *A Game at Chesse* (Cambridge: Cambridge University Press, 1929), p. ix. Also see T. H. Howard-Hill's introduction to his edition of *A Game at Chesse* (Oxford: Oxford University Press, 1990), pp. vii–xxii, for a discussion of the play's transmission.

72. Other transcriptions of the play were probably made but are no longer extant; as T. H. Howard-Hill argues, an "analysis of the relationships amongst the witnesses reveals that besides three non-extant manuscripts which must have existed by August 1624, at least seven more copies of the text must have been made subsequently in order to produce the six terminal copies which survive. Consequently, if publication of Q1 occurred quite shortly after the presentation of the Malone manuscript in January, at least thirteen copies of the play were made in the six months or so between performance and publication" ("The Author as Scribe or Reviser? Middleton's Intentions in *A Game at Chess,*" *TEXT,* 3 [1987], 307).

73. Zimmerman, "The Folger Manuscripts of Thomas Middleton's *A Game at Chesse:* A Study in the Genealogy of Texts," *Papers of the Bibliographical Society of America,* 76 (1982), 161.

74. Bald, for example, states of the Rosenbach manuscript that "it is the worst and *ipso facto,* probably the latest," with three hundred and fifty variants, "many of them obvious corruptions, which have found their way into the work of a careless scribe even though, as the evidence of the autograph title-page justifies us in concluding, he was, to some extent at least, working under the supervision of the author" ("A New Manuscript of Middleton's *Game at Chesse,*" *Modern Language Review,* 25 [1930], 474–475). Zimmerman similarly writes that "Middleton was not a careful scribe when he was writing fast; he was particularly prone to make mistakes in speech-prefixes and to omit passages. Thus texts derived from Middleton's papers are likely to contain such errors; in addition, they might well show evidence of awkwardness in those places where Middleton wrote in, or appended, his revisions" ("The Folger Manuscripts," p. 166).

75. For the stage history of the play and the reproduction of contemporary documents, including the letters to and from the Privy Council, see Bald, introduction and appendix

A, *A Game at Chesse,* pp. 19–22, 159–166. He lists this as the "first recorded 'run' in the history of the English theatre, for, as Henslowe testifies, it was the usual practice to have a different play from the company's repertoire each day, and no other series of consecutive performances is heard of until after the Restoration." As the *Dictionary of National Biography* (63 vols. [London: Smith, Elder & Co., 1894], vol. 37, p. 359) points out, there are only two unreliable sources of evidence to support the theory that Middleton was imprisoned: the first the manuscript note written in a contemporary hand in Dyce's copy of Quarto 1 (Victoria and Albert Museum National Art Library, pressmark 25.D.42), claiming that Middleton was "committted to prisson, where hee lay some Tyme, and at last gott oute upon this petition presented to King James"; and the second the six-line verse petition itself (which appears in variant form in four other contemporary miscellanies), in which Middleton pleads in part, "The White house wan: yet still the black doth bragg / they had the power to put mee in the bagge / vse but your royall hand. Twill set me free / Tis but remouing of a man thats mee." The crudeness and familiarity of the verse petition suggest that it would not have been addressed by an author such as Middleton to his royal patron. And as the note preceding the verse in the Dyce Quarto falsely states that the "chiefe actors" had also been imprisoned, both the story of Middleton's imprisonment and the verse written to celebrate it appear to be apocryphal.

76. G. E. Bentley, *The Profession of Dramatist in Shakespeare's Time,* p. 167.

77. T. H. Howard-Hill concludes that Middleton was "supervising the production of transcripts of the play for sale, for presentation to patrons, and for publication at the press" ("The Bridgewater-Huntington MS of Middleton's *Game at Chess,*" *Manuscripta,* 28 [1984], 145). As Middleton was preparing copies for public as well as private audiences (an activity contradicted by Middleton's comments in the Malone manuscript dedication to William Hammond in 1625, "This Which nor Stage nor Stationers Stall can showe"), he must have felt no need to obey the royal command which banned the play.

78. Bodleian Library manuscript Malone 25, F. vii.

79. Wilson, Review (*A Game at Chesse,* ed. R. C. Bald), *The Library,* 4th ser., 11 (1930–31), 111, 115. Wilson also suggests that the play may have had private performances after being banned. Jerzy Limon agrees that the "war party" headed by Buckingham sponsored the play's performance and offered protection to those involved in it, and that this play and several other 1623–24 works reflect the "ideology" of the war party, who were attempting to provoke war with Spain (*Dangerous Matter: English Drama and Politics in 1623–24,* pp. 98–129). See also Margot Heinemann, who in *Puritanism and Theatre: Thomas Middleton and Opposition Drama under the Early Stuarts* (Cambridge: Cambridge University Press, 1980), pp. 165–171, suggests that the Earl of Pembroke was the play's patron, and Thomas Cogswell, who, in "Thomas Middleton and the Court, 1624: *A Game at Chess* in Context," *Huntington Library Quarterly,* 47 (1984), 273–285, argues for the protection of Prince Charles, Buckingham, and Pembroke. Paul Yachnin argues in "*A Game at Chess:* Thomas Middleton's Praise of Folly," *Modern Language Quarterly,* 48 (1987), 107–123, that the play had no aristocratic sponsor except Middleton himself, yet Middleton could offer his own satire of the topical situation in the process of presenting a play to suit court sponsorship.

80. Wilson, Review, (*A Game at Chesse,* ed. R. C. Bald), p. 114. He suggests that the Malone manuscript may have been an abridged acting version of the play for the private

performances *before* or *after* its closing by the Privy Council, and it is possible that any of the versions' variants may have been due to some type of theatrical requirement. However, Middleton gave the Malone manuscript to William Hammond for New Year's, 1625; he thus had at least four months to correct it, but left it in its existing state.

81. Zimmerman, "The Folger Manuscripts," pp. 177–8. She also notes that the Rosenbach contains no corrections and thus was not proofread, which accounts for the "large number of corruptions" (p. 180). However, the play may have been quickly proofread without receiving corrections, and variants, which are sometimes classed as corruptions by Zimmerman, need not be considered corruptions unless the scribe has transcribed obvious errors such as nonsensical words.

82. Wilson, Review (*A Game at Chesse*, ed. R. C. Bald), p. 109.

83. Because the actors claimed in their defense to the Privy Council that they had acted the play exactly as licensed ("they confidently protested that, they added or varied from the same, nothing at all"; cited in Bald's edition, p. 162), the revisions either must have already been added to the copy originally licensed by Herbert, or Herbert must have licensed a second copy of the play with these revisions.

84. For discussions of the Archdall manuscript, see Bald, "An Early Version of Middleton's *Game At Chesse*," *Modern Language Review*, 38 (1943), 177–180, and Zimmerman, "The Folger Manuscripts," pp. 159–195. Zimmerman argues that nearly all of the revisions were additions by Middleton to passages in the play before or after stage clearances: "108 lines at the beginning of II.ii.; 82 lines at the beginning of III.i.; and 29 lines in mid-scene; 9 at the outset of V.i. and 44 at the end of the play (V.iii). Middleton did alter several phrases and add short passages of two to six lines in I.i., II.ii., III.i., and IV.v. in order to expand the characterization of the White King's Pawn" (p. 188).

85. T. H. Howard-Hill's investigation of the possibility of revision in the play places more emphasis on textual instability than on deliberate authorial change. For example, he argues that "unfortunately, in *A Game at Chess* those variations which may be suspected to reflect authorial revision, that is, Middleton's progress towards the accomplishment of his final intention for the work, are not concentrated but rather dispersed through various witnesses and are therefore to be distinguished from scribal corruptions or sophistications only with considerable difficulty and rarely with certainty" ("The Author as Scribe or Reviser? Middleton's Intentions in *A Game at Chess*," p. 307). My study does not challenge Howard-Hill's remarkable work on the transmission of *A Game at Chesse*, but questions whether the emphasis should be shifted back to revision and away from instability and the concept of "final" intention.

86. Zimmerman concludes that "Bridgewater's textual superiority is established by the presence of Middleton's hand as both scribe and reviser"; therefore its variants probably originated in an "authoritative copy-text" ("The Folger Manuscripts," p. 169, note 21). However, it is not entirely clear that any of the manuscripts is superior to the others, or that some derive from authoritative copy-texts and others do not. What is clear is that the versions are different; it is not necessary to establish and reconstruct the lost original but to examine the extant versions.

87. Howard-Hill argues that this manuscript received more correction than any other

manuscript because the two scribes who wrote out the first four acts were young and inexperienced ("The Bridgewater-Huntington MS," p. 151).

88. Howard-Hill was the first scholar to report that some four hundred corrections were in pencil ("The Bridgewater-Huntington MS," p. 146, 154), as Bald and Zimmerman had used microfilmed copies of the manuscript and believed that all corrections were in ink. Howard-Hill does not offer an identity for the pencil corrector. My collation of the penciled words in Bridgewater (Huntington Library manuscript EL. 34 B 17) with the same words as they appear in the holographic Trinity (Trinity College Library, Cambridge, manuscript O.2.66) and Bridgewater portions suggests that Middleton himself made some if not all of the Bridgewater penciled corrections, none of which appears in any portion of Act 5, which he transcribed (the portion which he transcribed in 2.2 does contain penciled corrections). The hand of some of the penciled words, sometimes exaggerated for clarity, does not resemble the hand of the same words as they appear in Trinity; however, certain words in Middleton's portion of Bridgewater do not resemble these same words in Trinity. Six of the nine penciled words (or single letter in one case), "best," "comes," "gratious," an "s" (added to "yonder,") "fice" (added to Orifex with the "fex" canceled), and "boades," are identical to the exact or nearly exact words as they appear in Middleton's portion of Bridgewater. I have not found exact parallels with three words, "againe," "ugh" (added above "throand" to make "through"?), and "thy," but as they are written in the same broad pencil strokes as the other words, I suspect that they are also in Middleton's hand. (For the penciled words, see Bridgewater, F. 8$^V$, 11, 11$^V$, 17, 21$^V$ [for an "s" added to "yonder"], 22, 26, 29, 32; for parallel words, see for example, Bridgewater, F. 48, 51, 51$^V$, 52$^V$.)

89. For example, "do's worke" (Trinity), appears as "ha's wrought" (Bridgewater); "it must bee strange cunning" (T), appears as "they must have cunning Judgments" (B); "Monster Impudence" (T), appears as "bloudie Villayne" (B). (See Bridgewater-Huntington Manuscript: F. 21$^V$, 47, 49; Trinity College Manuscript, F. 16$^V$, 41$^V$, 44.) Honigmann discusses first- and second-thought variants in this play in *The Stability of Shakespeare's Text* (pp. 59–62).

90. Price, "The Huntington MS of *A Game at Chesse*," *Huntington Library Quarterly*, 17 (1953), 86–87.

91. Bald, "'Assembled' Texts," *The Library*, 4th ser., 12 (1931–32), 247.

92. Bald, Preface, *A Game at Chesse*, p. ix.


3. Occasions and Occurrences of Revision in Shakespeare's Plays

1. Wells, "Revision in Shakespeare's Plays," pp. 67–97.

2. Bowers, "Establishing Shakespeare's Text," p. 195.

3. E. K. Chambers, *William Shakespeare: A Study of Facts and Problems*, vol. 1, p. 239; Greg, *The Shakespeare First Folio*, p. 151.

4. Both J. D. Wilson (introduction, *King Richard II* [Cambridge: Cambridge University Press, 1939], p. xxxiii) and Peter Ure (introduction, *King Richard II* [London: Methuen and Co. Ltd, 1956], p. xxv) argue that the scene was played in the theatre although it had been censored in print; yet the scene may also have suffered censorship on stage for particular performances.

5. A. R. Humphreys, introduction, *The Second Part of King Henry IV* (London: Methuen and Co. Ltd, 1966), p. lxxi.

6. J. D. Wilson argues that this scene was not shown to the censor. ("The Copy for *2 Henry IV*, 1600 and 1623," in *The Second Part of the History of Henry IV* [Cambridge: Cambridge University Press, 1948], p. 123.)

7. Andrew Cairncross, introductions, *The Second Part of King Henry VI* (London: Methuen and Co. Ltd, 1957), p. xlviii, and *The Third Part of King Henry VI* (London: Methuen and Co. Ltd, 1964), p. xii; J. H. Walter, *King Henry V* (London: Methuen and Co. Ltd, 1954), p. xxxv; Nosworthy, *Shakespeare's Occasional Plays*, p. 47.

8. Doran, *The Text of King Lear*, pp. 166ff.; Greg, *The Shakespeare First Folio*, p. 387.

9. Taylor, "Monopolies, Show Trials, Disaster, and Invasion: *King Lear* and Censorship," in *The Division of the Kingdoms*, pp. 104–105.

10. Patterson, *Censorship and Interpretation*, pp. 58, 71.

11. According to E. K. Chambers in *The Elizabethan Stage*, 4 vols. (Oxford: Clarendon Press, 1928), vol. 1, p. 40 and vol. 2, p. 195, Lord Hunsdon, the Lord Chamberlain until mid-1596, passed his company onto his son, the new Lord Hunsdon, who later became Lord Chamberlain after Lord Cobham's death in 1597.

12. J. H. Walter, introduction, *King Henry V*, p. xxxix.

13. For a discussion of Shakespeare's troubles with the Brooke family, see Gary Taylor, "The Fortunes of Oldcastle," *Shakespeare Survey*, 38 (1985), 85–100 and "William Shakespeare, Richard James, and the House of Cobham," *The Review of English Studies*, 38 (1987), 334–354.

14. Hibbard, textual introduction, *Hamlet* (Oxford: Clarendon Press, 1987), pp. 74–75.

15. Other, more subtle, forms of political censorship may have been practiced. Gary Taylor argues that the most famous crux of the 1609 Quarto 1 *Pericles*, the awkward and abrupt conversion of Lysimachus by Marina in the brothel in 4.6, resulted from censorship because the Master of the Revels was "particularly sensitive to allusions to the promiscuity of courtiers." Taylor cites the censorship of similar material in *The Second Maiden's Tragedy, The Honest Man's Fortune, Eastward Ho, Cynthia's Revels,* and possibly *The Two Noble Kinsmen* (*Textual Companion*, p. 559). It is possible that Shakespeare cut some of the necessary expository dialogue between the two characters to render Lysimachus, the governor of Mytilene, less corrupt than in the 1608 novella, *The Painfull Adventures of Pericles*. However, similarly abrupt moral conversions of characters can be found in other Shakespearian plays.

16. Taylor notes that the Chamberlain's Men may have attempted to raise capital by selling a number of their plays in 1599–1600, the time of their move into the Globe Theater (general introduction, *Textual Companion*, p. 33).

17. Bowers, "Establishing Shakespeare's Text," p. 192.

18. Bowers, "Establishing Shakespeare's Text," pp. 191, 194, and "The Copy for Shakespeare's *Julius Caesar,*" *South Atlantic Bulletin*, 43 (1978), 29–31.

19. J. D. Wilson, "The Copy Used for *The Tempest*, 1623," in *The Tempest*, ed. A. Quiller-Couch and J. D. Wilson (Cambridge: Cambridge University Press, 1921), p. 80. Also see Irwin Smith, "Ariel and the Masque in *The Tempest*," *Shakespeare Quarterly*, 21 (1970), 214–222.

20. J. D. Wilson, "The Copy for *The Two Gentlemen of Verona*, 1623," in *The Two*

*Gentlemen of Verona,* ed. A. Quiller-Couch and J. D. Wilson (Cambridge: Cambridge University Press, 1921), pp. 78–81.

21. J. D. Wilson, "The Copy for *Twelfth Night,* 1623," in *Twelfth Night,* ed. A. Quiller-Couch and J. D. Wilson (Cambridge: Cambridge University Press, 1930), pp. 100–101. Greg makes the same point in *The Shakespeare First Folio,* p. 297.

22. Greg, *The Shakespeare First Folio,* p. 358.

23. J. D. Wilson, "The Copy for *As You Like It,* 1623," *As You Like It,* ed. A. Quiller-Couch and J. D. Wilson (Cambridge: Cambridge University Press, 1926), p. 103.

24. See Eugene Waith, introduction, *Titus Andronicus* (Oxford: Clarendon Press, 1984), p. 11; J. D. Wilson, introduction, *Titus Andronicus* (Cambridge: Cambridge University Press, 1948), p. xxxvi; Greg, "Note on *Titus Andronicus,*" *Modern Language Review,* 14 (1919), 322–23.

25. David George, "Shakespeare and Pembroke's Men," *Shakespeare Quarterly,* 32 (1981), 306.

26. Greg, *The Shakespeare First Folio,* p. 208, note B.

27. Opinion remains divided about the relationship of *A Shrew* to *The Shrew.* For a summary of modern theories, see Wells, *Textual Companion,* pp. 169–70.

28. Ann Thompson, introduction, *The Taming of the Shrew* (Cambridge: Cambridge University Press, 1984), pp. 2–3. However, Wells argues that *The Shrew* may represent the early version and *A Shrew* the later version with the additions of the concluding Sly material (*Textual Companion,* p. 169). Also see Wells and Taylor's essay, "No Shrew, A Shrew, and The Shrew: Internal Revision in *The Taming of the Shrew,*" in which they argue that the only revision in the play that needs to be postulated "is such as might be expected to occur in the heat of composition, and so to be preserved in foul papers" (in *Shakespeare: Text, Language, Criticism: Essays in Honour of Marvin Spevack,* p. 353).

29. The Folio text of *The Taming of the Shrew* contains a number of foul-paper characteristics such as confusion in speech prefixes, false starts, loose ends, gaps, and inconsistencies in plotting, particularly in the functions of Hortensio and Tranio, perhaps due to Shakespeare's uncertainty about how to proceed with the subplot of the wooing of Bianca. Greg argues that Shakespeare was recasting the subplot, which he took from the existing version of the play (*The Shakespeare First Folio,* p. 215). Wells notes among other signs of revision during composition that "the speeches assigned to Tranio in 3.2/Sc. 7 were originally given to Hortensio, to whom they are far more appropriate in his capacity as Petruccio's old friend," and that "it has been generally assumed that an entry for Lucentio was carelessly or accidentally omitted at the beginning of the scene, but his presence is not required till 3.3.1/1435, and we assume rather that an entry has been omitted at that point, and that it would have marked the start of a new scene" (*Textual Companion,* p. 169). Along with second-thought changes in composition, the Folio text also contains numerous cuts and corruptions, suggesting that the printed version does not accurately represent the play as it was originally written or possibly later revised. Henslowe's *Diary* (p. 22) records a performance of *The tamynge of A shrowe* by the Admiral's and the Chamberlain's Men at Newington Butts in 1594, and it seems plausible that Shakespeare reworked his own play (or even his source play) after it had changed hands from Pembroke's to the Chamberlain's Men in 1593/4, as he did in the case of *Titus Andronicus,* incorporating changes made after the printing of the reported Quarto.

What appear to be second-thought or later revisions in the play are haphazard and show no particular pattern, as do those, for example, in *Titus Andronicus*, with the possible exception of the reworking of the subplot to give Hortensio the disguised role of the music teacher, Litio (see H. J. Oliver, introduction, *The Taming of the Shrew* [Oxford: Clarendon Press, 1982], p. 33, and Ann Thompson, textual analysis, *The Taming of the Shrew* [Cambridge: Cambridge University Press, 1984], pp. 160–174).

30. This is the opinion of both Andrew Cairncross and Scott McMillin; see Cairncross's introductions to his editions of the plays, and McMillin, "Casting for Pembroke's Men: The *Henry VI* Quartos and *The Taming of A Shrew*," *Shakespeare Quarterly*, 23 (1972), 149.

31. A. Cairncross, "Pembroke's Men and Some Shakespearian Piracies," *Shakespeare Quarterly*, 11 (1960), 349.

32. Greg, *The Shakespeare First Folio*, p. 244. Editors disagree on the significance of this stage direction to characterize Blackfriars' performances: see for example R. A. Foakes, textual analysis, *A Midsummer Night's Dream* (Cambridge: Cambridge University Press, 1984), pp. 142–143.

33. Greg, *The Shakespeare First Folio*, p. 242. E. K. Chambers argues that the masque, perhaps performed by children, may have contained personal allusions to the bride and groom which were altered for theatrical presentation by an adult company (E. K. Chambers, *William Shakespeare: A Study of Facts and Problems*, vol. 1, pp. 360–361).

34. J. D. Wilson, "The Copy for *As You Like It*, 1623," *As You Like It*, p. 108; Greg, *The Shakespeare First Folio*, p. 413; J. D. Wilson, "The Copy Used for *The Tempest*, 1623," *The Tempest*, p. 80.

35. *Henslowe's Diary*, ed. Foakes and Rickert, p. 21, and introduction, pp. xxx–xxxi.

36. Wilson, introduction, *Titus Andronicus*, p. xvii. Wilson cites as support an early essay by Greg; however, Greg does not discuss a preexisting play in his later commentary on the play in *The Shakespeare First Folio* (pp. 203–209).

37. Nosworthy, *Shakespeare's Occasional Plays*, pp. 93ff.

38. Greg, *The Shakespeare First Folio*, pp. 186–188. Andrew Cairncross argues instead that Shakespeare was the sole, original author of the three plays (see the introductions to his editions).

39. Wilson, introduction, *King John* (Cambridge: Cambridge University Press, 1936), p. xxff. Greg also considers this possibility in *The Shakespeare First Folio*, pp. 248–249.

40. Edwards, introduction, *Hamlet* (Cambridge: Cambridge University Press, 1985), p. 8. See also G. I. Duthie, *The 'Bad' Quarto of "Hamlet"* (Cambridge: Cambridge University Press, 1941).

41. S. Musgrove, "The First Quarto of *Pericles* Reconsidered," *Shakespeare Quarterly*, 29 (1978), 399ff.; also see Taylor, *Textual Companion*, pp. 557–560.

42. For the most recent discussion of Fletcher's participation in *Henry VIII* and *The Two Noble Kinsmen*, see Fredson Bowers, textual introductions, to both plays, in *The Dramatic Works in the Beaumont and Fletcher Canon*, vol. 7, pp. 3–20, 147–168.

43. For a discussion of the Shakespeare-Middleton collaboration on this play, see David J. Lake, *The Canon of Thomas Middleton's Plays: Internal Evidence for the Major Problems of Authorship* (Cambridge: Cambridge University Press, 1975), pp. 279–286; Macd. P. Jackson, *Studies in Attribution: Middleton and Shakespeare* (Salzburg: Institut für Anglistik und Amerikanistik, 1979), pp. 54–66; and Jowett, *Textual Companion*, p. 501.

44. J. W. Lever, introduction, *Measure for Measure* (London: Methuen and Co. Ltd, 1965), p. xiv.

45. Jowett, *Textual Companion,* p. 468.

46. Wells disagrees; see *Textual Companion,* p. 543.

47. Jowett, *Textual Companion,* p. 289.

48. Jowett and Taylor, "Sprinklings of Authority: The Folio Text of *Richard II,*" *Studies in Bibliography,* 38 (1985), 162.

49. Greg offers possible candidates for editor of the First Folio in *The Shakespeare First Folio,* pp. 77–83.

50. Honigmann, *The Stability of Shakespeare's Text,* p. 12.

51. This is also Stanley Wells's final point in "Revision in Shakespeare's Plays," p. 97.

52. Brents Stirling, "*Julius Caesar* in Revision," *Shakespeare Quarterly,* 13 (1962), 190–192.

53. Taylor, "*King Lear:* The Date and Authorship of the Folio Version," in *The Division of the Kingdoms,* p. 428.

54. For a differing perspective on the status of "bad" Quartos, see Urkowitz, "Good News about 'Bad' Quartos."

55. Honigmann, *The Stability of Shakespeare's Text,* pp. 2–3.

56. Richard Hosley argues that "since there is no evidence that any of these revisions was added to the text after the original writing of the manuscript, the presumption that they were made by the author at the time of originally writing the manuscript is suggested by the fact that in all the revisional duplications in Q2 the original version stands first and its revision second. This would be the situation if the revisions had been written directly after or below their original versions during the original writing of the manuscript, whereas if they had been inserted at a later date in the margin some of them might appear in print ahead of the original versions. From this we may conclude in passing that the second version of a revisional duplication in Q2 is generally to be preferred as giving the author's intention in the matter of his revised text but that the position of the earlier version is to be preferred as giving the author's intention regarding the location of the revision" ("The Corrupting Influence of the Bad Quarto on the Received Text of *Romeo and Juliet,*" *Shakespeare Quarterly,* 4 [1953], 29–30). But there is significant evidence that the revisions were made after some time had elapsed and that some of the duplications which stand second in the passages are not the revisions but the original versions.

57. Brian Gibbons, introduction, *Romeo and Juliet* (London: Methuen, 1980), p. 2.

58. S. W. Reid, "The Editing of Folio *Romeo and Juliet,*" *Studies in Bibliography,* 35 (1982), 43, 60.

59. See Brian Gibbons's discussion of the emendation of this passage in the note to 3.3.40–43 on p. 177 of his edition.

60. Randall McLeod (Random Cloud), "The Marriage of Good and Bad Quartos," *Shakespeare Quarterly,* 33 (1982), 425.

61. Greg, *The Shakespeare First Folio,* pp. 110–111, 233.

62. G. I. Duthie discusses the "case for regarding not Q1 but Q2 as giving the first version, and for regarding Q1 as giving a reflection (admittedly distorted, but at a given point possibly accurate owing to good reporting) of a Shakespearian revision" in "The Text of Shakespeare's *Romeo and Juliet,*" *Studies in Bibliography,* 4 (1951–2), 21–22.

However, Jowett ascribes the Quarto 1 inconsistencies to the presence of Henry Chettle as the main reviser (*Textual Companion,* pp. 289–290).

63. G. Blakemore Evans, textual analysis, *Romeo and Juliet* (Cambridge: Cambridge University Press, 1984), p. 207. Lord Hunsdon later became the Lord Chamberlain in 1597, and Shakespeare's company again took this name at that time.

64. Evans, textual analysis, *Romeo and Juliet,* pp. 208–209.

65. For example, Gibbons states that the title page advertises "that it is a replacement of the first edition, not a revision of an earlier version of the play," (introduction, *Romeo and Juliet,* p. 1), while Evans asserts that the title-page formula "is now considered a publisher's device for asserting the authority of his text and distinguishing it from Danter's Q1 . . . Ironically, Q2 is on the whole less carefully printed than Q1 and reveals no evidence of significant press correction" (textual analysis, *Romeo and Juliet,* p. 208). Evans's comment on the fact that the text was *not* corrected helps support the theory that the term "corrected" was merely used to signify that the edition had not been reported as the previous one had.

66. Jowett also discusses the revision of this passage in *Textual Companion,* p. 292.

67. J. D. Wilson, preface, *Love's Labour's Lost* (Cambridge: Cambridge University Press, 1923; rev. 1962), p. xxi; Richard David agrees, arguing that the play provoked "a battle in a private war between court factions" (introduction, *Love's Labour's Lost,* [London: Methuen and Co. Ltd, 1951], p. l).

68. J. D. Wilson, "The Copy for *Love's Labour's Lost,* 1598, 1623," *Love's Labour's Lost,* p. 106.

69. For a discussion of the "metrical virtuosity and inventiveness" of the language of *Love's Labor's Lost,* see G. R. Hibbard, *The Making of Shakespeare's Dramatic Poetry* (Toronto: University of Toronto Press, 1981), pp. 104–113.

70. Richard David, introduction, *Love's Labour's Lost,* pp. xxiii–xxiv.

71. Dual speech prefixes with a character's name and his function appear often in other Shakespearian plays printed from foul papers; see Greg, *The Shakespeare First Folio,* pp. 113–114, and Randall McLeod (Random Cloud), "The Psychopathology of Everyday Art," in *The Elizabethan Theatre IX,* ed. G. R. Hibbard (Port Credit, Ontario: P. D. Meany, 1981), pp. 131–167.

72. Printer's copy for Quarto 1 has recently occupied the attention of several critics. George Price argues that the hypothesis that any pages of Quarto 1 were set from the nonextant Quarto (implied in the title-page advertisement of Quarto 1) is "untenable" and argues instead for foul-paper copy ("The Printing of *Love's Labour's Lost* (1598)," *The Papers of the Bibliographical Society of America,* 72 [1978], 434). Paul Werstine concludes in "The Editorial Usefulness of Printing House and Compositor Studies" (in *Play-Texts in Old Spelling: Papers from the Glendon Conference,* ed. G. B. Shand with Raymond C. Shady [New York: AMS Press, 1984], pp. 35–64), that Quarto 1 was set from the nonextant Quarto 0, a "good" rather than a "bad" Quarto. Manfred Draudt asserts in "Printer's copy for the Quarto of *Love's Labour's Lost* (1598)" that "the beginning of *Love's Labour's Lost* was set from the Bad Quarto, whereas the rest was set from foul papers" (*The Library,* 6th ser., 3 [1981], 127). Stanley Wells agrees with Werstine that the hypothesis that the Quarto was reprinted from a lost "good" Quarto, "itself set directly from Shakespeare's foul papers" is the most plausible (*Textual Companion,* p. 270).

73. Kerrigan, "Shakespeare at Work: The Katharine-Rosaline Tangle in *Love's*

*Labour's Lost," The Review of English Studies,* n.s. 33 (1982), 134–136; also see his essay "Love's Labor's Lost and Shakespearean Revision," *Shakespeare Quarterly,* 33 (1982), 337–339, and the Correspondence section of *The Library,* 6th ser., 5 (1983), 399–404, for conflicting views by Kerrigan, Wells, and Draudt on this and other cruxes in the play.

74. Manfred Draudt, in his essay, The 'Rosaline-Katherine' Tangle of *Love's Labour's Lost* (*The Library,* 6th ser., 4 [1982], 381–396) also suggests this possibility; however, he does not examine it, as I do, in the context of Shakespeare's revision of Berowne's character.

75. J. D. Wilson and others have argued that the Katherine-Rosaline tangle resulted from Shakespeare's decision to move the plot device of mistaken identities caused by masking to Act 5, and his imperfect cancellation of both of the 2.1 passages ("The Copy for *Love's Labor's Lost,* 1598, 1623," p. 121 in his edition of the play). However, these changes are too similar to those in the duplicated passages to be anything other than part of Shakespeare's reshaping of Berowne's role.

76. If, as E. A. J. Honigmann has recently argued from the evidence of the passages attributed to Shakespeare in *Sir Thomas More* ("Do-It-Yourself Lear," p. 59), Shakespeare sometimes wrote in the speech prefixes after having written the dialogue, his revisions in speech prefixes in the Berowne-Katherine-Rosaline passages could have been made even later than the lately added original prefixes.

77. Stanley Wells argues that the copy for the Folio text was the Quarto collated with a manuscript closer to the performance version than the foul papers (the copy for the Quarto); see "The Copy for the Folio Text of *Love's Labour's Lost,*" *The Review of English Studies,* n.s. 33 (1982), 146.

78. Kerrigan, "Shakespeare at Work," pp. 129–136.


4. Revising Shakespeare Before and After 1596

1. Taylor, *Textual Companion,* p. 229. Taylor and the other editors of the Oxford Shakespeare *Complete Works* (Wells, Jowett, and Montgomery) agree that only post 1596 plays were heavily revised.

2. See Joseph Bolton, "The Authentic Text of *Titus Andronicus,*" *Publications of the Modern Language Association of America,* 44 (1929), 776–780, and Eugene Waith's introduction to his edition of *Titus Andronicus,* pp. 39–43.

3. Wilson, introduction, *Titus Andronicus,* p. xxv. Wilson also argues that in *Titus* we have "a play specially written for a travelling company and afterwards adapted for London production" (p. xxxvi).

4. Waith, introduction, *Titus Andronicus,* p. 20. The play may also have been performed privately by the Chamberlain's Men in 1596 at Burley-on-the-Hill. Gustav Ungerer conjectures that Jacques Petit's mention of a private performance of the play at the home of Sir John Harrington at Burley suggests that it was performed by the Chamberlain's Men ("An Unrecorded Elizabethan Performance of *Titus Andronicus,*" *Shakespeare Survey,* 14 [1961], 105). However, Petit merely states that the tragedy of *Titus Andronicus* was presented after a masque without explaining who performed the play, which was by this time already in print.

5. Waith, introduction, *Titus Andronicus,* p. 39.

6. This is also the theory of Joseph Bolton in "*Titus Andronicus:* Shakespeare at Thirty," *Studies in Philology,* 30 (1933), 221–224.

7. Greg's theory (*The Shakespeare First Folio,* p. 203) that the centered speech prefixes resulted from the compositor setting from an added and inserted sheet is more plausible than other possible causes, such as the compositor erring in casting off or deleting a portion of the text for some reason and therefore centering the speech prefixes in order to use up more lines.

8. Waith, introduction, *Titus Andronicus,* pp. 11, 43.

9. Wells, *Re-Editing Shakespeare for the Modern Reader,* p. 108. John Cranford Adams argues that the "differences, omissions, contradictions, additions, redundancies" and other textual problems of the early texts of the play result from Shakespeare's revision of an existing play designed for a different theatre: "the original *Titus* appears to have been written for a stage of two units (the Platform and Gallery), whereas the revised *Titus* was written for three (Platform, Gallery, and Inner Stage). As a consequence three scenes were radically recast and others modified to take advantage of improved stage resources" ("Shakespeare's Revisions in *Titus Andronicus,*" *Shakespeare Quarterly,* 15 [1964], 190).

10. J. D. Wilson, in "The Copy for *A Midsummer Night's Dream,* 1600," in *A Midsummer Night's Dream,* ed. A. Quiller-Couch and J. D. Wilson (Cambridge: Cambridge University Press, 1924), pp. 96–100, argues that the play was "first handled by Shakespeare in 1592 or before, rehandled in 1594, and rehandled once again in 1598," and that the 1598 performance celebrated the marriage of Southampton to Elizabeth Vernon; in 1594 Shakespeare "revised not only the Bottom scenes but the fairy scenes as well, leaving however the lovers' scenes very much as they had been in the first draft." Although later critics, including Greg (*The Shakespeare First Folio,* p. 242), agree that the play was revised, they have rejected the notion that it was originally written by someone else.

11. See Harold Brooks on this point in *A Midsummer Night's Dream* (London: Methuen and Co. Ltd, 1979), p. 127, note on 5.1.416.

12. Wilson, "The Copy for *A Midsummer Night's Dream,* 1600," in *A Midsummer Night's Dream,* p. 85.

13. See Greg, *The Shakespeare First Folio,* p. 242, and R. A. Foakes, who argues that "the obvious way of accounting for confusions in lineation in the quarto is to suppose that they result from alterations and reworkings made by the author in the course of composition. Later revisions would need to be made, if at all, in the copy used in the theatre, and though it is possible that Shakespeare revised his manuscript for publication in 1600, the only serious grounds for so arguing are that the revisions show a much more mature style" (textual analysis in *A Midsummer Night's Dream,* pp. 137–138).

14. J. D. Wilson argues that Theseus's two lines in this passage, "The best . . . amend them," were inserted at a later date along with the marginal additions on the poet in the lunatic/lover/poet speech ("The Copy for *A Midsummer Night's Dream,* 1600," p. 85). However, there is no bibliographical evidence to support this claim.

15. See Michael Warren on the problems of regarding revision as "replacement rather than as multiplication" in "The Theatricalization of Text," p. 41.

16. Barbara Hodgdon argues that the change in 5.1 from Philostrate in Quarto to Egeus in Folio helps to "shape a sense of familial and community harmony that extends and strengthens the possibilities suggested in the Quarto" and "illuminate character,

quicken rhythms of action and reaction, suggest a firmer resolution of discord, and deepen retrospective connections within the play," revealing the influence of "Shakespeare's own revising mind" ("Gaining a Father: The Role of Egeus in the Quarto and the Folio," *The Review of English Studies,* 37 [1986], 541–542).

17. Gary Taylor also discusses these revisions in "Revising Shakespeare," pp. 285–304.

18. Robert K. Turner, Jr., "Printing Methods and Textual Problems in *A Midsummer Night's Dream* Q1," *Studies in Bibliography,* 15 (1962), 55. Turner's support for the theory is based upon evidence in *reproductions* of delayed distributions, which he interprets to indicate difficulties in setting from a heavily revised manuscript; but Adrian Weiss, in "Reproductions of Early Dramatic Texts as a Source of Bibliographical Evidence," *TEXT,* 4 (1989), 237–268, argues that typographical evidence demonstrates a perfectly normal sequence of distributions.

19. Greg, *The Shakespeare First Folio,* p. 289; also see Jowett, *Textual Companion,* pp. 386–387.

20. Jonson, *Discoveries,* p. 29; Jonson also puns on this line in the induction to *The Staple of News.* For commentary, see *The Staple of News,* ed. Anthony Parr (Manchester, Eng.: Manchester University Press, 1988), p. 66.

21. See Wilson, "The Copy for *Julius Caesar,* 1623," *Julius Caesar* (Cambridge: Cambridge University Press, 1949), p. 95, and Dorsch, introduction, *Julius Caesar* (London: Methuen and Co. Ltd, 1955), p. xxiv.

22. See Stirling, "*Julius Caesar* in Revision," Bowers, "Establishing Shakespeare's Text," pp. 191, 194, and "The Copy for Shakespeare's *Julius Caesar,*" pp. 29–31, and Jowett, *Textual Companion,* pp. 386–387 for discussions of revisions made as a result of theatrically doubled roles and/or authorial changes in intention.

23. Fredson Bowers suggests that the difference in spelling in the speech prefix demonstrates that Shakespeare wrote out the revisions in 4.3 and 2.1 with *Cass.* and turned them over to the bookkeeper, who inserted them into the scribal transcript of the play, which had used *Cassi.,* this transcript and the added leaves served as copy for the promptbook ("The Copy for Shakespeare's *Julius Caesar,*" pp. 28ff.). Yet variant spellings in speech prefixes do not necessarily imply revision; instead, they may reveal Shakespeare's forgetfulness of the abbreviated form of the character's name that he had previously used, or his immediate second-thought changes. Spelling changes in speech prefixes may even stem from compositorial requirements, for, as John Jowett asserts, the change from *Cassi.* to *Cass.* may simply have been due to the compositor's shortage of *ssi* ligatures in his type case rather than to the author's revisions ("Ligature Shortage and Speech-prefix Variation in *Julius Caesar,*" *The Library,* 6th ser., 6 (1984), 252. Jowett also argues that speech-prefix variants should not be used to support theories of revision in the duplicated passages on Portia's death, and argues, as Thomas Clayton does ("Should Brutus Never Taste of Portia's Death But Once?: Text and Performance in *Julius Caesar,*" *Studies in English Literature,* 23 [1983], 237–255), that the two passages do not appear contradictory in performance. However, the coexistence of the duplicated passages, with conflicting reports of the contents of Brutus's letters, portrays Brutus as a man of conscience *and* as a man who has no scruples about baiting one of his men into revealing painful news.

24. Arthur Humphreys, introduction, *Julius Caesar* (Oxford: Clarendon Press, 1984), p. 78.

25. Bowers, "Establishing Shakespeare's Text," pp. 191–195.

26. That original promptbooks were not generally used for Folio copy is, according to Fredson Bowers, supported by evidence that printing from a manuscript, whether foul papers or a promptbook, entailed its destruction ("Authority, Copy, and Transmission in Shakespeare's Texts," in *Shakespeare Study Today,* ed. Georgianna Ziegler [New York: AMS Press, 1986], pp. 15ff.). However, Bowers's point has proved controversial; what seems certain is that acting companies would not part with a promptbook in order to allow it to be used for printer's copy if it contained the censor's license and/or if they intended to perform the play in the future.

27. Greg, *The Shakespeare First Folio,* p. 334.

28. Other variants in the Folio masque present problems in theatrical staging. See John H. Long, "Another Masque for *The Merry Wives of Windsor,*" *Shakespeare Quarterly,* 3 (1952), p. 40.

29. The Revels Accounts of 1604 record this entry for the King's Men: "Hallamas Day being the first of Nouember A play in the Banketinge house att Whithall called The Moor of Venis. The Sunday ffollowing A Play of the Merry Wiues of Winsor" (cited by E. K. Chambers in *The Elizabethan Stage,* vol. 4, p. 171).

30. William Green, in *Shakespeare's Merry Wives of Windsor* (Princeton: Princeton University Press, 1962), p. 25, followed Leslie Hotson (*Shakespeare Versus Shallow* [Boston: Little, Brown and Co., 1931]) in believing the occasion for revision to be the 1597 installation of Hunsdon; both Nosworthy (*Shakespeare's Occasional Plays,* pp. 121–124) and Taylor ("William Shakespeare, Richard James, and the House of Cobham," pp. 346–354) argue that the Garter passages were part of the original version, written to celebrate a Garter feast. John H. Long, in "Another Masque for *The Merry Wives of Windsor,*" 39–42, asserts that the Folio masque was added for a performance early in 1604 before James "at Windsor Castle," citing Chambers (*William Shakespeare,* vol. 1, p. 435) as the source for the date and place of performance. However, Chambers cites only a performance "at court on 4 November 1604" in this work, and in *The Elizabethan Stage* reprints the Revels Accounts giving this date, so it is unclear how Long arrives at the earlier date and place of performance.

31. On this point see Edmond Malone, "An Attempt to Ascertain the Order in Which the Plays of Shakspeare Were Written," in his 1821 edition of Shakespeare, vol. 2, pp. 373–380.

32. H. J. Oliver, introduction to *The Merry Wives of Windsor* (London: Methuen and Co. Ltd, 1971), p. xxxii.

33. Jowett, *Textual Companion,* p. 341.

34. G. Blakemore Evans has recently discussed the seventeenth-century Folger Manuscript of this play, suggesting that it may derive from a theatrical manuscript (see "*The Merry Wives of Windsor:* The Folger Manuscript," in *Shakespeare: Text, Language, Criticism: Essays in Honour of Marvin Spevack,* pp. 57–79).

35. Greg, *Shakespeare First Folio,* pp. 389–390, 392. Greg suggests that the copy used to print the Folio represented the play as it was presented in abbreviated fashion before James I, because Shakespeare's editors "thought it good policy to print a version prepared for court presentation. It may be that to this bit of snobbery we owe the loss of the authentic text" (p. 395).

36. W. W. Greg and F. P. Wilson, in the introduction to their Malone Society Reprints

edition of *The Witch* (Oxford: Oxford University Press, 1950), from which all citations from this play are taken, p. vii, argue for the earlier date of 1609 for the play, while Kenneth Muir, in the introduction to *Macbeth* (London: Methuen and Co. Ltd, 1977), p. xxx, argues for the later date of 1616. Both R. C. Bald ("The Chronology of Middleton's Plays," *Modern Language Review*, 32 [1937], 41) and Anne Lancashire (*"The Witch*: Stage Flop or Political Mistake,"* in *"Accompaninge the players"*: *Essays Celebrating Thomas Middleton, 1580–1980*, ed. Kenneth Freidenreich [New York: AMS Press, 1983], pp. 161–181) assert that *The Witch* alluded to the sensational Essex-Howard divorce case and subsequent scandal involving the murder of Sir Thomas Overbury from 1610–1616; Bald dates the play around 1616 while Lancashire dates it around 1613. Lancashire suggests that Middleton complained that the play was "ill-fated" because its allusions provoked political censorship rather than theatrical unpopularity. Yet Middleton's remark that his play was "ignorantly" ill-favored implies that the play failed because of its audience's ignorance of its topical allusions and therefore belies any claim that the authorities were completely aware of the play's real message. If the play had been censored, the authorities would have been far from "ignorant," and indeed worried enough about the play's satiric presentation of a current political scandal to encourage its censorship. Middleton's remark appears to be a petulant complaint about the play's theatrical failure and possibly a jab at the more successful *Macbeth.*

37. Wilson, introduction, *Macbeth* (Cambridge: Cambridge University Press, 1947), pp. xxiiiff.; Wells, *Textual Companion*, p. 543.

38. See for example David L. Frost's argument in *The School of Shakespeare* (Cambridge: Cambridge University Press, 1968), pp. 262–267, which assigns the *Macbeth* Hecate scenes to Middleton on the grounds that she is represented in these passages and in *The Witch* as a witch rather than as a goddess; also see Taylor's arguments in *Textual Companion*, p. 129. David J. Lake, who presents linguistic evidence of Middleton's share in *Timon of Athens* (in *The Canon of Thomas Middleton's Plays*, p. 279), states of *Macbeth* that "the interpolated passages do not contain any usable evidence of authorship" by Middleton. MacD. P. Jackson comments on linguistic evidence of Middleton in Shakespeare's plays in "The Additions to *The Second Maiden's Tragedy:* Shakespeare or Middleton?" (*Shakespeare Quarterly*, 41 [1990], 402–405), listing *Macbeth* as one of "the seven latest plays by Shakespeare alone."

39. Muir, introduction, *Macbeth*, p. xii, xxxi.

40. See Nosworthy, *Shakespeare's Occasional Plays*, pp. 24–31, for other parallels in "subject, phrasing and rhyme" between the Hecate passages in *Macbeth* and passages in other Shakespearian plays.

41. Nosworthy, *Shakespeare's Occasional Plays*, pp. 44–47, 31.

42. Taylor, *Textual Companion*, p. 306.

43. Taylor, "The Fortunes of Oldcastle," and "William Shakespeare, Richard James, and the House of Cobham", see also Jowett, "The Thieves in *1 Henry IV*," *The Review of English Studies*, 38 (1987), 325–333. The 1634 remark about the "first shewe of Harrie y$^e$ fift" could easily allude to the *Henry IV* plays as the "first shewe" of Henry V, to differentiate them from the "second" show, the play *Henry V.* Only if the allusion were to "the first shewe of Harrie the fourth" could it be used to confirm that Oldcastle did not appear in *2 Henry IV.* Taylor also argues that "when *Part One* was entered in the Stationer's Register on 25 February 1598, it was not called 'Part One,' which has led

most scholars to doubt that *Part Two* had yet been performed" ("Shakespeare and the House of Cobham," p. 344). Yet the first play was published as *The Historie of Henrie the Fovrth* in 1598 and the second as *The Second part of Henrie the fourth,* so that even after the completion of the second play, Shakespeare and his company may have continued for some period of time to refer to the first play as *The Historie of Henrie* without attaching "the first part" to it. In any case, if the hurried publication of *1 Henry IV* was made to please the offended Brooke, Harvey, and Russell families, Shakespeare's company may have not have been as eager to release or to refer to *2 Henry IV* in 1598.

44. Wilson, "The Copy for *2 Henry IV,* 1600 and 1623," in *The Second Part of the History of Henry IV* (Cambridge: Cambridge University Press, 1946), p. 123.

45. Jowett and Taylor, "The Three Texts of *2 Henry IV,*" *Studies in Bibliography,* 40 (1987), p. 36. Their argument is supported by evidence in the manuscript of *King Johan,* in which John Bale marked with crosses and ampersands the place of insertion of passages written out on added leaves (see chapter 3).

46. Greg, *The Shakespeare First Folio,* p. 267.

47. Jowett and Taylor, "The Three Texts of *2 Henry IV,*" p. 40; also see their article, "Sprinklings of Authority: The Folio Text of *Richard II.*"

48. Jowett, in *Textual Companion,* similarly argues that "Shakespeare seems to have begun to expand the historical matter of the play, and in particular the links with the events he had dramatized in *Richard II* and *I Henry IV,* whilst still working on the foul papers. He evidently continued this process of expansion and consolidation, perhaps shortly afterwards when preparing or by adding to the fair copy which was to serve as the promptbook, a direct or indirect transcript of which must accordingly have eventually served as the printer's copy for F" (p. 351). I argue that the bulk of the expansion took place in the fair rather than the foul papers after the original composition.

49. A. R. Humphreys, in his introduction to *The Second Part of King Henry IV* (London: Methuen and Co. Ltd, 1966), p. xvii, asserts that both *Henry IV* plays were completed by 1597; Taylor, in *Textual Companion,* p. 120, assigns Part 1 to 1596–97 and Part 2 to 1597–98.

50. Giorgio Melchiori argues in the textual introduction to his recent edition (*The Second Part of King Henry IV* [Cambridge: Cambridge University Press, 1989], p. 199) that "we can conclude not only that the eight major passages missing in the quarto were actually present in the foul papers on which the edition is based, but also that they were crossed out or otherwise marked for deletion by a reviser acting upon the players' instructions, with a view to preparing the copy for the book-keeper in charge of getting the prompt-book ready. The foul papers retained the typical signs of authorial inadvertency, such as unmarked exits, permissive or incomplete stage directions, entrances for characters who never speak because the author has changed his mind about their presence in the scene." This implausible argument posits that Shakespeare turned over his foul papers to another reviser "who heavily tampered with" the manuscript at the actors' request, in the process botching passages and scenes while allowing other inconsistencies and loose ends to stand. We can conclude only that this theory would not be consistent with Shakespeare's treatment of any of the other plays in the canon; he appears to have been more than capable of handling revisions of his plays himself, especially at this point in his career. Melchiori also argues in his edition (introduction, pp. 9–14) and in "Reconstructing the Ur-*Henry IV*" (in *Essays in Honour of Kristian Smidt,* ed. Peter Bilton et al. [Oslo: University of Oslo, 1986], pp. 59–77) that Shakespeare reworked his original single

play of *Henry IV* into two parts (the extant two plays), but the structural coherence and unity of *1 Henry IV* belie this hypothesis.

51. Gary Taylor, "Three Studies in the Text of Henry V," in Stanley Wells and Gary Taylor, *Modernizing Shakespeare's Spelling, with Three Studies in the Text of Henry V* (Oxford: Clarendon Press, 1979), pp. 39, 104. See Annabel Patterson, "Back by Popular Demand: The Two Versions of *Henry V*," *Renaissance Drama*, 19 (1988), 29–62, and Kathleen Irace, "Reconstruction and Adaptation in Q *Henry V*," *Studies in Bibliography*, 44 (1991), 228–253, for differing discussions of Quarto 1.

52. Greg, *The Shakespeare First Folio*, pp. 282–285.

53. J. H. Walter, introduction, *King Henry V* (London: Methuen and Co. Ltd, 1954), p. xxxvi.

54. Gary Taylor, introduction, *Henry V* (Oxford: Clarendon Press, 1982), p. 16.

55. On the sources of these revisions see Cairncross, introduction, *The Second Part of King Henry VI*, p. xxvii; McMillin, "Casting for Pembroke's Men: The *Henry VI* Quartos and *The Taming of A Shrew*," *Shakespeare Quarterly*, 23 (1972), 149, and Montgomery, *Textual Companion*, pp. 175–178.

56. Cairncross, introduction, *The Third Part of King Henry VI*, p. xl.

57. McMillin, "Casting for Pembroke's Men," p. 149.

58. See Montgomery's discussions of these points in *Textual Companion*, pp. 176, 198.

59. Montgomery, *Textual Companion*, pp. 175–177, 197.

60. Madeleine Doran asserts that the Folio restores passages cut from the play when Shakespeare originally abridged it while also showing signs of later revision, evidenced by "verse-fossils" in the text (*"Henry VI," Parts II and III: Their Relation to The "Contention" and the "True Tragedy"* [Iowa City: University of Iowa, 1928], pp. 27–28, 48, 75).

61. See Montgomery, *Textual Companion*, p. 217.

62. See Greg, *The Shakespeare First Folio*, pp. 186–188; Cairncross, introduction, *The First Part of King Henry VI* (London: Methuen and Co. Ltd, 1962), p. xiv; and Taylor, *Textual Companion*, pp. 217–218.

63. Taylor, *Textual Companion*, p. 230.

64. Antony Hammond, introduction, *Richard III* (London: Methuen, 1981), pp. 20, 48; also see Kristian Smidt, *Memorial Transmission and Quarto Copy in "Richard III": A Reassessment* (New York: Humanities Press, 1970), pp. 44–47, 80.

65. Greg, *The Shakespeare First Folio*, p. 190.

66. Taylor, *Textual Companion*, pp. 228–229.

67. Kerrigan, "Revision, Adaptation, and the Fool in *King Lear*," in *Division of the Kingdoms*, p. 195.

68. Honigmann, "Shakespeare's Revised Plays: *King Lear* and *Othello*," p. 156.

69. McLeod (Cloud), "The Marriage of Good and Bad Quartos," p. 249.

## 5. Revising *Hamlet, Troilus and Cressida*, and *Othello*

1. Greg, *The Shakespeare First Folio*, p. 299.

2. Wilson, *The Manuscript of Shakespeare's Hamlet and the Problems of Its Transmission*, 2 vols. (Cambridge: Cambridge University Press, 1934), vol. 1, p. 22.

3. Duthie, *The 'Bad' Quarto of "Hamlet,"* p. 149.

4. Duthie, *The 'Bad' Quarto of "Hamlet,"* p. 206.

5. Greg, *The Shakespeare First Folio,* p. 307.

6. Hibbard, textual introduction, *Hamlet,* pp. 74–75.

7. Hibbard, textual introduction, *Hamlet,* p. 74.

8. Steven Urkowitz discusses other changes in Gertrude's characterization in these texts in "Five Women Eleven Ways: Changing Images of Shakespearean Characters in the Earliest Texts," in *Images of Shakespeare,* ed. W. Habicht, D. J. Palmer, and R. Pringle (Newark: University of Delaware Press, 1988), pp. 292–304, and in "'Well-sayd olde Mole': Burying Three *Hamlets* in Modern Editions."

9. Philip Edwards, introduction, *Hamlet, Prince of Denmark* (Cambridge: Cambridge University Press, 1985), p. 8.

10. Nosworthy, *Shakespeare's Occasional Plays,* p. 215.

11. Edwards, introduction, *Hamlet,* p. 10.

12. Wilson, *The Manuscript of Shakespeare's "Hamlet,"* vol. 1, p. 30.

13. Kerrigan, "Shakespeare as Reviser," p. 259.

14. Edwards, textual notes, *Hamlet,* p. 196, note on 4.5.74–76.

15. Greg, *The Shakespeare First Folio,* p. 315.

16. Jenkins, "Playhouse Interpolations in the Folio Text of *Hamlet,*" *Studies in Bibliography,* 13 (1960), 42.

17. Urkowitz, in "Well-sayd olde Mole': Burying Three *Hamlets* in Modern Editions," pp. 49–59; Werstine, in "The Textual Mystery of *Hamlet,*" pp. 3–6; and Taylor, in *Textual Companion,* pp. 400–401, also discuss the dramatic impact of the excision of these passages.

18. Kerrigan, "Shakespeare as Reviser," p. 261.

19. Edwards, textual notes, *Hamlet,* p. 133, note on 2.2.333.

20. Greg, *The Shakespeare First Folio,* p. 338.

21. Kenneth Muir, introduction, *Troilus and Cressida* (Oxford: Clarendon Press, 1982), p. 3.

22. Foakes, commentary, *Troilus and Cressida* (New York: Viking Penguin, 1987), p. 161.

23. Greg, *The Shakespeare First Folio,* pp. 445–451.

24. Greg, *The Shakespeare First Folio,* pp. 348–349.

25. Taylor, in *"Troilus and Cressida:* Bibliography, Performance, and Interpretation," *Shakespeare Studies,* 15 (1982), 99–136, was the first to argue that the Quarto was printed from foul papers; my research agrees with his conclusion.

26. Palmer, introduction, *Troilus and Cressida* (London: Methuen, 1982), p. 17.

27. Honigmann, "The Date and Revision of *Troilus and Cressida,*" in *Textual Criticism and Literary Interpretation,* ed. Jerome McGann, pp. 38–54.

28. For a discussion of Shakespeare's fluency in legal language and his knowledge of English law, see Mark Edwin Andrews, *Law Versus Equity in "The Merchant of Venice"* (Boulder: University of Colorado Press, 1965); O. Hood Phillips, *Shakespeare and the Lawyers* (London: Methuen and Co. Ltd, 1972); W. Nicholas Knight, "Equity and Mercy in English Law and Drama (1405–1641)," *Comparative Drama,* 6 (1972), 51–67.

29. Taylor, *"Troilus and Cressida:* Bibliography, Performance, and Interpretation," pp. 120–121.

30. Muir, appendix, *Troilus and Cressida,* p. 193.

31. *The Second Part of the Return from Parnassus,* in *The Three Parnassus Plays (1598–1601),* ed. J. B. Leishman (London: Ivor Nicholson & Watson Ltd, 1949), p. 337, 4.3.1772–3.

32. As Josiah Penniman pointed out in his study, *The War of the Theatres* (Boston: Ginn and Company, 1897) p. 146, one passage in the play within the play of *Histriomastix* apparently puns on Shakespeare's name: Troylus remarks to Cressida that her knight "shakes his furious speare." Penniman conjectures that Shakespeare responds by satirizing Marston as "rank Thersites."

33. See Kenneth Palmer, introduction, *Troilus and Cressida*, p. 19, and Muir, introduction, *Troilus and Cressida*, p. 5. The *Troilus and Cressida* prologue contains other puns on *Poetaster* and allusions to the War of the Theatres. For example, Envie, who speaks Jonson's induction, remarks, "Marke, how I will begin: The *Scene* is, ha! / ROME? ROME? and ROME?" (Folio, sig. Z6$^v$), while the speaker of Shakespeare's prologue begins, "In Troy there lyes the Scene."

34. In addition, the three characters who speak Jonson's "Dialogue" (Nasutus, Polyposus, and Author) use a number of terms which appear in the epistle to *Troilus and Cressida;* they ponder the degree of "salt" and "wit" in the play and the reaction of the "Multitude" to Marston's attacks on Jonson. Author also defends himself against his rival dramatists: "Sure I am, three yeeres, / They did prouoke me with their petulant stiles / On euery stage," while the epistle writer of *Troilus and Cressida* chides the "grand censors" who now "stile them [comedies] such vanities."

35. Rowe, *Distinguishing Jonson: Imitation, Rivalry, and the Direction of a Dramatic Career* (Lincoln: University of Nebraska Press, 1988), pp. 173–174.

36. Palmer, appendix I, *Troilus and Cressida*, p. 304.

37. Coghill argues that *Troilus and Cressida* was first publicly performed at the Globe in 1602–03 as a tragedy, without the "fierce" prologue or "salacious" epilogue (represented in part by the Quarto 1 text, which does not contain the epilogue), and was adapted for a private performance at the Inns of Court in 1608 by the addition of a prologue and epilogue which rendered the play a comedy (as printed in the Folio text); *Shakespeare's Professional Skills*, p. 78. Taylor, however, takes the opposite view: he argues that Shakespeare altered his original version, first written for a private performance, to a public play for the Globe by omitting the original epilogue ("*Troilus and Cressida*: Bibliography, Performance, and Interpretation," 125–126).

38. The summary nature of the prologue resembles the late additions to the English history plays, which narrated previous action in order to give the audience perspective about the current events, and the remote possibility that the play was acted or was planned to have been acted with a preceding play portraying some of these events cannot be ruled out. Kenneth Muir notes that at least three other plays on the subject of the Trojan War, *Troyelles and Creasse*, *Agamemnone*, and *Troye*, were performed in the late 1590s (introduction, *Troilus and Cressida*, p. 7).

39. William Drummond recalled of Jonson in 1619, "He had many quarrells with Marston beat him & took his Pistol from him, wrote his *Poetaster* on him the beginning of ym were that Marston represented him in the stage in his youth given to Venerie" (Jonson, *Conversations with William Drummond*, p. 13).

40. Shakespeare may have intended to provide a satiric parody of Jonson or Dekker, if not Marston, in his revised portrayal of Thersites.

41. Nosworthy, *Shakespeare's Occasional Plays*, pp. 81, 84–85; Taylor, "*Troilus and Cressida*: Bibliography, Performance, and Interpretation," 125–126.

42. Jonson, *Conversations with William Drummond*, p. 13.

43. Foakes, "An Account of the Text," *Troilus and Cressida*, p. 232.

44. Bevington, "Determining the Indeterminate: The Oxford Shakespeare," p. 510.

45. Ridley, introduction, *Othello* (London: Methuen and Co. Ltd, 1958), p. xliii.

46. Coghill, *Shakespeare's Professional Skills*, pp. 164, 167, 198–199, 200–201.

47. Honigmann, "Shakespeare's Revised Plays: *King Lear* and *Othello*," pp. 162–171.

48. Sanders, "Note on the Text," in *Othello* (Cambridge: Cambridge University Press, 1984), p. 52. Daniel Amneus, in *The Three "Othellos"* (Alhambra, Calif.: Primrose Press, 1986), less persuasively argues for three Shakespearian versions of the play.

49. Stanley Wells argues for a scribal transcript of foul papers and of Shakespeare's revised manuscript as Quarto and Folio copy (*Textual Companion*, pp. 476–477).

50. Wells, "Revision in Shakespeare's Plays," p. 77.

51. Greg, *The Shakespeare First Folio*, p. 358. Alice Walker also argued that the Quarto's variants "fairly certainly represented cuts for performance, motivated, like those of the F. *Lear*, by practical rather than artistic considerations" and that the Quarto represents "a licentious transcript of a late acting version of *Othello* further mangled in its printing" ("The Copy for *Othello*, 1622 and 1623," in *Othello*, ed. J. D. Wilson [Cambridge: Cambridge University Press, 1957], pp. 123–125).

52. E. K. Chambers notes that the Willow Song may have been borrowed from other sources, as a text of it with musical notation was printed from a 1615 manuscript and the music appears in a 1583 lute book (*William Shakespeare: A Study of Facts and Problems*, vol. 1, p. 462.)

53. Sanders, introduction, *Othello*, p. 1.

54. Coghill rejects Walker's argument that the cuts were made to shorten the play by demonstrating that these cuts save only eight minutes in playing time (*Shakespeare's Professional Skills*, p. 178).

55. Sanders, textual analysis, *Othello*, p. 203.

56. Honigmann, "Shakespeare's Revised Plays: *King Lear* and *Othello*," p. 162.

57. Coghill, *Shakespeare's Professional Skills*, p. 197.

58. Ridley, introduction, *Othello*, p. xxviii.

59. As M. R. Ridley points out in his edition, the difference between "your weapon" in Quarto and "this weapon" in Folio is "important for stage business" (p. 190, note on 5.2.240). Some critics have also debated whether Othello's lines, "So, so," imply that he stabs Desdemona after strangling her; see Ridley's edition, p. 182.

60. Wells argues that the Quarto was printed from a transcript of foul papers in which "a scribe" attempted to make sense of difficult readings, *Textual Companion*, p. 477.

61. Kerrigan, "Shakespeare as Reviser," p. 263.

## 6. Revising *King Lear* and Revising "Theory"

1. Howard-Hill, "The Challenge of *King Lear*," p. 161.

2. Wells, "The Once and Future *King Lear*," in *The Division of the Kingdoms*, p. 6.

3. Taylor discusses the transmission of the Quarto and Folio texts in *Textual Companion*, pp. 509–542. Howard-Hill argues for an intermediate transcript derived from the promptbook and Quarto 2 as Folio copy in "The Challenge of *King Lear*," pp. 170–179.

4. Doran, *The Text of "King Lear"*, pp. 137, 128–129.

5. Greg, *The Shakespeare First Folio*, pp. 379–381.

6. Duthie, "The Copy for *King Lear,* 1608 and 1623," in *King Lear,* ed. J. D. Wilson and G. I. Duthie (Cambridge: Cambridge University Press, 1960), pp. 136, 124; Walker, *Textual Problems of the First Folio* (Cambridge: Cambridge University Press, 1953).

7. Smidt, "The Quarto and the Folio *Lear:* Another Look at the Theories of Textual Deviation," *English Studies,* 45 (1964), 162.

8. Warren, "Quarto and Folio *King Lear* and the Interpretation of Albany and Edgar," pp. 96–97.

9. Stone, *The Textual History of King Lear* (London: Scolar Press, 1980), pp. 64–65. Stone's hypotheses do not appear to take into account theatrical practices demonstrated in other texts of Shakespeare's plays. For example, it is difficult to imagine that the King's Men would bother to collate and correct their existing theatrical manuscript with the Quarto if it was a pirated edition, even if they had lost their original promptbook in the Globe fire of 1613.

10. Taylor, "The War in *King Lear,*" p. 34.

11. Urkowitz, *Shakespeare's Revision of King Lear,* pp. 129, 147.

12. Blayney, *The Texts of "King Lear" and their Origins: Volume 1, Nicholas Okes and the First Quarto* (Cambridge: Cambridge University Press, 1982), pp. 5–6. Also see Howard-Hill, "The Challenge of *King Lear,*" pp. 166–167 for a discussion of theories about the provenance of the Quarto text.

13. Warren, "The Folio Omission of the Mock Trial: Motive and Consequences," in *The Division of the Kingdoms,* p. 49.

14. Warren, "The Diminution of Kent," p. 59; Clayton, "'Is this the promis'd end?' Revision in the Role of the King," p. 122; Goldring, "*Cor.*'s Rescue of Kent," p. 149; McLeod, "*Gon.* No more, the text is foolish," p. 171; Kerrigan, "Revision, Adaptation, and the Fool in *King Lear,*" p. 230; all in *The Division of the Kingdoms.*

15. Taylor, "Monopolies, Show Trials, Disaster, and Invasion: *King Lear* and Censorship," and "*King Lear:* The Date and Authorship of the Folio Version," both in *The Division of the Kingdoms,* pp. 106, 428–429.

16. Werstine, in "Folio Editors, Folio Compositors, and the Folio Text of *King Lear,*" in *The Division of the Kingdoms,* pp. 287–288, asserts only that not all of the variants derive from compositorial or editorial origin.

17. Thomas, "Shakespeare's Supposed Revision of *King Lear,*" pp. 506–511; John L. Murphy, "Sheep-Like Goats and Goat-Like Sheep: Did Shakespeare Divide *Lear's* Kingdom?" *Papers of the Bibliographical Society of America,* 81 (1987), 53–63; Marion Trousdale, "A Trip Through the Divided Kingdoms," *Shakespeare Quarterly,* 37 (1986), 218–223; see also Brean S. Hammond, Review, *Theatre Research International,* 9 (1984), 231–234.

18. Muir, *Shakespeare: Contrasts and Controversies,* pp. 51–52.

19. Honigmann, "The New Lear," p. 18; Howard-Hill, "The Challenge of *King Lear,*" pp. 161–179; also see Richard Knowles, "The Case for Two *Lears,*" *Shakespeare Quarterly,* 36 (1985), 115–120.

20. Howard-Hill, "The Challenge of *King Lear,*" p. 164.

21. Warren, "Quarto and Folio *King Lear* and the Interpretation of Albany and Edgar," pp. 98–99.

22. Foakes, "Textual Revision and the Fool in *King Lear,*" *Essays in Honour of Peter Davison, Trivium,* 20 (1985), 40.

23. Taylor, *Textual Companion,* p. 529.

24. Taylor, "The War in *King Lear,*" pp. 29–30.

25. Howard-Hill, "The Challenge of *King Lear,*" p. 173.

26. Warren, "The Diminution of Kent," in *The Division of the Kingdoms,* p. 63.

27. Geoffrey Bullough, *Narrative and Dramatic Sources of Shakespeare,* 8 vols. (London: Routledge & Kegan Paul, 1973), vol. 7, pp. 318–319.

28. Granville-Barker, *Prefaces to Shakespeare,* 2 vols. (Princeton: Princeton University Press, 1946), vol. 1, p. 273.

29. Doran, *The Text of "King Lear,"* p. 73.

30. Taylor, "Monopolies, Show Trials, Disaster, and Invasion: *King Lear* and Censorship," in *The Division of the Kingdoms,* pp. 75–79.

31. Taylor, "*King Lear:* The Date and Authorship of the Folio Version," in *The Division of the Kingdoms,* pp. 417–418.

32. Goldring, "*Cor.*'s Rescue of Kent," in *The Division of the Kingdoms,* p. 149.

33. Goldring, "*Cor.*'s Rescue of Kent," in *The Division of the Kingdoms,* pp. 143–145; Urkowitz, *Shakespeare's Revision of "King Lear,"* p. 39.

34. Warren, "The Diminution of Kent," in *The Division of the Kingdoms,* p. 61.

35. Greg, "Time, Place and Politics in *King Lear,*" *Modern Language Review,* 35 (1940), 443.

36. Urkowitz, *Shakespeare's Revision of "King Lear,"* pp. 72–73.

37. Goldring, "*Cor.*'s Rescue of Kent," in *The Division of the Kingdoms,* pp. 148–149.

38. Mack, *"King Lear" in Our Time* (Berkeley: University of California Press, 1965), p. 9.

39. Warren, "The Diminution of Kent," in *The Division of the Kingdoms,* p. 66.

40. Ibid., p. 67.

41. Granville-Barker, *Prefaces,* vol. 1, p. 332; Urkowitz, "The Growth of an Editorial Tradition," in *The Division of the Kingdoms,* p. 27.

42. Urkowitz, *Shakespeare's Revision of "King Lear,"* p. 94.

43. Muir, introduction, *King Lear* (London: Methuen and Co. Ltd, 1972), p. lii.

44. Taylor, "*King Lear:* The Date and Authorship of the Folio Version," in *The Division of the Kingdoms,* p. 426.

45. Granville-Barker, *Prefaces,* vol. 1, p. 277.

46. Elton, *"King Lear" and the Gods* (1966; rpt. Lexington: University Press of Kentucky, 1988), p. 75.

47. See Dusinberre, *Shakespeare and the Nature of Women* (New York: Barnes and Noble, 1975), p. 215, in which she argues that Cordelia's refusal to *speak* in 1.1 "salutes a rule of femininity in a context which gives her bluntness masculine strength"; and Novy, *Love's Argument: Gender Relations in Shakespeare* (Chapel Hill: University of North Carolina Press, 1984), p. 89, in which she argues that Shakespeare "includes" 4.3 as a choral scene to comment on Cordelia's expression of her feelings of love for her father. Novy, like Dusinberre, bases her interpretation of Cordelia on the fact that she "initially attempts to say nothing." Also see Edward W. Tayler's discussion of how "Shakespeare actually obliges Cordelia to *say* 'nothing,' and to say it again, which is quite a different thing from having her say nothing" ("*King Lear* and Negation," *English Literary Renaissance,* 20 [1990], 23).

48. Honigmann, "Shakespeare's Revised Plays: *King Lear* and *Othello,*" p. 155.

49. Kerrigan, "Shakespeare as Reviser," p. 256. Taylor also cites Jonson's lines as evidence of authorial revision ("Revising Shakespeare," pp. 297–298). Honigmann links Jonson's lines to lines in Horace's *Ars Poetica,* translated by Jonson, which commend the poet who blots "all" and brings his verses to the "anvile . . . to new hammering" (*The Stability of Shakespeare's Text,* p. 31).

50. Taylor, *Textual Companion,* p. 509.

51. Kerrigan, "Shakespeare as Reviser," p. 269.

52. Wells and Taylor, in "The Oxford Shakespeare Re-viewed," share this view.

53. Eric Sams, Letter, *TLS,* 1 February 1985, 119.

54. As R. A. Foakes has suggested, the conception of Shakespeare as the "artist who never needed to blot a line" will die hard partly because "we want to preserve all that Shakespeare wrote, and are reluctant to accept as cuts what he may willingly have omitted for the sake of theatrical coherence" (Review [*William Shakespeare: The Complete Works,* ed. Wells and Taylor], *Modern Language Review,* 84 [1989], 437.

55. Jerome McGann, "The Theory of Texts," *London Review of Books,* 18 February 1988, 21.

56. Warren, "Textual Problems, Editorial Assertions in Editions of Shakespeare," in *Textual Criticism and Literary Interpretation,* p. 35.

57. Wells, "Revision in Shakespeare's Plays," pp. 95, 88.

58. Bevington, "Determining the Indeterminate: The Oxford Shakespeare," p. 503.

59. Honigmann, "Do-It-Yourself Lear," p. 60.

60. McKenzie, *Bibliography and the Sociology of Texts* (London: British Library, 1986), pp. 4–5, 28.

61. Kerrigan, "Shakespeare as Reviser," pp. 260–261.

# INDEX

*Folios in bold refer to illustrations*